Theatre with a Purpose

CULTURAL HISTORIES OF THEATRE AND PERFORMANCE

The Bloomsbury series of *Cultural Histories of Theatre and Performance* recognizes that historical knowledge has always been contested and revised. Since the turn of the twenty-first century, the transformation of conventional understandings of culture created through new political realities and communication technologies, together with paradigm shifts in anthropology, psychology and other cognate fields, has challenged established methodologies and ways of thinking about how we do history. The series embraces volumes that take on those challenges, while enlarging notions of theatre and performance through the representation of the lived experience of past performance makers and spectators. The series' aim is to be both inclusive and expansive, including studies on topics that range temporally and spatially, from the locally specific to the intercultural and transnational.

Series editors:
Claire Cochrane *(University of Worcester,* UK)
Bruce McConachie *(University of Pittsburgh,* USA)

George Farquhar: A Migrant Life Reversed, David Roberts
The Polish Theatre of the Holocaust, Grzegorz Niziołek
A Century of South African Theatre, Loren Kruger
Alternative Comedy: 1979 and the Reinvention of British Stand-Up,
Oliver Double
Soviet Theatre during the Thaw: Aesthetics, Politics and Performance,
Jesse Gardiner
*Theatre, Performance and Commemoration: Staging Crisis, Memory and
Nationhood,* Edited by Miriam Haughton,
Alinne Balduino P. Fernandes and Pieter Verstraete

Forthcoming titles
*Performing Modernity: Culture and Experiment in the Irish Free State,
1922–1937,* Elaine Sisson
*German Amateur Theatre and Social Change in the
Early Nineteenth Century,* Meike Wagner

Theatre with a Purpose

Amateur Drama in Britain 1919–1949

Don Watson

methuen | drama

LONDON · NEW YORK · OXFORD · NEW DELHI · SYDNEY

METHUEN DRAMA
Bloomsbury Publishing Plc
50 Bedford Square, London, WC1B 3DP, UK
1385 Broadway, New York, NY 10018, USA
29 Earlsfort Terrace, Dublin 2, Ireland

BLOOMSBURY, METHUEN DRAMA and the Methuen Drama logo are trademarks of
Bloomsbury Publishing Plc

First published in Great Britain 2024

Series design by Adriana Brioso
Cover image: Hartfield Road, Chalk Farm. 30th September 1944.
(© Staff / Mirrorpix / Getty Images)

Library of Congress Cataloging-in-Publication Data.

Names: Watson, Don, 1954– author.
Title: Theatre with a purpose : amateur drama in Britain 1919-1949 / Don Watson.
Description: London ; New York : Methuen drama, 2024. | Series: Cultural histories of
theatre and performance | Includes bibliographical references and index.
Identifiers: LCCN 2023028310 (print) | LCCN 2023028311 (ebook) |
ISBN 9781350232044 (hardback) | ISBN 9781350232082 (paperback) |
ISBN 9781350232068 (pdf) | ISBN 9781350232051 (ebook)
Subjects: LCSH: Amateur theater—Great Britain—History—20th century.
Classification: LCC PN3169.G8 W38 2024 (print) | LCC PN3169.G8 (ebook) |
DDC 792.02/220941082—dc23/eng/20230830
LC record available at https://lccn.loc.gov/2023028310
LC ebook record available at https://lccn.loc.gov/2023028311

A catalog record for this book is available from the Library of Congress.

ISBN: HB: 978-1-3502-3204-4
       ePDF: 978-1-3502-3206-8
       eBook: 978-1-3502-3205-1

Series: Cultural Histories of Theatre and Performance

Typeset by RefineCatch Limited, Bungay, Suffolk

To find out more about our authors and books visit www.bloomsbury.com
and sign up for our newsletters.

Contents

Illustrations

Acknowledgements

My thanks are due to the following institutions who have kindly given permission for the images they hold in their collections to be reproduced in this book. The front cover picture of the St. Pancras Theatre in a bombed area of wartime London is from the Getty Images Collection. The image of Gateshead ILP Amateur Drama group in *The Hill-Top* in Chapter 1 is from the Ruth Dodds papers in Gateshead Archives: The People's Archive. The performance of *Peer Gynt* in Chapter 2 and the British Drama League Festival programme in Chapter 4 are from the Bensham Grove Settlement collection held by the Tyne and Wear Archives Service. The image of the performance of *Blackleg* used in Chapter 3 is from the Manchester University Settlement Archive at the University of Manchester. The rehearsal of *On Guard for Spain* in Chapter 5 and the performance of *Buster* in Chapter 6 are images from the Bristol Unity Players collection in the Modern Records Centre at the University of Warwick.

Some of the research material used in Chapter 4 first appeared in *New Theatre Quarterly* vol. 36 part one 2020, and some of the material used in Chapter 5 first appeared in *North East Labour History* no. 23 in 1989. My thanks to Keith Armstrong for permission to quote from his two edited collections, *But the World Goes On the Same: Changing Times in a Durham Pit Village* (Strong Words Collective, 1978) and *Homespun: The Story of Spennymoor and its Famous Settlement, told by Local People* (Northern Voices, 1992).

I would like to thank Ella Wilson and all on the team at Bloomsbury Academic who saw this project through from proposal to production. In particular the two series editors at Bloomsbury, Claire Cochrane and Bruce McConachie, who provided important comments and suggestions both at the initial proposal stage and again after submission. A good deal of the research for this book took place during the Covid pandemic of 2020. Besides the usual thanks to the archivists and librarians who made my research possible I offer my additional thanks for their efforts to maintain a service and to provide a safe environment during that time.

When the book was at the ideas stage I had invaluable discussions about it with Colin Chambers, Ben Harker and Mick Wallis. Later Mick was also kind enough to comment on one of the chapters in its draft form. Along the way I had useful discussions too with Angela Jackson, Peter Lathan, Fiona Macpherson and the late Nigel Todd. Peter Brabban and Maggie Thacker were also helpful with the illustrations. Needless to say the mistakes are all my own work.

Finally, I would like to record my thanks to these former enthusiasts for the amateur stage, now no longer with us, who helped me with earlier research and who would have been interested in this book: Dave and Iris Atkinson, Dave Ross, and Vince and Betty Waddington.

Abbreviations

BL/LCP	British Library, Lord Chamberlain's Plays collection
CUSC	Cardiff University Special Collections
DA	Derbyshire Archives
GA	Gateshead Archives: The People's Archive, Gateshead Central Library
GUSC: STA	University of Glasgow Special Collections: Scottish Theatre Archive
LHASC	Labour History Archive and Study Centre, People's History Museum, Manchester
LUSC	University of Leeds Special Collections
MRC: BUP	Modern Records Centre, University of Warwick: Bristol Unity Players collection
NA	Nottinghamshire Archives
NORTH	Northumberland Archives
PGL: SPE	Palace Green Library, Durham University: Spennymoor Settlement Archive
SUSC	University of Sheffield Special Collections
TWAS	Tyne and Wear Archives Service, Newcastle upon Tyne
V&A	Victoria & Albert Museum Theatre and Performance Archives

Introduction

Amateur Theatre and History

Our Theatre Company began with a small group of women – miners' wives and mothers and sisters. Such Theatre Companies always do begin with women. Then they cajoled a man to come in. He, with me, was the only other man in the play, *The Cradle Song*, which was the first thing we did in public ... Our theatre has never been thought of as a place where amateurs play. It's a place where a real job has to be done by actors, poets, painters, singers, dancers, carpenters, electricians, and seamstresses.[1]

This, in a broadcast at the end of the Second World War, was how Bill Farrell described the Spennymoor Community Players, the amateur company which he and his wife Maggie had formed in County Durham in the 1930s. This is one example of how the inter-war and Second World War years were the heyday of British amateur theatre, with contemporary estimates of anything from 20,000 to 30,000 performing companies in every part of the country. This leads the Shakespeare scholar Michael Dobson to observe that, 'By the end of the 1930s, a higher proportion of the British population had practical experience of putting on plays than at any time before or since ...'[2]

Nevertheless until comparatively recently amateur drama was largely ignored by theatre historians. This neglect appears to have been for three main reasons. As Helen Nicholson, Nadine Holdsworth and Jane Milling state, the post-war policy of the Arts Council of Great Britain was to support the professional arts and to purposefully exclude the amateur. This policy originated during the Second World War when state funding for the arts began, and after 1942, with limited budgets, high-quality work by professionals was prioritized over widening participation. When this policy continued after the war it was additionally justified by a belittling of amateur drama by Arts Council members. In the theatre itself at the time Norman Marshall, a critic with a good knowledge of the amateur stage, concluded – a view that will be contested in due course – that although 'the growth of the amateur movement in the years before the war was awe-inspiring', nonetheless 'it had contributed little of importance to the theatre as a whole'.[3] The conviction that this work did not warrant public funds probably signalled to historians that amateur drama did not warrant their attention either. Similarly, a recurrent feature of amateur work at the time, particularly in festival and competition, was the one-act play. This form had a low status in theatrical and educational circles during these years and in Britain the one-act play has never attracted the same critical interest as its literary equivalent, the short story. Arguably a third reason is the assumed character of the amateur stage in the inter-war period, a time when the professional and lower-middle classes in secure employment experienced a real growth in living standards. One feature of this was the increased leisure time which underlined the opportunity to participate in amateur drama, the 'genteel interest' in it noted by Claire M. Tylee, Agnes Cardinal and Elaine Turner.[4] This would be the affluent milieu described in R. C. Sherriff's account of the genesis of his own writing career. This was in the amateur theatre of Richmond, London, in the 1920s, where the expectation was for 'pleasant stories that fitted neatly into a village hall and satisfied a friendly, undemanding audience'.[5] Thus a recollection by an important post-war playwright that amateur dramatics were the preserve of the comfortably placed in search of a pleasant recreation. As such there would seem to be little of historical interest.

In contrast there were the Spennymoor Community Players described by Farrell, whose account foregrounds both the social class origins of the company and the seriousness with which they approached their activity. Nor was the Spennymoor group unique at the time, as this book will demonstrate; another example will be Kathleen Edwards's commedia dell'arte-inspired tours with casts of unemployed workers. The historical narrative needs to be widened to accommodate these types of play-making, and an entry point for this comes through the recent scholarship on amateur drama. Here the absence from the history is increasingly coming to be filled as research explores neglected areas and challenges dismissive verdicts.

The comprehensive survey of modern British theatre by Rebecca D'Monte gives a legitimate place, as a matter of course, to the growth of the amateur theatre movement in Britain during the period covered by this book. In Scotland and Wales before the Second World War most theatrical activity was amateur, and this is the focus of Linda Mackenney's history of Scottish popular theatre since 1900. One theme is how aspirations for a drama of Scottish life (as seen by some) collided with portrayals of the urban working class. In her examination of Welsh drama in the twentieth century Alyce Von Rothkirch gives important space to the amateur movement, which as she describes was the dominant theatrical presence outside the cities. She concludes, however, that although it had an important social function it was too reliant on popular plays to develop the dramatic arts in Wales. The continuing studies of English rural amateur drama by Mick Wallis demonstrate how it was recognized as a potential vehicle for community development and rural reconstruction, particularly after 1919, and often in alliance with adult education. In the historically informed analysis of British amateur theatre by Nicholson, Holdsworth and Milling, theatre is understood to be an eco-system of inter-dependent elements. Their approach confirms the massive contribution that the amateur theatre has and continues to make to British theatre as a whole. This includes, to take just some examples, the large numbers of professional actors and theatre workers who were inducted through amateur theatre, the movement to establish a National Theatre, and commercial support to playwrights and publishers through permissions and royalties. Their survey demonstrates, as other the writers do, that theatre is a complex industry and the boundaries between the amateur and professional sectors of it have always been fluid, to the benefit of both. They also demonstrate how amateur players build audience knowledge of different theatrical genres and performance styles, thus contributing to the understanding and sustainability of live performances among both audiences and participants.[6]

Claire Cochrane's analysis of British theatre in the twentieth century includes an account of the many and varied models of amateur drama which were created. She covers some similar ground to this book, albeit within the understandable restrictions of a general survey.[7] Her discussion includes the early years of the British Drama League and its festival competitions, the Village Drama Society, adult education and the growth of the Little Theatres; also the significant presence of amateur drama in Wales between the wars and how it sustained cultural identity and social cohesion. In covering the socialist theatres she notes that they are the exception to the lack of attention paid to amateur drama by historians. She identifies what she terms a 'binary opposition' in the historical understanding, not only between the amateur and the professional stage but also between amateur theatre groups with an explicitly political purpose and those pursuing more conventional amateur drama. It can be added that the fact that this one aspect of the amateur stage has attracted serious historical interest is probably because in the inter-war years it pioneered new forms such as documentary theatre and living newspapers, mass declamations and political pantomime. It also nurtured a major theatre director in Joan Littlewood.[8]

One connecting thread between these recent accounts is that each of them uses historical evidence to trace the different ways in which amateur theatre was valued before and during the Second World War. As these writers demonstrate important practitioners believed that the amateurs could invigorate, if not actually save, the theatre as a whole. Their freedom from the pressure of market forces meant that they could perform the quality dramas the commercial stage would avoid. Amateur drama was held to promote an active participation in cultural life as opposed to the passive consumption of ready-made entertainment. Thus participation in drama was seen as a parallel with participation in active citizenship generally, and there was a consensus too that it had an important role in adult education. The co-operation involved in play-making was considered to be a potential class-leveller and thereby a force for social cohesion and development. At the same time some practitioners used amateur drama to challenge existing social arrangements and to refashion the relationship between theatre and society. In short, amateur drama could be a theatre with a purpose well beyond the simply recreational.

This book builds on the foundation of this scholarship to study five interrelated examples of such amateur theatre practice, all during the years when participation in amateur theatre was at its most extensive. Each deserves a detailed examination in its own right, as this account intends to show. Any demarcation by date in an historical narrative risks being arbitrary but here it seems appropriate to select one bookmarked by two major national theatre conferences. These were held in 1919 and 1948. Both took place in the aftermath of cataclysmic wars which had left no aspect of society untouched and in the context of widespread debate about social change and reconstruction. Both featured prominent figures from the stage, and the consensus of both was that theatre, including amateur drama, had an important role to play in post-war life.

In 1919 the founders of the British Drama League (BDL), supported by major figures in the theatre, asserted the value of drama in the social reconstruction made necessary by the war. They also saw the need, faced by what they believed to be the failures of the commercial stage, to build a popular base for it. They intended to promote 'a theatrical revival on democratic lines'. The theatre with a purpose they sought involved using drama at every level of the education curriculum, promoting both the study of and participation in drama through adult education, and supporting amateur theatre companies in every locality and major workplace. Chapter 1, largely contextual, examines this and the often networked organizations which offered an infrastructure for amateur drama: also the economic realities they faced in the absence of state support, and some of the issues involved in extending the social base of audiences and participation.

The BDL was allied with the national network of educational settlements and the Workers' Educational Association. Although the role of the educational settlements in adult education has been discussed by historians their theatre practice has largely been neglected. Chapter 2 deals with a selection of settlement theatre companies: those from nineteenth-century initiatives, like Manchester; those founded immediately after the First World War, such as in Gateshead and Sheffield; and those established in response to the unemployment crises of the 1920s and 1930s in South Wales, Scotland and County Durham. Each example functioned in a deprived area. The chapter examines the important role assigned to participation in drama as an adult education practice, the repertoires and performances of the settlement drama groups, and their contribution to the social class diversity of amateur theatre.

It was during the years following the foundation of the BDL that some areas of the country experienced a growth of employment in new industries, substantial rises in wages and living standards, and a housing boom. However, as John Burnett observes, 'one's view of the inter-war period depended on where one stood geographically, occupationally and socially'.[9] Other areas of the country reliant on heavy industry endured persistent structural unemployment and poverty. Chapter 3 discusses the National Council for Social Service centres and clubs for the unemployed in the 1930s. These were controversial at the time and criticized as simply palliative measures. Amateur drama groups of unemployed people were established in these clubs and they performed in overwhelmingly working-class communities. This chapter is the first detailed examination of the work of these groups. It covers performances and performance spaces, gender relations, some innovative practice, and whether unemployed drama groups were marginalised or part of mainstream amateur theatre. It also covers if these initiatives were indeed solely palliatives or also an opportunity for groups to create an independent space of their own.

During the inter-war period a major activity in amateur drama was the festival or competition, and their expansion is one of the metrics of the growth of the movement. Chapter 4 examines the contemporary discussions about the effects of competitions on playmaking, and some attempts, influenced by cinema techniques and American political theatre, to expand the potential of the maligned one-act play. The role of the amateurs in building a drama of national life in Scotland and Wales was an issue for critics at the time, and the chapter reviews this through playwrights with a working-class perspective. The rise of fascism and the threat of another world war were features of these years and so it is legitimate to enquire whether the amateur theatre world reflected these themes and concerns and played any role in addressing them. The chapter discusses the presence of political and socially conscious amateur theatre in festival activity in the 1930s, as evident among companies which were unconnected to the political left. In this respect it queries any simple binary opposition between political and amateur theatre during these years.

Chapter 5 extends this in a way through examining the Left Book Club Theatre Guild (LBCTG) between 1936 and 1939. Unlike other aspects of the left theatre of the 1930s the LBCTG has not been considered in detail, even though the Guild was acting as a hub for more than 200 affiliated local groups by 1939. This was the time of the 'popular front', often understood in terms of the machinations of political parties but in this chapter, continuing a theme of the previous one, the focus is the interface between the social movements concerned with the rise of fascism and the drift towards war, the political left and the amateur theatre world. The chapter discusses the work of the Guild, its relationship with the amateur theatre in general and what effect it may have had on the political landscape of the time.

The final chapter explores how the movements and initiatives examined in the previous chapters did not finish with the outbreak of war in 1939. Essentially, they continued under different circumstances, adapting to new conditions and demonstrating their resilient roots. Wartime amateur dramatic activity has to be understood in terms of its pre-war basis. Historians have examined the role of state sponsorship of the arts during the Second World War through the Council for the Encouragement of Music and the Arts. Government sponsored tours of professional theatre were introduced, a prequel to the Arts Council of Great Britain. A far less examined aspect is how amateur companies worked to confirm a popular audience for drama, asserted the value of theatre in wartime, and promoted participation across every aspect of the home front and the services. It also helped to articulate the hopes for a better society following the war.

The 1948 British Theatre Conference provides an almost thirty-year marker since the establishment of the British Drama League. This conference too attracted major figures in the theatre: J. B. Priestley, Sybil Thorndike and Basil Dean, for example. The concluding chapter discusses the issues raised there and considers the disengagement by the Arts Council of Great Britain from what the amateur theatre had achieved. However much of what the 1919 Conference and the BDL had advocated was now mainstream. Therefore the concluding discussion centres on how far, in terms of the examples examined in the book, 'a theatrical revival on democratic lines' had taken place. It considers the negative evaluations which have been made and attempts a balanced assessment of the contribution the amateur theatre with a purpose made to British drama and theatre studies.

Source material

David Coates believes that the traditional lack of academic attention paid to amateur theatre is reflected in the lack of archive holdings related to it, or the lack of catalogue identification where archives do hold relevant material.[10] This raises the question of the nature and availability of the documentary material about amateur theatre to be discussed here. The records of some, by no means all, of the local groups associated with the Left Book Club Theatre Guild are held in university collections. Possibly this reflects the fact that political theatre at least has attracted academic interest, but in practice these records were secured because one of the activists involved took responsibility for collecting and storing them before they were eventually deposited for professional curation. Most of them are identified as belonging to amateur groups but they vary in size and range, with the Bristol Unity Players material being particularly extensive, simply because the original compiler was particularly meticulous. The intention of this book to widen the narrative about the amateurs required widening the range of source material to sustain it. This involved tracing amateur drama in the records and journals of organizations which were established for different purposes altogether. Thus this account draws on local authority and rural community council minutes, the annual reports of educational settlements, miscellaneous newsletters, social service journals, reports from councils of social service and even Women's Land Army bulletins. This range reflects the intersection of amateur drama and the social history of the period, and it reflects too how seriously it was taken by diverse organizations and how routinely it was present in their operations.

Nevertheless, these sources bring their own issues of completeness and detail. The available records of the educational settlements covered in this book range from the comprehensive in one case through varying degrees of sparseness to actual non-existence in others. Those of the Spennymoor Settlement, for example, are extensive and complete, whereas when historians acquired the records of the Sheffield Settlement they found that those covering 1931–44 had been destroyed by rodents. Records for the Rock House Settlement consisted largely of a now-vanished compilation of press cuttings, of the four annual reports for the Harkness House project only one has survived and existing reports of the Welsh settlements are sparse.[11] The haphazard availability of the records of non-statutory bodies of the period reflects, as with the political theatre groups, the haphazard availability of someone to take responsibility at the time for their collection and preservation. As regards play texts, the Lord Chamberlain's Plays collection is an archive of every script submitted to be licensed for public performance, a legal requirement until 1968. As such it is a source for plays that were written for amateur performance but which were never published. However, where a play was intended for private performance, for example restricted to audiences of club members only, then licensing was not required and no submission was made. In these cases if the script was never published it has more than likely disappeared. The minutes and annual reports of organizations not principally concerned with amateur drama understandably vary in the coverage they devote to it. This of course can be complemented by the coverage in contemporary journals, and again not necessarily just those of the theatre.

The expanding digitization of local newspapers offers a tremendous resource for the historian of amateur theatre. During the inter-war years 'an extraordinarily high proportion of households' in the larger provincial towns took local newspapers which publicized and regularly reviewed amateur theatre performances. Detailed coverage often continued even during the Second World War when newsprint was scarce. Amateur drama groups, their performances and their success in festivals, were considered to be among the cultural assets of their localities. However a critique of much of this coverage came in the 1930s from Lawrence du Garde Peach, a national figure in the amateur drama at the time.[12] In his opinion the local press was nowhere near critical enough, reviews being the province of junior reporters whose priority was simply to record the names of everyone connected with the performance. Every effort would receive fulsome praise regardless of quality and this generated a 'completely inappropriate self-satisfaction' among the performers. These were the unserious and self-congratulating circles described by R. C. Sherriff. Another important limitation with reviews as a source has been discussed by Helen Freshwater, albeit largely in terms of reviews by professional theatre critics.[13] As she identifies, they normally record the responses of an individual reviewer and not usually those of the audience. Press reviews frequently give little or no information about an audience although paradoxically it is the presence of the audience which makes the theatre the art form it is.

Nevertheless for a theatre historian newspaper reports are often the only source material available and, whilst bearing these caveats in mind, they are a crucial record of what was being performed, by whom and where. They make it possible to trace the different appearances by a particular drama group, individual, or of a particular play. They can provide information not readily available elsewhere, if at all. For example, press reviews of the tours by the Old Vic in County Durham and South Wales in the 1940s suggest that their famous success owed much to the prevalence of amateur drama in adult education before the war, something unexplored in the histories. Du Garde Peach's critique has some accuracy but it is not universally applicable, particularly where newspapers serving major urban centres had critics who were knowledgeable commentators on the local amateur movement.

As the reader will see, the arrangement of the material into chapters is somewhat arbitrary and largely for convenience. The separation into sections is intended to provide an easier focus for examination. There are no discrete divisions between several of the examples, and this reflects the interrelated nature of what is discussed, the purposes with which significant practitioners at the time believed amateur theatre could have. By examining these different examples, and building on existing scholarship, the book contributes to understanding amateur theatre as a popular cultural practice during the inter-war years and those of the Second World War. This in turn offers a contribution to the social history of British theatre in general.

1

'A theatrical revival on democratic lines'

Drama and the People after the Great War

Drama and social reconstruction

As the First World War drew to a close national attention moved to the shape society should take after the conflict. The Ministry of Reconstruction was established in 1917 and it initiated a series of policy discussions and recommendations across many issues, including the future of adult education. These last recommendations gave drama a formal role in the future well-being of the nation. The *Report of the Adult Education Committee* was published in 1919. It sought to lift the profile of adult education and underpin it by a commitment to public funding. It argued that the issues facing the democracies could only be appreciated by a more educated electorate, educated in the duties of citizenship and the active participation which was the essence of democracy. Therefore adult education was not to be a luxury for the few but, as 'a permanent national necessity' and 'an inseparable aspect of citizenship', it should be 'both universal and lifelong'. The sacrifices of the war should be justified by the better nation that had emerged from them.[1]

The Committee included a covering letter, addressed to Prime Minister Lloyd George, stating: 'There is stirring through the whole country a sense of the duty we owe to our children, and to our grandchildren, to save them not only from a repetition of such a world-war and from the obvious peril of civil dissension at home.'[2] The 'peril of civil dissension at home' would indeed have been 'obvious' to the government at the time. In extreme form in Europe 'civil dissension' had, in Eric Hobsbawm's words,[3] 'swept away all the regimes from Vladivostok to the Rhine' – the Bolshevik Revolution of 1917 in Russia and the abrupt demise of the old monarchies of the warring nations. In Britain itself in 1918 the Representation of the People Act extended the franchise to all men (and some women) and on offer to working people now was a Labour Party whose 1918 constitution committed it to the public ownership of the key industries. Therefore it is plausible to see the '1919 Report', as it became known, in terms of containment; an attempt to steer a new, appropriately educated, electorate in the direction of seeking consensual approaches to redressing grievances and social issues. However this argument in the covering letter is not recurrent in the document, the thrust of which demonstrates an idealism and drive for a better society than the one that had gone to war in 1914.

The *Report* recognized practical modes of learning through the arts, and the value of participation in them both for individuals and communities. Drama was important as an informal route to education because it could draw in those who were deterred by traditional tutorial teaching. At the same time the *Report* advocated cheap, accessible performances of good drama – 'few reforms would do more for the reality of education'. Drama was the form of literature with 'the greatest popular possibilities' and it had been shown during the war that good drama at an accessible price would be met by an 'overwhelming response', a phenomenon that will be discussed below. This trend had been ignored by most theatre managers who seemed to assume that 'the public positively demands imbecility'. As a result drama, 'the type of literature with the widest popular appeal is also that which has sunk to the lowest depths'. However, in the hands of commercial management its potential would not be realized. As we shall see, this view of the theatre was widely shared at the time. The *Report* believed that a way forward should be through the role of drama in adult education, in alliance with the local amateurs in the Little Theatres, the name applied when an amateur company had a theatre building of its own and a regular season.[4]

In other words the recommendations to the post-war government for the future of adult education valued drama, and indeed believed that it should be a normal part of the educational activity of the nation. The active participation in drama which educational classes and amateur theatre could offer were in parallel with the active participation in society on which democracy and progress would now depend. Therefore amateur theatre should be central and not peripheral in the post-war British landscape.

Separately, but almost simultaneously, the theatre world was making its own contribution to the discussions about the role of drama in society and social reconstruction after the war. The British Drama League was formed in December 1918 and held an initial public meeting in June the following year. The advance publicity was in a similar vein to the Adult Education Committee report, stating that for many people 'self-expression is a need that would find a natural satisfaction in the writing and acting of plays'. Unfortunately there had been 'a divorce of the drama from the intimate life of the people' and this 'had been a mistake'.[5] The British Drama League (BDL) initiative had important supporters, and this first meeting, as the stage press noted, attracted 'some notable persons in dramatic circles'.[6] They included messages of support from Harley Granville Barker, Ellen Terry and Lilian Baylis, whose presentations of Shakespeare at cheap prices at London's Old Vic Theatre had attracted popular audiences. A consistent theme of the meeting and indeed one of the principal motives behind the League itself was a belief in the dire state of the British commercial theatre. In particular, there was a gulf between the quality of drama that it was known ordinary people would respond to and the quality of what was actually on offer to them. The experience of the war had brought this into focus, as the BDL Secretary Geoffrey Whitworth explained at that first public meeting of the League. His experience with drama and adult education at an armaments factory during the war had 'corroborated all that one had heard about the interest aroused among war workers in the best theatrical art wherever it was provided'.[7] This had also been the experience of another founder of the League and its Vice-President, the actress, producer and theatre manager Lena Ashwell, who had led theatrical tours to front-line troops during the war.[8] She had been impressed by the appetite of ordinary soldiers, men mainly unused to conventional theatre-going, for serious drama as well as musical entertainments. This had included new work as well as the classics of Greek tragedy and Shakespeare. Ashwell decried the 'present degradation' of the commercial theatre and declared, 'We mean the workers to have the right kind of entertainment, for the foundation of the future does not lie with the West End, it lies with the workers'.[9] Although this statement was reported by the Labour newspaper the *Daily Herald*, Ashwell actually had a conservative perspective on the symmetry between cultural renewal and preventing national decline. In declaring that no other nation would allow its people to eat mentally what this nation was eating, the 'rotten, low, suggestive' entertainment provided around the country, she warned that if this continued 'we should not long remain one of the greatest Empires the world had ever seen'.[10]

In part these views were a reaction to the shows that had become common during the war in London and other major cities: bawdy entertainments aimed at troops on leave or awaiting embarkation. Such was the cultural authority of the capital that the situation in the West End theatres and the behaviour of its managers was held to be the apex of the commercial theatre. As a characterization of the state of British theatre this was shared in the 1919 Report as we have seen. It should not be taken as a complete representation, however, as theatre historians have demonstrated. The key issue was the economy of the theatre industry and the necessity to concentrate on productions that were guaranteed a commercial success.[11] Whitworth went on to explain that the contrast between the 'decadence' of the London stage and 'the promise of vitality outside it' suggested that in these days after the war a scheme to 'stimulate a theatrical revival on democratic lines' was possible. After all, 'drama was the art par excellence of the people'. What he had in mind was similar to the definition of the democratization of art and literature that has been put forward by Christopher Hilliard: sharing a sense of the entitlement to participate, in this case both to enjoy good drama as audiences and to take part as performers.[12] Harley Granville Barker, another early catalyst in the BDL whose own experience of the war had sharpened his perspective on theatre and society, made a link between this and democratic participation. The need for self-expression, he argued, be that personal, communal or national, would have to be met 'if democracy is not to be a by-word, for the fooling of the people, if the voice of the people is to be anything more than a parrot-cry'.[13] Three principals of the BDL – Whitworth as Secretary, Granville Barker as Council Chairman and Ashwell a Council member – thus believed that participation in theatre had a social purpose beyond recreation for the participants.

The decline of theatre

One consequence of the movement of the theatre away from the people, in the eyes of some, was that through the inter-war years the cinema came to dominate the world of mass entertainment. England alone made up a tenth of the world market for films with attendances through the 1930s reaching between eighteen and nineteen million per week. It was particularly popular with working-class people who appreciated the cheapness and comfort of the well-appointed buildings. Audiences also appreciated the Hollywood productions; contemporary surveys showed that the classless nature of the American accents, in marked contrast to their British film equivalents, made them more popular with working-class cinema-goers.[14] Film and cinema could be seen as a threat on two levels. Firstly and obviously the opportunities for audiences to attend plays were substantially reduced as theatre buildings were converted into more profitable cinemas. This was particularly the case in suburbs and towns, so that the amateur dramatic societies and the Little Theatres alone were making live performances available. The other level was a cultural one. Patrick Carleton was a popular novelist, critic and participant in the British Drama League during the 1930s and his hostility to popular cinema was vehement. He believed that the average American film shown in Britain was 'not only aesthetically worthless but socially pernicious, a menace as well as an affront'. In his view 'our cultural outlook will be black indeed' if the 'poor and under-educated' were left with this as their only exposure to drama. Given the output of the professional stage, and the loss of theatre buildings as the cinemas supplanted them, only the amateur drama networks could meet the need. Any recruit to the audience for good plays would be 'another soul saved from celluloid'. Lena Ashwell persistently made the case for municipal theatre as a counter-balance to what was likely to be performed in theatres run purely on commercial lines, and to help resist the 'Americanization' of British culture 'due to sensational films from Hollywood'. [15]

Such attitudes could be found across the political spectrum. In Gateshead, County Durham, Ruth Dodds was a political activist in the town and active too with the Gateshead Independent Labour Party Amateur Dramatic Club. She confided in her diary (admittedly whilst depressed at the failure of the rail and transport unions to support the miners during their dispute of 1921), 'The stunt press, & the kinema, because they distract our minds with trivialities, will be the mainstays of a foolish aimless people, who will afford these things when they cannot afford to feed body and mind properly'. In this she was following the tradition among British socialists at the time of encouraging the working class to rise above the mass commercial culture on offer to it, and take up higher and more demanding pursuits. Such encouragement had a political motive. Popular magazines, music-hall theatre and later the cinema were believed by socialists to encourage a lack of reflection among the masses and thereby acquiescence in the current arrangement of society. On the other hand, the promotion of good literature and drama among the working classes, and the more serious levels of cultural activities generally, were more likely to encourage critical thought, and thus critical reflection on the conditions in which working people found themselves.[16]

Although it was accepted by most that film acting had an important role in drama an attitude persisted, in some theatre and educational circles, that there was something fundamentally less authentic about what was referred to as 'mechanical entertainment' such as film. The experience it offered was assumed to be a passive one in contrast to the active one encouraged by engagement with a live performance, and demanded by the requirements of actual participation in plays.

Gathering allies

The BDL organized the first British national theatre conference in 1919 and it attracted the full spectrum of the theatre industry: producers, actors and managers both professional and amateur, scene designers, but also social workers and adult education staff. As Whitworth later recorded, this was quite likely the first ever gathering for a 'free discussion on problems confronting the theatre in its artistic and social aspects'.[17] The conference endorsed the aims of the BDL and the core activities which were to provide the focus of the organization until the end of the Second World War. These were to lobby government to establish a National Theatre to showcase British dramatic culture, and to include drama in the education curriculum in school, college and university. In these cases drama should, as in American universities, be linked to practical performance and not just literary study. The overall objective was to promote 'both individual and collective efforts to develop Acting, Drama and Theatre as forces in the Life of the Nation'. This was also to include giving local authorities the power to finance municipal theatres as was the case in France and Germany. This would support drama unrestricted by the need for commercial appeal.[18]

A primary focus was practical support for the local amateur drama companies which affiliated to the League. In different parts of the United Kingdom organizations with similar aims affiliated to or worked in parallel with the BDL: the Scottish Community Drama Association was formed in 1926, the Drama Association of Wales in 1934, and the Northern Drama League, established in 1923, facilitated amateur theatre activity in Northern Ireland. Mary Kelly founded the Village Drama Society in 1919 to support participation in local amateur drama as a community theatre movement, recovering rural self-expression as a route to cultural revival. The Society was absorbed into the BDL during the 1930s. As Milling, Holdsworth and Nicholson state, it is with the foundation of the League (and, it should be added, these other organizations) that we can identify the rise of British amateur theatre as a *movement*. As we have seen, this was to be a movement with a purpose.[19] Alongside its potential role in education for democracy the amateur movement had the potential to revitalize the theatre as a whole, an objective which, as we shall see, was to underlie the promotion of festivals and competitions.

The BDL comprised elements which were outward-looking and inclusive. Guest speaker at the 1934 annual meeting was Ernst Toller, the German Expressionist playwright and refugee from Nazi Germany. He reiterated that the standard repertoires of the commercial theatre avoided dealing with 'the problems of the times' and that the amateur stage should provide an alternative, and a forum for young dramatists.[20] In 1934 Una Marson, the Jamaican feminist and activist in the League of Coloured Peoples in London, produced her own play *At What a Price* at the Scala Theatre and then a YMCA. It concerned the inter-racial and sexual workplace politics in a Caribbean office where a young black woman has a white employer. The play had an amateur cast of black West African and Caribbean students, and the performance led to discussions with Mary Kelly at the BDL who urged Marson to encourage more play-making from the African and Caribbean communities. According to Marson's biographer this was thwarted by the transient nature of the African and Caribbean student population in London who would have provided the performers.[21]

Building the movement

The BDL came to be popularly associated with amateur drama. It established, following a major grant from the Carnegie Trust United Kingdom in 1925, a comprehensive library from which groups could borrow printed plays and acting copies. Small groups might be unable to afford to pay an author's copyright fee and so the BDL negotiated a system of royalty payments for copyright plays. A monthly journal on all aspects of theatre, *Drama*, was published from 1920 and in keeping with the BDL's outward-looking stance it always included international material. Importantly, and due to the support which professional theatre workers were willing to offer the amateur movement, lecturers and producers could be available to advise affiliates on all aspects of play-making. For example in 1928 Edith Craig was a principal tutor at a weekend School of Drama for Amateurs in Gateshead, arranged by a committee representing a number of local amateur dramatic societies in conjunction with the League. Alongside Margaret Macnamara, a playwright active in the Independent Labour Party (ILP), she taught acting and production and conducted auditions.[22] In this way any binary opposition between the amateur and the professional spheres was eroded.

Lena Ashwell built on her wartime experience to pioneer municipal theatre in working-class London, a continuation also of pre-war efforts to offer accessible quality theatre there. A consortium of Labour mayors, co-ordinated by the Mayor of Stepney and future Prime Minister Clement Attlee, undertook to provide halls at a nominal rate for performances by her 'Once-a-Week Players'. Their presentations of quality drama in return for their expenses were intended to build the case for supporting local theatres through the rates in the same way that public libraries were supported.[23]

In another post-war initiative the Adult Education Committee of the Board of Education for England and Wales had been commissioned to promote the development of liberal education for adults. One report, *The Drama in Adult Education*, was published in 1926 after consultation with a number of organizations and individuals involved in amateur theatre. It provides a wide survey of the amateur drama world of the 1920s. Reinforcing the 1919 Report, it characterizes the amateur movement as 'a dramatic revival of national scope' and reiterated its value in adult education. The report's recommendations echoed the objectives of the BDL: public funding for municipal theatre and Little Theatres, since quality drama could not be left to the commercial sector; teachers qualified in drama in all schools; and the study of performance as well as dramatic literature in the universities. These teachers would be one means to make available the professional producers that amateur societies needed but could not afford. As far as the BDL was concerned this report was an important chapter in the history of post-war reconstruction and provided a 'chapter and verse' endorsement of its efforts.[24] The chapter will now examine some of the examples covered by the report, together with others, their contribution to a new popular basis for theatre through the amateur movement and some of the issues involved.

Little Theatres

The 1926 report drew attention to the role of the Little Theatres in offering quality drama outside cities and major towns, often providing the only opportunity to experience it. Claire Cochrane has described how the exponential growth of these theatres was a feature of suburban expansion and the development of new towns, especially in those parts of the country experiencing economic success rather than recession. It could also be the case in towns experiencing recession: Sunderland Drama Club, formed in 1925 with thirty-six subscribing members, had 1,141 by 1933; the town's staple shipbuilding industry was in decline throughout this period. Subscribing members provided a steady income for Little Theatres, and according to Cochrane they were largely drawn from the professional middle classes. Sunderland Drama Club bears this out, given that it had repaid a substantial amount from the mortgage for its theatre by 1930. Similarly its neighbour in Newcastle, the People's Theatre (originally founded by Edwardian socialists), was financially secure enough in 1929 to take out a large loan for new premises. This suggests that as with other Little Theatres their audience catchment areas were better positioned to weather economic crises than their wider localities.[25]

Several Little Theatres were re-purposed buildings whose original function was redundant. As Rebecca D'Monte points out this could affect staging: the small performance spaces necessitated by the size of many buildings presaged the intimate production techniques more associated with the contemporary theatre. In addition a small venue would probably have made audiences more conscious of themselves as a group. At the same time there were other Little Theatres, such as Southport, with a seating capacity of 400. The programmes were taken seriously. At the inaugural meeting of Sunderland Drama Club, for example, they were advised by the Newcastle People's Theatre that 'the plays the club ought to produce were plays with a purpose, plays in which the authors felt they had a truth to express'. In both of these cases the programmes included both classics and modern drama, fulfilling the potential to offer alternatives to the mainstream commercial stage: works by Ernst Toller and the Capek brothers alongside plays by Clemence Dane and Susan Glaspell.[26] Sunderland experienced pressure from members to include more popular works for the sake of the box office, but apparently this attempt for additional income was not a success although the policy for varied programmes continued.[27]

Some Little Theatres encouraged new authors through play-writing competitions, the best of the entries awarded with a performance by a local amateur company and possibly publication too. Aberdare Little Theatre in Wales did so during the inter-war period, with a competition held every year for one-act plays in Welsh and English. Although generally only three or four plays would reach the stage out of thirty or forty entries the exercise introduced at least two serious Welsh writers to the amateur theatre. One was Florence Howell, a Pembrokeshire farmer whose plays such as *Castle Garth*, *Ann Marlowe* and *Jane Wogan* featured strong independent female leads. Another was a bus driver, E. Eynon Evans, who eventually followed a career as a screenwriter.[28] In 1932 Sunderland Drama Club's competition was judged by Whitworth who considered that around a third of the entries 'were well worth acting'. This was followed by occasional 'experimental nights' where programmes of one-act plays by members were performed – one of these, *While of Unsound Mind* by Nan Richenbeg, was performed by the Club in the finals of the BDL Community Theatre Festival in 1937.[29]

The aspiration for a local Little Theatre was a widespread one across the urban amateur movement in the inter-war years. It was taken as evidence that a local movement was serious, confident and had achieved a status. It was believed too that that use of a permanent base offered continuity in production and that this would help to maintain quality.[30] A Little Theatre certainly established the amateur movement as a presence in the area and helped to build a regular audience. As Nicholson, Holdsworth and Milling conclude, many Little Theatres believed in their responsibility to build the public taste, whilst recognizing the pragmatic necessity to sustain their audience through a varied repertoire.[31]

Women's Institute drama

The National Federation of Women's Institutes in England and Wales and the Scottish Women's Rural Institutes had been formed during the First World War as an initiative to revitalize rural communities. By 1928 there were four thousand branches in the smaller villages comprising more than a quarter of a million active members. Meetings offered talks, classes and entertainment, and during the inter-war years campaigns to improve the circumstances of local families over housing and water supplies.[32] They were an opportunity for women to develop self-confidence in their own space and thus drama groups were a frequent activity.

Many of the local branches had all-female casts for their performances with women playing men's parts, while others recruited some local men for particular roles. Nora Ratcliff, a prolific author for the amateur stage and producer for village theatre in Yorkshire, was ambivalent about this development which some of the groups concerned claimed would expand their scope. Ratcliff was concerned that in doing so they might 'throw away a very precious birthright – their identity as a women's organisation'. She pointed out that if there was a market for plays for amateurs with all-women casts then authors would provide them; in this, as we shall see in a later chapter, she was proved to be correct.[33]

As with BDL affiliates the most active Women's Institute (WI) groups held training weekends where theatre professionals advised them. Mick Wallis observes that although WI leaderships were from the affluent classes they were concerned not to exclude any of their members, those restrained by domestic responsibilities and transport, from attending courses and participating in drama.[34] Therefore they obtained Carnegie Trust UK funding to develop their own local drama training and for the temporary appointment of advisers where rural populations were too dispersed to sustain regular teachers.[35] In addition theatre professionals were hired to develop play-making. For example, in 1927

Miles Malleson, an actor, author and producer involved with the ILP Arts League, attended a WI drama school at Lewes in Sussex. There he advised on 'producing and acting in modern plays' and rehearsed scenes with different volunteers from the audience. A year later Edith Craig taught at a WI event in north-east England where she advised them to focus on plays 'with characters they can get hold of' and avoid attempting 'superficial comedies of manners', in keeping with the aspiration for quality drama in the amateur sector.[36] Malleson's advice was obviously followed the next year when one of the Sussex village groups performed *The Price of Coal* by Harold Brighouse. Here the action centres on a group of miners' wives in Lancashire waiting for their men at the pit where an accident has taken place. Clearly the creative potential of representing someone entirely different from themselves had been grasped by some cast members. That much is clear from the press review: 'Mrs. Mabel Godfrey-Fawcett was very convincing as the mother who has already lost her husband in a pit disaster' and Lady Beatrice Swift was praised too for her performance as a miner's wife.[37] There are a number of questions here, such as how parts were allocated and indeed why the play was chosen: was it due to an interest in social-issue drama or simply the scope of the acting opportunities this play offered? If the more confident, educated upper-class members were taking the lead roles did this not reinforce the existing social hierarchies? The WI was a very diverse federation and so these questions would bear further local research.

The WI held its own drama festivals which were consciously non-competitive. Each county organization chose a team to represent it from those entering its own festival, and then inter-county festivals were held. Initially at least there were no trophies other than the prize of being selected to represent the county. The first national WI Drama Festival was held at the organization's annual general meeting in 1928. The entry from the village representing Somerset was a comedy written by one of the local members and the cast included two women who had never before been inside a theatre or seen a play performed.[38]

The ILP Arts Guild and Gateshead Progressive Players

Another national organization of the time, seeking to develop amateur theatre among other cultural activities, was definitely outside the establishment milieu and sought to challenge social hierarchies. The Independent Labour Party Arts Guild was formed in 1925 to formalize and support different local initiatives by the ILP to appeal to a wider range of people through social activity. In addition, as we have seen, it was part of the tradition of offering an alternative to the commercial mass culture that the ILP believed left acquiescence in the current arrangements of society unquestioned. Ros Merkin notes that there is a firm narrative now that ILP theatre groups abandoned socialist theatre in favour of promoting classic drama.[39] For example, in his account of the ILP drama groups of the 1920s Raphael Samuel comments that 'Propaganda was subordinate to the more general aim of making "great art" available to working people'.[40] Merkin has clarified that in fact the ILP Arts Guild, or at least some affiliated drama groups, did in fact perform propaganda material. It should be added, as we have seen, that the ILP believed that there was a political dimension to performing the classics to working-class audiences that went beyond addressing cultural impoverishment. For them, cultivating an appreciation of good drama in impoverished towns was part of the process of encouraging critical reflection. Thus there was little distinction between addressing cultural impoverishment and socialist politics in the amateur drama of the time.

By 1930 the Guild had 130 affiliated branches and at least two of its drama groups, in Sheffield and Gateshead, were affiliated to the BDL. The example of Gateshead is particularly interesting. The Gateshead ILP Amateur Dramatic Club – renamed during the 1920s as the Gateshead Progressive Players – outlived both the Arts Guild and the ILP itself to mutate into a well-regarded amateur theatre company with a Little Theatre.[41] It provides a useful case study because two of its active members during the inter-war years, the sisters Hope and Ruth Dodds, left articles and diary entries that illustrate the practicalities of sustaining a working-class amateur theatre society at the time. The performance space used by the Players until the Second World War was a hall that functioned as the hub for local labour movement activity, and the performances were also an important element in the networks, what Raphael Samuel described as 'the whole galaxy of social institutions', which activists created for themselves in Gateshead as elsewhere. These included a Socialist Sunday School, whose children's choir sang at meetings; regular lectures and educational classes, and social activities such as concerts and dances.[42]

Hope Dodds published a contemporary account of the Progressive Players which was perceptive about the covert hegemonies serving to exclude working-class people from the theatre. As she maintained in the BDL journal, 'We laugh at the Russians for prohibiting bourgeois drama, but the restriction of plays in England to one class of society is as strong in practice as any legislation could make it'. She observed of the Gateshead ILP drama group that these 'hard working men and women will spend their brief leisure in learning, rehearsing, producing and acting in plays without the smallest wish to go to the professional theatre'. They were 'blankly indifferent to the ordinary round of social comedy' that was on offer. This was because the stratum of society within which so many plays were set was completely unfamiliar to them: 'Witty dialogue depends very much upon analogies and references to a certain way of living and thinking of which our members know nothing, and lacking that experience it sounds pointless. The situations seem to them weak and artificial, or improper . . .'[43]

Shakespeare was popular but the company needed plays that could be done in everyday clothes with plain settings, and preferably on themes to which working people would respond. In terms of such a repertoire, however, there was very little. Andrew Davies summarizes the repertoire of such progressive theatre groups at this time as 'the ubiquitous Shaw plays'. If this is accurate Hope Dodds helps to explain the popularity of Shaw. His works were in modern dress, were simply set and took working people seriously.[44] The Gateshead programmes followed a similar pattern throughout the inter-war years. The works traditionally popular with progressive audiences: Shaw and Ibsen, the socially conscious dramas of Galsworthy and Barrie, and also an annual Shakespeare production. Each season included at least one performance of a play of the left, if possible a new work. Ruth Dodds wrote two overtly political plays for the group: *The Pitman's Pay*, which will be discussed below, and an 'industrial comedy', *The Hill-Top*. Other examples are Margaret Macnamara's *Mrs. Hodges*, in which members of the housing committee come up against the realities of slum conditions and the plays of Harold Brighouse, such as *The Price of Coal* and *The Northerners*, which dealt with pit disasters and cotton industry disputes in Lancashire. Thus a claim made of the 1938 season seems accurate enough for the whole two decades:

Figure 1 Gateshead ILP Amateur Drama Club perform *The Hill-Top* in 1924. Reproduced with the permission of Gateshead Archives: The People's Archive, Ruth Dodds Papers.

'four plays representing a varied choice . . . all except the farce throw light on the social conditions of past days or of today'. [45]

These programmes included classics and comedies, but perhaps this combination of the political with the mainstream demonstrates a strategy rather than a confusion of purpose, and one based on practicalities. The Players, like any Little Theatre, needed to sustain a presence to become a recognized feature in their towns and to establish the regular attendance needed to cover costs. Again this required a pragmatic approach to their repertoire.

Play-making in the workplace

Workplace drama clubs are an important feature of the popularity of amateur theatre in the inter-war years. As Nicholson, Holdsworth and Milling note, these drama groups were encouraged by the employers and were integral both to the culture of the workplace and their local communities. In addition Robert Snape has shown how in the inter-war period 'scientific' management linked employee welfare with productivity, and so support for clubs, sports teams and drama groups across the divides of the workplace were encouraged. The BDL established an advisory service for industrial welfare supervisors who intended to set up drama groups in their workplaces and reported on initiatives in the field.[46] Throughout the inter-war period there are reviews and references to workplace amateur companies: the Birkenhead Tramwayman's Amateur Dramatic Society, or the Hull Corporation Electricity Board Drama Club, and in Belfast the Ministry of Labour Dramatic Society; the Welwyn Stores Staff Association Players, and the Glasgow Corporation Transport Players; these are just some examples. Groups like these were obviously more common where the workplaces were major ones. In Birmingham the factory at Fort Dunlop employed, by the mid-1930s, some eight thousand people. The Dunlop Works Dramatic Society was drawn from all sections and performed in their own well-equipped Little Theatre. The annual works drama festival showcased entries by teams from the different sections of the factory.[47] In Liverpool the Littlewoods Drama Society had a membership of 250 and a theatre space seating 300. The annual works drama festival was described as 'the biggest of its kind in the world' with twenty-seven entries and five finalists.[48]

A drama club could be one of several sporting or welfare amenities to attract workers, for example in Bristol where three major factories competed for female employees. Thus the Robertson's Golden Shred Dramatic Club, established in

1927 and for which the company employed Joan Tuckett, a locally known performer and producer for the amateur stage. Apparently performances were traditionally in the works canteen for 'guaranteed audiences of fellow workers, their parents, children and retired employees'. However, Tuckett managed to organize performances further afield, intending to expand her casts' horizons and experience. Quaker employers already had a long tradition of promoting welfare, sporting and educational opportunities for their employees. One example is the Cadbury's factory at Bournville, Birmingham, an important development outside the city where the recreational and leisure facilities provided amounted to a complete environment for the workforce. One of these was the Bournville Dramatic Society, 'whose acting members represent all grades or workers at Cadbury Brothers' Works', and which established a reputation for excellent Shakespearian productions. Jonathon Rose observes that there were sound practical reasons behind the popularity of Shakespeare among workplace drama groups. The plays required large casts and therefore offered a range of parts that could accommodate the enthusiastic but less skilful members. The costumes, sets and lighting could be made in different sections of the factory without recourse to specialist outside theatrical departments.[49]

In the early 1920s the manufacturing areas of Yorkshire were hosting some significant examples of working-class participation in amateur theatre. The Reverend Gough in Heptonstall responded to interest among local mill workers by organizing readings and then performances of scenes from Shakespeare plays. His view, which as we have seen was widely shared at the time, was that active participation was a more productive use of leisure time than the more passive modes of spectating.[50] One of their performances in Leeds helped to initiate an interesting example of theatre with a purpose, the Leeds No. 1 Industrial Theatre. Warrender Dow ran a manufacturing enterprise that employed around a thousand people in the city. As a contribution to the welfare and education of his employees he had organized visiting lectures on literature and drama as well as trips to see performances of classic plays. The lectures, apparently, 'appealed more to the members of the clerical staffs than to factory or works hands'. When his employees saw the Heptonstall Village Players perform 'the working-class audience was attentive and roused to imitation' – they had witnessed people like themselves who spoke like themselves, and this dissolved some of the covert hegemonies which had separated them from theatre.[51]

Workers at Dow's plant progressed to producing plays with all the sets, lighting and costumes made by the factory workers. Like Tuckett in Bristol, James Gregson was paid as the producer for this group. Gregson had left school in Leeds aged twelve for work in the cotton factories before the First World War, later becoming a railway clerk. He received his later education through the local chapel, the ILP and the Workers' Educational Association (WEA). This had been established in 1903 to provide student-led adult education for working people up to university entrance level. Whilst working in Manchester Gregson was introduced to drama through Annie Horniman's Gaiety Theatre and in particular the plays in the Lancashire idiom by writers like Harold Brighouse. These were to inspire Gregson's own plays of Yorkshire life.[52] Dow and Gregson took different approaches. Dow was primarily concerned with the role of the drama in the education and welfare of his employees; for him, the process rather than the dramatic product was the main concern. Gregson, by contrast, with his recent background as an actor, writer and theatre manager, was focussed on the quality of what was going to be presented to the public. Writing many years later and from the standpoint of a theatre professional, he described the preparations for the first attempt to perform before an audience with a production of *The Merchant of Venice*. Forty or fifty would-be actors – 'managers, machinists, joiners, fitters, blacksmiths, painters' – were assembled. His recollection of the early rehearsals would probably be recognized by many schoolteachers:

> When we got down to actual rehearsals, I found myself facing a bigger snag than their inability to read – their terrible self-consciousness which made them giggle at each other's efforts whilst resenting the amusement they aroused in their parts. Coupled with a rough shyness which made them chary of any display of emotion and made them afraid of 'looking soft' when attempting speech a little nearer English than their Leeds dialect, this self-consciousness made the going very hard at first. Unthinking laughter would provoke quarrels . . .[53]

Gregson's memoir reveals that Dow, and quite likely other employers like him, had more prosaic motives for supporting workplace theatre groups. The novelty of the Industrial Theatre intrigued newspaper reporters, who were skilfully managed by Dow to present favourable publicity for the company and this in turn generated new orders. Membership of the Industrial Theatre was open to employees of all the local factories and according to Gregson it was 'a workers' theatre run from top to bottom by working people'. Member subscriptions covered the cost of the hall and any materials needed for costume and scenery, which the members made themselves, and any member wishing to act would be found a part. The management was through a committee with a representative for each factory with fifty or more subscribers.[54]

Shakespeare and repertoire

Gregson recommended Shakespeare for novice actors and was clearly not deterred by the challenges he described. He believed it gave them something to 'encourage them to be larger than life, something on which they can cut their teeth and loosen their jaws, something in which they have to act, not merely behave'. The project was ambitious. As Gregson said they performed 'lots of Shakespeare, and we've tackled Ibsen and Galsworthy and Shaw'. Further, by 1922 they had performed the little-known verse play *The Cenci* by Shelley, and a production of Ibsen's *Peer Gynt* which involved a cast of 150 and a Leeds orchestra. The local press reviews were encouraging although it is clear that the performance standard among those who had never acted before was understandably variable.[55] The factory workers were not able to produce more than one play a month and to make full use of the hall the Leeds No. 1 Industrial Theatre became a hub for the amateur movement in industrial Yorkshire. For example, the Leeds Arts Club Dramatic Society, forerunner of the Leeds Arts Theatre, was among the companies whose programmes made up a winter season: performances of Shakespeare, Pinero, Russian plays and 'works by local amateurs' were held.[56]

Valuing workplace theatre

For Gregson and many like him performing was compensation for the sterile rote-learning experienced at school, and an antidote to the repetitive, routine tasks of factory and junior clerical work. He described the appeal of acting to a journalist: 'Honestly, we love it. It takes us right out of ourselves. We become other people when we are acting – other people miles away from the factory. It is the most restful recreation in the world … And it necessitates the study of history, literature, and the manners of other ages.' He was one of the amateur theatre practitioners who gave evidence to the Committee on Adult Education for their Report in 1926, and Jonathon Rose believes that for Gregson there were also issues of reclaiming culture for his class, who had been denied it along with opportunities for education and self-expression.[57]

One query that could be raised about workplace drama groups is whether there was a class-based division of labour in which the manual workers were responsible for the sets, props and costumes while the more formally educated clerical and managerial staff took on the principal stage roles. Gregson's account of the Leeds Industrial Theatre in the 1920s suggests a socially diverse cast at all levels but the question remains as to what extent this was typical.

These developments in workplace drama were valued in other respects. Steve Nicholson points out that *The Drama in Adult Education* was published in 1926, the year of the General Strike and an escalation of class conflict in Britain. It must be added that 1926 too was the year of major defeat for the Miners' Federation after its long lockout following the General Strike itself.[58] It is probably unsurprising therefore that the report, discussing good practice in workplace drama groups, was particularly appreciative of examples of co-operation across the different hierarchies in large workplaces, promoting harmony at a time of social division. It expressed the hope that these activities would promote a 'greater understanding and sympathy between classes and heal social disorders which were so often caused by a failure to know each other'. Activities which cut across the social classes, all trades and departments of the factory, such as participation in amateur drama productions clearly might meet these criteria. Such hopes were also expressed elsewhere. One egregious example is the right-wing paper *John Bull*, in a review of a Mansfield House Players' production of Galsworthy's *The Pigeon* in London. Observing that these amateurs were 'drawn from all walks of life' in a 'non-class effort', the reviewer commented that 'a young dock labourer made as good a judge as ever sat on a bench in real life. The more of this sort of thing the less we shall hear of Bolshevism.'[59] However, noting that there were these varied expectations over the purpose of workplace play-making is to acknowledge its diversity and not to dismiss its value.

Rural Community Councils and adult education

Another network formed after 1918, again in an effort to counter the perceived decline of rural England, were the Rural Community Councils (RCCs), of which there were twenty-nine by the outbreak of war.[60] These were county-wide panels of voluntary organizations acting in liaison with statutory authorities and part of their remit was to promote adult education. Funding from the Carnegie Trust UK was secured for drama and arts work, with co-ordination frequently through the National Council for Social Service (NCSS), itself a creation of post-war reconstruction. Nottinghamshire and Derbyshire are interesting examples because in these cases the villages they covered included those in their coalfields as well as traditional rural areas.

By 1929 the Nottinghamshire Rural Community Council was seeking additional funding to meet the demand for adult education work, and this was obtained from University College Nottingham, the first university in England to establish an extra-mural department of adult education. The additional support for the drama classes entailed, to meet the University requirements, devoting time to studying the history and development of dramatic literature as well as to practical work. The practical work in the village drama classes included exercises in facial expressions, movement, gesture, mime and characterization as well as understanding the functions of the producer. Here the objective was 'to bring out capabilities and develop the imagination'. In turn the groups would produce one-act plays under supervision.[61] Nottinghamshire RCC, through its staff tutor in drama, successfully took drama work into small rural villages, many with populations of under 400 people. The twelve drama classes established by 1930 had led to eight permanent amateur drama groups affiliated to the Nottingham Drama League when it was founded that year. By 1934 there were seventy-four village drama societies recorded as active with most of them deriving from the adult education classes. The Director of Education – in an echo of the 1919 Report – recommended drama classes 'where few if any other subjects could be offered'; besides their own intrinsic value such classes introduced the study of motive, emotion and characterization, and stimulate the student into 'taking up other studies'.[62]

The numbers of entries to the Nottinghamshire Drama League festivals provide a measure of the growth of the movement: seven entries in 1930, forty-five entries in 1934 and fifty in 1937. By this time the press were reporting that there were almost a hundred village drama groups in the county, mainly formed following village meetings and generally involving people who had no theatrical experience. Groups affiliated to the League could receive classes in acting and production, sessions from experts in lighting, make-up and so forth, as well as opportunities to attend BDL training schools and make use of its play library.[63]

Derbyshire Rural Community Council established a Music and Drama Sub-Committee in 1926 and, following a survey of local amateur theatre societies, set up lecture courses 'combining production with literary treatment', and organized weekend schools for village hall producers in conjunction with the WI. One prominent tutor was Lawrence du Garde Peach, a local playwright and director of the well-established and successful amateur company the Great Hucklow Village Players. This support helped to give rise to the Derbyshire Drama League in 1931. The RCC gained practical support from other organisations promoting amateur theatre, such as the Derbyshire Co-operative Society which paid for its members to attend the drama classes.[64] In 1936 this Rural Community Council was one of those who appointed a full-time drama advisor, George Makin, who was an experienced amateur theatre actor and producer as well as a WEA tutor. Funding had been obtained from the NCSS and the Carnegie Trust UK which both recognized the strength of the Derbyshire Drama League, numbering as it did nearly a hundred local amateur companies by 1938.[65]

Makin gave talks and lectures on theatre history and ran training courses and schools on every aspect of play-making: production, lighting, make-up, speech training and acting. The students were groups affiliated to the Derbyshire League, new societies starting out, and Women's Institutes, Townswomen's Guilds and WEA classes. He also organized festivals and competitions for amateur groups and acted as a general resource for advice and training. His case, made to as many organizations as possible, was that it was up to the amateurs to keep the theatre alive in Derbyshire because it was too expensive for professional companies to tour there. The objective of the League was to promote productions that would be worth seeing for their own sake and not because they were fund-raising for charity.[66] He appears from this work to have been on the more progressive side of the political spectrum. However, he was accused in a letter to the local press of crass naivety when he returned from a Youth Hostels Association drama group tour of Germany and praised life under the regime there. It seems he had been taken in by the welcome and propaganda the group had received. His naivety about Germany did not last, however, as by the outbreak of war he was supporting Czech refugees and helping them to produce an expressionist play about Nazi persecution.[67] As we shall see Makin's more progressive credentials are confirmed by his important work with drama groups for the unemployed in the coalfields.

The 1919 Report had recommended that all universities establish extra-mural departments to support adult education initiatives in their areas. In the British university sector at the time, however, courses in drama which combined literary study with practical stage work were an innovation. This was not the case in the USA, where the links between the college and the stage were admired by some British theatre commentators.[68] Until the encounter with adult education British university drama courses had focussed on the literary. As a professor at University College Hull explained to a BDL conference, 'the teaching of drama had been carried out in the past far too much as a literary study. But plays were meant to be acted and even a University course should provide a certain amount of practical work.'[69] This theme of drama and adult education will be considered in the next chapter. If these examples of adult education and drama practice did achieve at least a precarious stability during the inter-war period this was not to be the case with several others. The aspirations of the 1919 Report as a whole were thwarted by the economic recession which followed it.

Recession and industrial crisis

The 'social disorders' noted by the liberal members of the Adult Education Committee arose from the bitterness generated by the coalfield disputes of the 1920s. The optimism of post-war reconstruction had been short-lived. The unemployment in traditional industrial areas with which the 1930s are associated was already clear by 1921.[70] The aspirations for national adult education envisaged in 1919 did not survive the austerity programme that was the government's response to recession. In the coal industry enforced wage cuts caused a lengthy lockout for the miners' union in 1921 and another longer one took place after the failure of the General Strike in 1926, itself called in support of the miners' struggles. The amateur theatre movement produced two plays in the 1920s, one by Ruth Dodds and the other by Joe Corrie, which responded to the miners' lockouts. It achieved this because it contained writers and casts who were either directly involved in or very close to the events themselves.

The Pitman's Pay, by Ruth Dodds, was performed by the Gateshead Progressive Players to revive morale after the miners' defeat in 1921. In three acts it recounts the story of Tommy Hepburn, who founded the first miners' union in County Durham in the 1830s, and the struggles against spies and informers, repression, strikes for recognition, and the eventual defeat and destruction of the union by the coal owners. Nevertheless the central theme is hope; the pitmen and their families are building something that will eventually succeed. As Hepburn says when he is forced to concede that the coal owners have won: 'Hepburn's Union is done, but there'll be another yet, a stronger and a better. And if that goes down they'll be another, and after that another. This thing we've started is going on, and the bairns will reap what we've sown.' Thus again in the final scene Hepburn's younger sister Bessie, after two years (the time scale covered by the play), announces her pregnancy and hopes for a girl, 'a scalding, unchancey woman like myself . . .'. Through this symbolism of forthcoming new life she can see, like Tommy, a future, optimism and hope for the days that are coming.[71] The general story would have been known to the more politically conscious audiences and the play was well received in Gateshead. A working miner played the role of Hepburn, miners and their families were in the audiences, and a reviewer described how 'pioneers in the local movement were deeply moved at the portrayal of the struggles, comparable to those which they took part in, years back'. The play was taken on tour, albeit a tour confined to the areas within easy reach for the cast. Ruth Dodds's diary recorded both high and low points of the tour. On one hand March 1923 saw 'a large and intelligent audience' in the pit village of Chopwell. An entry in the same month about a Bill Quay show describes the exigencies of touring non-theatrical venues: 'a horrible dirty inconvenient picture hall … every possible difficulty in entrances and exits, dressing accommodation, stage space and sitting generally'. Further, at this performance to raise funds for a new Labour Party branch, they played to 'a huge, noisy, ill-mannered audience' although 'I afterwards heard that it made a deep impression on the more serious-minded members'.[72]

Whereas Ruth Dodds was an affluent supporter of socialism Joe Corrie began his working life as a miner in Fife, where he had written and performed for his local amateur theatre group. He went through the lockout of 1926 after which he was unemployed, but the experience provided the material for his most overtly political play, *In Time O' Strife*. This three-act play takes place in the living room of a miner's cottage and concerns two families and their friends towards the end of the lockout. It is an entirely realistic description of the pressures exerted on such families at the time: dependent on communal soup-kitchens and meagre payments of parish relief, the consequences of malnutrition, and the aggression and violence shown to strike breakers who are undermining the solidarity required. In the course of the play a young strike breaker, engaged to the main family's daughter, has to flee the community, whilst another character is gaoled after making speeches to the pickets and an ill woman who has been putting her children's feeding before her own dies as a consequence.

In marked contrast to the unremitting seriousness of *The Pitman's Pay*, Corrie uses humorous one-line comments and light incidents to balance the action. Jean Smith, Jock Smith the miner's wife, is a particularly strong character with several pointed political remarks to make about newspapers biased against the miners and the need for active, not passive, union members. She is frank too about life in the colliery community even without the dispute:

Jean … It's been a hard time, richt enough, and mony a nicht I have lain doon wonderin' where oor breakfast was to come frae, but Jock, it's nae mair he'rt-rendin' than watchin' they wheels turnin' every day, and never lookin' oot the windie but dreadin' to see some o'yee cairrit hame a corpse or maimed for life …[73]

As with *The Pitman's Pay* the piece ends with optimism despite the defeat, as background voices are heard singing *The Red Flag*; as Jean declares, 'Keep up your he'rts, my laddies, you'll win through yet, for there's nae power on earth can crush the men that can sing on a day like this'.[74] Both plays respond to defeat with hope, providing their audiences with a coping mechanism as well as a dramatically coherent resolution.

Unlike the Dodds play which had a second limited tour during the 1926 lockout itself *In Time O' Strife* toured the mining villages of Fife when the dispute was over, although it too had a confirmatory function for audiences who had themselves been part of the events portrayed. The cast were amateurs and each and every one was from Corrie's own mining community so that there was a close relationship between performers and audience. Whereas James Gregson in Leeds as we have seen wanted his cast to act and not to 'merely behave' Corrie's approach has been described by his historian as 'behaviourist'. He rehearsed them to do on stage just what they would have done at home, something that would have been grasped and appreciated by the audiences. In contrast to Lady Beatrice Swift's no doubt creditable effort to play a miner's wife with the WI in Sussex, this cast were enacting a lived experience. As the Bowhill and then the Fife Miner Players Corrie's group toured the play in the north of England too, and aspired to develop a professional company.[75]

The onset of economic depression in the 1920s exposed the vulnerability of a drama movement aimed at or involving working-class people. The 'Once-a-Week Theatre' proved unviable; Ashwell's biographer notes that it had faced the prejudice that drama, even of educational value, should be financially self-sustaining and not a charge on the rates. Surely it must be added too that these projects faced greater obstacles when it came to funding through the rates. Poor Law Relief for the unemployed also had to be provided from the rates, and accusations by central government of excessive spending had led to legal clashes with local authorities. Poplar in London became a famous example. This together with all the other demands on service provision in impoverished areas thwarted efforts to establish municipal theatres in the absence of support from national legislation.[76] In 1929 the effects of recession on both casts and audiences for the Gateshead Progressive Players were such that the group survived financially for a time by hiring costumes to other amateur groups around the country. This is a contrast to the neighbouring People's Theatre in Newcastle, which as we have seen was financially secure enough in 1929 to take out a large loan for new premises – suggesting a more affluent audience catchment area than Gateshead.[77] In Leeds economic pressures severely curtailed the activities of the Industrial

Theatre and Dow's business could no longer afford to pay Gregson as a producer: trade recession reduced numbers of staff and hence subscribers.[78] Joe Corrie's Fife Miner Players had successful tours of his material around variety theatres and music halls but by 1929 these tours, and their project for a professional company, were coming to an end as their venues were rapidly changing over into cinemas.

This chapter has demonstrated how some of the prime movers behind the amateur theatre movement after 1919 invested it with a purpose beyond that of a recreation for the participants. Amateur drama had the potential to be a vehicle for social action and improvement. It was a viable means to build a popular basis for theatre given that it could present the public with quality drama, whereas the theatre dependent on commercial success was much less likely to take the necessary risks. It had a role in community development, rejuvenating village life and thus contributing to the sustainability of rural areas. Efforts were made to express working-class experience on stage and through this to confirm the values of politically engaged audiences. The importance of participation in drama as an educative experience, enhancing personal development through self-expression and as an entry point for further study was recognized by statutory agencies. In the liberal educational sector it was believed that participation could promote social cohesion in contentious times through communication across the social classes and collaboration on mutually valued projects. The following chapter examines one aspect of these motivations in the detail required to appreciate what was attempted and achieved. Educational settlements could be important providers of adult education in deprived areas, along with the WEA, and both were allies of the BDL. Both too shared the motivation to rebuild a better society after the war. Therefore the next focus is on some examples of how the impetus to promote amateur drama and the impetus to provide access to lifelong learning opportunities were often in partnership.

2

'A co-operative community effort'

Educational Settlement Theatre

The educational settlement movement

Victorian Britain saw the development of a network of university settlements, residential establishments attached to universities and situated in deprived areas. In them younger people from the affluent classes had the opportunity to study social conditions, train for social work and help with the provision of local services. In many respects they were a classic example of Victorian philanthropy and as such open to a range of criticism, voiced at the time, that they were an inappropriate vehicle to effect change.[1] Educational settlements, which began to emerge after 1905, had several important differences. Initially they were largely a Quaker initiative and were supported through Society of Friends philanthropy such as the Joseph Rowntree Charitable Trust. They followed a similar model of institutions for social action in particular communities, but they were mostly not residential (apart from a manager, 'the warden') and their focus was almost exclusively on adult education. They hosted Workers' Educational Association (WEA) classes, three-year courses organized by University Joint Committees, and shorter ones they established themselves. Besides courses they offered a range of activities and provided meeting places for different local organizations. Educational settlements were firmly in the tradition of education for a democracy of active citizens.[2]

The role played by educational settlements in British adult education has had some examination by historians but their role in promoting community play-making has not been explored in detail. This is despite the fact that in a number of cases at least it was an important part of their activities during the inter-war period. The 1926 report *The Drama in Adult Education* noted approvingly that the residential and educational settlements between them 'number some hundreds of dramatic groups', and that drama was regarded by the settlements as an essential element of cultural education. The students in those with their own theatre spaces were producing several plays a year, whilst those without them organized play-reading groups to study texts.[3] Given where the students were often drawn from and the audiences they often played to this can be seen as part of the movement to build a popular base for theatre. The 1919 Report, in fact, expressed hopes that such work would spread the appreciation of good drama and increase the public demand for it.[4] This chapter does not attempt a complete history of the role of British educational settlements in amateur theatre, nor does it attempt to cover all the settlements and their different theatrical initiatives. It will focus on several which represent a range as regards their terms of origin but which all faced the challenge of providing their services to communities that were being severely damaged by the unemployment of the inter-war years. A number, especially in the mining areas, were created as specific responses to such conditions. All were committed to the value of drama as an educational force and as a vehicle for both individual and community development. Some also had a vision for theatre and society which derived to a large extent from the aspiration for social and cultural renewal that followed the end of the First World War.

Foundations

Sheffield Educational Settlement was established in 1919 and the Bensham Grove Settlement in Gateshead opened for classes in 1920. Beechcroft Settlement in Birkenhead on Merseyside was earlier, opening in 1914. Taking Bensham Grove as an example, Gateshead was an overwhelmingly working-class community, and one of the worst boroughs in England for overcrowded housing and the associated problems of poor health.[5] The opening ceremony for Bensham Grove emphasized the 'intended non-political and non-sectarian character' of the new facility, and that 'we do not wish to identify the Settlement with any political party, nor to do anything of the nature of propaganda'. Nevertheless, the groups holding their meetings there included engineering trade union branches, the Irish Labour Party and Irish Self-Determination League, reunions of conscientious objectors and the League of Nations Union, as well as local Labour Party branches. As was the case at Beechcroft the management committee included members from the Labour Party and Trades Union Council and the Co-operative movement as well as the WEA and the students' elected representatives. Its aims included 'to promote systematic study of social, industrial and international conditions with a view to furthering plans for their improvement', reflecting the idealism for social reconstruction after the war. It emphasized purposeful citizenship in this new society and how Bensham Grove would contribute:

> An Educational Settlement must seek to *unsettle* those whose lives are limited by narrow personal aims, or who are content with the injustices and inequalities of the social system in which they live. Its aim must be continually to awaken a reverence for human potentialities, often so tragically underdeveloped, to arouse a sense of personal responsibility and to urge purposeful participation in a new way of life.[6]

Horace Fleming, the first warden of Beechcroft, believed that 'the task of the modern Settlement is the quickening and deepening of the personal life of the individual and the social life of the community, the central purpose being growth from the nascent to the mature'. A similar idealism was on display at the Sheffield Settlement, situated in a district seriously affected by the recessions of the inter-war period. Not short of ambition, the aim of the Settlement was to establish nothing less than the 'Kingdom of God' in the city. The definition of the 'Kingdom of God' included streets along which it would be pleasant to walk; workplaces in which people enjoy working; an environment where people 'may have life and have it in abundance' and education by means of which 'people may become more spiritual; everything that enriches human beings'. Enrichment was what its later supporters saw in its aim to 'give to people who would otherwise be destitute of them the treasures of the world's literature, drama, music, knowledge, art'.[7] Manchester University Settlement was of the traditional residential model, founded in the 1890s for the purposes of social work in the district of Ancoats. Alongside social work went the conviction that 'humanity has a great inheritance of ancient and world-wide culture, and that this should be shared by all ...'. Ancoats was a densely populated area whose residents, by the early 1920s, were described as living on the precarious edge of destitution. The Settlement had a long tradition of presenting concerts and plays in an annexe adapted as a theatre and known locally as the Round House. The producer Joan Littlewood, whom as we shall see had some influence on a producer at the Settlement theatre, described the Round House of the 1930s as 'the best theatre space in Manchester'.[8]

Accommodation, purpose and performance space

Access to and the good use of a performance space was believed to be an important element of these educational projects, and this reflected the place of drama in adult education. In Sheffield warden Arnold Freeman believed that 'the supremely educational thing – it might perhaps be regarded as the consummation of the activities of the Settlement – is the production of a play'. He earmarked a hall as a Little Theatre, with a hundred seats and a stage area 'little bigger than an average dining room'. At Beechcroft the Settlement Players performed in the grounds until a theatre area was built in 1924, and Bensham Grove used an interior rehearsal space which was later refurbished as a theatre. At York the Settlement Community Players, again from one of the long-established settlements, had access from 1935 to the Rowntree Theatre, although they also performed in local Co-operative Society halls and in what was obviously a large dining block at the York Cocoa Factory.[9] An important position for drama was also true of the later projects. The Rock House Settlement in Seaham Harbour, County Durham, was opened in 1932 as what was hoped to be a permanent centre for adult education in a town experiencing the high unemployment that had come to define the north-east of England by that time. It was linked to Durham University and intended to provide a community for adult education students. This too was a large house and grounds with rehearsal space; the Rock House Players were performing in local miners' halls and clubs within three months of opening, and by 1936 funding had been raised for a new building whose functions included a theatre.[10]

The establishment of the Spennymoor Settlement in 1931, also in County Durham, was a direct response to the unemployment in a mining area. A German artist who later taught at the Settlement described her first visit to the town in 1936: 'Rows and rows of men were standing in the drizzle. They stood there with drawn shoulders rather like birds perched on a bough on a wet day. So they stood, crouched, squatted, hundreds of them. Unemployed miners. Quite a number of them had nowhere to go ...'. Bill Farrell was an actor and theatrical producer and his wife Maggie was a teacher, although like all married women teachers at the time legally barred from practising her profession. The Farrells were encouraged to go to the area by the Educational Settlements Association to investigate the possibility of establishing a settlement. Funding was obtained through the Pilgrim Trust, a charity which funded initiatives to research and address the effects of sustained unemployment around Britain. There was very little property available in a colliery town like Spennymoor and so the Settlement had to manage with empty shop premises in the centre. The main room could function as a rehearsal space, the Spennymoor Settlement Players performing in local halls although by the end of the decade they had opened their own theatre building. This – a disused warehouse converted by settlement members – was partially grant-aided from central government sources with the balance of the funding raised by the local community. This was no mean achievement in an impoverished area, and it reflected the status the project had gained in Spennymoor. As Farrell emphasized, 'When the wives of unemployed men, and the men themselves will make toffee and cakes and other articles, raffle them, and hand the proceeds over to a particular fund no one will question their enthusiasm'.[11] Thus the origins of this Little Theatre (Spennymoor Everyman Theatre) are a contrast to those in more affluent areas. Jonathon Rose notes that the settlements such as Mansfield House in London and cities like Sheffield functioned as or supported 'fringe theatres' for local amateurs. It should be added that the later settlements such as Rock House and in particular Spennymoor functioned as the theatres in their communities and contributed to what would later be known as place-making, helping to define the identity of a place and its activities.[12]

As another Christian on the progressive end of the political spectrum Bill Farrell shared the philosophical sentiments expressed around the Gateshead and Sheffield Settlements. Amongst the aims of the project were the objectives to 'encourage tolerant neighbourliness and voluntary social service and give its members opportunities for increasing their knowledge, widening their interests and cultivating their creative powers in a friendly atmosphere'. Writing during the Second World War, however, Farrell positioned its role in terms of a war against the effects of persistent unemployment on the community:

> a war that might never end, a war that killed children slowly, that turned men and women to dullness, despair, degradation, in some cases to death by their own hands, a war waged by those who would preserve a social and economic system, which, the longer it lived, could by the very nature of its structure, perpetuate the War ...[13]

In Scotland Harkness House at Bellshill in Lanarkshire, like Spennymoor and Rock House in County Durham, was opened as a response to unemployment, and was formally launched in 1931. The buildings consisted of a former pub and a one-time bank branch which were obtained at a low rent from the local authority. The warden Katherine Dewar had the view that too many people in both education and industry in Britain suffered from what she called 'the gaffered mind': an undeveloped capacity for independent thought and action, something that the Settlement sought to promote. Accommodation was limited but there was a sufficient area to serve as rehearsal space for the Harkness House Players, who had begun performing by 1934. Later in the decade most of their public performances took place in local venues such as miners' institutes.[14] Bellshill like Spennymoor was a mining town and as in County Durham and South Wales the closure of the local sources of colliery employment had profound effects, particularly when the dismantling of the mines made the situation permanent. As Katharine Dewar put it, 'During this spring two more pits were closed and dismantled, and something very close to despair seized many of our members. They went about like creatures with an inward bleeding wound, or they disappeared for a bit, almost as if they could not even bear companionship.'[15] Again, the Settlement was dependent on grant aid from the Pilgrim Trust, and by 1934 the Harkness House Players represented an active theatre section of the Settlement. Elsewhere in Scotland the Edinburgh University Settlement was gifted an empty cinema for use as a hub for adult education and other activities with the unemployed in mind. This, the Kirk O'Field College, opened in 1933 and its drama class was performing publicly by 1935.[16]

Settlements in Wales

The new wave of British educational settlement projects after 1920 were based in the coalfields rather than impoverished city areas. As responses to the effects of long-term unemployment they were pioneered in South Wales, and the specific circumstances are noteworthy. After 1926, following the national lockout in the coal industry, widespread pit closures and part-time working, poverty in the Welsh valleys were known to be acute. During the 1926 lockout Quakers had organized relief work for the mining families in the Rhondda: managing the distribution of food, boots, clothes and money donated by national appeals, and organising local people in boot repair groups and networks to re-purpose clothes. As the lockout was drawing to an end A. D. Lindsay, the Oxford academic who had chaired the 1919 report on the future of adult education, and Horace Fleming of the Beechcroft Settlement, supported the proposal to build on these contacts to establish an educational settlement with two English Quakers on site.[17]

They had use of a detached house called Maes-yr-haf and its grounds near Trelaw; the grounds included a large barn with an improvised stage which provided a rehearsal and performance space for the early years. The impact of Maes-yr-haf was such that a similar project was established at Merthyr Tydfil in 1930, and by 1937 there were eight more settlements in the Rhondda Valley. Most had a drama group performing in popular, central local venues such as miners' institutes and the Judges Hall near Tonypandy railway station. This, according to Barrie Naylor, meant that plays had to be arranged so that the intervals coincided with the arrival of the 'up' trains, because the engine noise from departing trains would have drowned the voices of the actors. Eventually a Little Theatre was opened in the grounds of Maes-yr-haf in 1937 and for many years it served as a hub for the local amateur network.[18]

In all British educational settlements activity with amateur drama should be seen in the context of their adult education activity in general. Again, in the mining areas of Wales there were specific circumstances: a tradition of independent working-class education, a militant one in which 'independence' meant no influence from the state, universities or trade union hierarchies. The Central Labour College (CLC) had developed during the industrial unrest in the years leading up to the First World War and extended by 1922 into the National Council of Labour Colleges (NCLC), an implacable opponent and rival to the WEA. NCLC courses in Wales were dominated by politics and economics and the study of literature had never taken root. Those who advocated the study of culture and politics had been marginalized in the movement, and by the later 1920s teaching methods were being criticized for being 'dogmatic' and 'catechetical'.[19] By the later 1920s, however, the Quaker reconnaissance had identified weaknesses in their approach, both regarding the curricula and the methods of instruction adopted by many of the volunteer teachers.

A report prepared by Horace Fleming of the Beechcroft Settlement had noted the strength of the Marxist-oriented adult education, an issue for the pacifist Quakers because they associated Marxism and class war with the violence of revolution. Fleming's proposal though, if reminiscent of the deflection of 'civil dissension' suggested in the 1919 and 1926 Reports, did not involve rejecting progressive politics. The constituency was to be those critical of the 'extremists' whilst 'sensitive still to the best side of Communism', amongst whom, 'The desire for an education that is more ample and more generous than that of the CLC is even more apparent, and the contribution of a movement which, while not opposing present loyalties, would provide something fuller and lead to creativeness rather than to destructiveness, is certain of a wide acceptance'.[20] Fleming was convinced too that the participative arts could overcome political division amongst students, something he had witnessed during an historical pageant at Beechcroft when political rivals had worked together in a common project: 'drama can serve as a useful agent in bridging gulfs, and in drawing together in friendship men and women of diverse points of view and so aid the growth of the community spirit'. By 'not opposing present loyalties' the settlements across South Wales in the 1930s offered, as did settlements elsewhere, student-led courses which a Welsh historian has described as taking 'the principles and forms of independent working-class education and blending them with popular recreation and leisure'.[21]

Curricula

By 1931 most settlements, certainly all those considered in this chapter, received funding through the National Council for Social Service and the Pilgrim Trust to provide schemes for the unemployed. These, and the role they had with amateur drama, will be discussed in the next chapter. At this point it is important to understand that the amateur drama that was promoted by the settlement projects represented an integral part of their adult education curricula.

Lecturers from the WEA, local universities, or volunteer teachers like Maggie Farrell taught courses on economics, politics, science, philosophy, history, literature and foreign languages. There were of course some local variations and specialities, such as at Harkness House where Katherine Dewar and her artist sister De Courcey organized courses on arts and crafts, or at the Rhondda settlements where courses on Welsh literature and social history were held. Understandably economics was a popular subject – as Barrie Naylor comments, 'the unemployed wanted to know why they were out of work'. Linked to this were the related topics of 'Industrial Problems of To-day' and 'Problems of the Coal Industry'. The settlements of the Rhondda Valley and indeed elsewhere in South Wales offered an adult education that was clearly both wider and richer than the curriculum offered by Central Labour College lecturers and their success was notable. The WEA principle of student-led education was largely followed; at the opening of Rock House, for example, it was stated that, 'The programme of its work will be shaped in a large measure by its members – that is, by Seaham folk and not by outsiders'.[22] Harkness House provided courses of lectures on fascism, and communism and the Russian Revolution ('which attracted our Communist Neighbours') and an occasional speaker was the Glasgow anarchist Guy Aldred on the subjects of art criticism and the work of William Morris. As the 1930s wore on and international events increasingly occupied political thinking most of the settlements were hosting lectures and courses to reflect this.[23]

Courses of lectures on 'The Stage as a Means of Expression' were held at Bensham Grove and a one-year WEA class on 'Drama and the Arts of the Theatre' was held at Spennymoor. Both used the established WEA method of exploring drama through play reading and discussion. The Bensham Grove lectures were also 'arranged to meet the needs of people engaged in amateur dramatic work who feel the necessity of thinking over their aims and methods' and aimed at securing co-operation between them in the future. Visiting lecturers on drama at the Merthyr Tydfil Settlement included Michel Saint-Denis on 'The Actor – The Principal in the Theatre'. Saint-Denis had recently established the London Theatre Studio with its focus on innovative actor training absorbed from Europe. His involvement in a course for amateur actors drawn largely from unemployed miners and their families suggests a high calibre of adult education was being provided.[24] At Spennymoor students in the Social Science and Local Government History courses also received, at their request, classes in public speaking 'so that they might become more useful members of their other organisations', presumably political and labour movement bodies. Effective public speaking was a transferable skill from practical drama classes and it is likely that there was some interrelation between those sessions and classes that could provide speakers with argument and information.[25]

Mark Freeman states – based on a report of 1921 from the St Mary's Settlement in York – that in adult education as a whole there was 'a marked divide between the WEA students with their taste for economics, industrial history and other subjects on the one hand, and the settlement students with their preference for "aesthetics" (literature, music, art and drama) on the other'.[26] There is evidence to query this generalization, certainly as regards the settlements discussed here and during the inter-war period. Economics and related subjects were popular but not defining. Courses for railwaymen at Beechcroft, for example, included French as well as 'Economic Problems of To-day'; Newcastle railwayman Tommy McCulloch recalled being taught French at Bensham Grove by Eric Barber, the settlement drama tutor, who offered to teach morning classes in order to fit in with shift patterns. Barber also tried to encourage his group to think in terms of university. Similarly a County Durham miner explained during a WEA drama course that he and his fellow students were 'fully appreciative of the value of matters literary'. George Thompson, a former student at the Spennymoor Settlement, recalled that classes on economics and politics were indeed popular but the unemployed miners could have a wider focus: 'Some asked for history, for literature, as well as economics. Even the literature had to have a political bias – Dickens, Shaw, HG Wells, and people like that. We'd read and discuss them.' Among students such as these it did not necessarily follow that drama was separate from political interests. Farrell reported, in a point that will be discussed in a later chapter, that the Settlement Players had recruited some members from the social science class, who believed that 'the theatre has a function other than entertainment'. In the six years of the Harkness House Settlement some unemployed students won scholarships to Glasgow School of Art, having followed art courses at the settlement as well as social science ones.[27] The Spennymoor Settlement became known locally as the 'Pitman's Academy' and its classes nurtured the painter Norman Cornish and the novelist Sid Chaplin among the colliery worker students. It also tutored miners and women domestic servants for courses at trade-union funded adult education colleges such as Ruskin or Fircroft. In South Wales, where as we shall see the settlements functioned as educational hubs for unemployed clubs, literature and languages were popular options too. The balance of evidence, certainly as regards the post-1930 settlements in the mining areas, is towards participation by working-class students in cultural as well as social science courses; and the cultural included participation in drama.[28]

Funding, resources, contacts

Membership of an educational settlement and its courses and activities was open to all for an annual subscription, usually two shillings a year and payable by instalments if necessary. Examples of the numbers involved are that Harkness House initially catered for seventy-nine men and sixty-six women students, and Spennymoor around 400 men and fifty women students. By 1939 the settlements across the Rhondda Valley were reaching a combined number of nearly four thousand men and three thousand women students.[29]

The settlements each depended on grants from charitable trusts and the funds they could raise locally, always a problem during recessions and particularly difficult in deprived areas where the local sources for donations were overstretched. In practice they each had a financially precarious existence during the inter-war years and responded by making full use of their networks and, with the drama groups, creative approaches to costumes and stage properties. Manchester, for example, used black cardboard top-hats and advised that torches for procession scenes could be fashioned from 'small round tins mounted on broomsticks and filled with spirit-soaked cotton wool'.[30] Such props would have been in common use for community pageants and processions at the time. It enlisted the resources both of local factories, the university and local orchestral musicians as well as settlement residents: Frida Stewart, producer there between

1934 and 1936, relied on electricians from the Ferranti factory for help with lighting, musicians from the College of Music, and the Settlement historian notes that Stewart's Cambridge family background enabled her, when the occasion required, 'to mobilize her own family and their wide circle of friends to produce visiting musicians for Ancoats'.[31]

The opportunities presented by the Carnegie United Kingdom Trust are an example of the use of temporary funding by the settlements. During the 1920s the Trust had been looking to provide financial support to music and drama projects aimed at people who had no opportunity to see them or who could not afford to pay for them. Typically, the support took the form of guarantees against loss for a touring company, particularly where there was an objective to stimulate an interest in drama and to encourage the formation of amateur societies.[32] By 1929 the Bensham Grove Community Players had already performed in Durham mining districts on this basis. In 1931 Eric Barber at the Rock House Settlement seems to have built on this initiative; he had secured a two-year grant for him to work as an organiser and producer to establish amateur drama groups specifically in colliery villages, just as the Trust had supported drama work in agricultural ones. By 1932 eight amateur theatre companies were functioning in Durham and Northumberland colliery villages as a result of his efforts. Of these at least two were formed from WEA classes, beginning with play readings and then moving on to casting and eventually public performances of what had been read. The Trust paid for incidentals such as stage curtains, and any profits from performances were normally donated to local charities in order to conform to the charitable status of the Trust itself. The programmes favoured Shaw, both *Androcles and the Lion* and *The Showing Up of Blanco Posnet* being favourites, Shakespeare and adaptations of Dickens – particularly *Oliver Twist* – with the addition of Sheridan's *The Rivals* and *The Critic*.[33] In colliery villages the social dynamics differed from the rural. For example J. G. Wetherburn, an active member of one of these groups – and a radio broadcaster of Shakespeare – was a Labour member of Durham County Council and an official of the Durham Miners' Association, placing him in two important working-class networks with influence in the county.[34] Wetherburn promoted Shakespeare among these groups in the mining villages and in some cases the first ever performances were given in the welfare halls. *The Merchant of Venice* was popular either as a full-length play or just the trial scene as part of a wider programme.[35]

In Wales local schoolteachers like Margaret Copland at Bargoed were volunteer drama producers for the settlements, and advice also came from experienced amateur actors in the Rhondda Valley. In addition there was some input across the settlements from appointed drama organizers like Glyn Jones and the theatre professional Christine Bradshaw. Katharine Dewar at Bellshill seems to have used her networks to secure voluntary help from a Glasgow theatre producer and a newspaper critic to advise the Settlement Players, and to act as critical friends for their rehearsals and performances. The Kirk O'Field College had the services of playwright Catherine Orr as a producer.[36] Their national body, the Educational Settlements Association, was affiliated to the British Drama League (BDL) and the Scottish Community Drama Association (SCDA). Bill Farrell, and Lettice Jowitt, the warden at Bensham Grove and then Rock House, took part in BDL activities as competition adjudicators and training school lecturers and organizers. Freeman, Farrell and Jowitt each sometimes acted in their settlement productions as well as producing them, as did Warden J. A. Hughes in York. Farrell was a regional representative on the BDL National Council and he also chaired the Durham County Drama Association. He was closely involved with the amateur theatre movement in the county generally and acted as an adviser and producer for groups outside the Settlement. There was also cross-current between settlements: Eric Barber, for example, worked as a producer and teacher with Freeman at Sheffield before moving to Bensham Grove in the 1920s and then to Rock House; his last employer before the Second World War was University College Hull, which also employed Frida Stewart for outreach drama work when she left the Manchester Settlement in 1936. The Principal of University College Hull, A. E. Morgan, had a background in adult education and was Vice President of the Village Drama Society.[37]

Performances and education

The programmes of educational settlement drama groups were definitely ambitious and for the most part certainly seem to have avoided the easiest options. The 1926 Board of Education Report had observed 'a very high standard in the choice of plays' by settlement groups and this was generally the case. As we saw in the previous chapter the advice given to amateur companies by sympathetic professionals and the BDL was to be ambitious. Thus the York Settlement Community Players established a reputation for the quality of their material and the fact that they would not produce a play merely because it was likely to be a box-office draw. Lettice Jowitt explained to a WEA class, meeting to form a drama group, that she was against them performing one-act plays, believing that 'They are seldom good, and far too short'.[38]

This opinion of the one-act plays available was not uncommon in the early 1930s. Actor, writer and producer Norman Marshall, reviewing a very large collection of them in 1931, described them as 'workmanlike dramatisations of excessively trivial incidents' offering little opportunities to the actor, and the one-act play as 'the choice of the author with nothing to say'.[39] As we shall see in a later chapter as the 1930s progressed the quality of the one-act dramas available to amateur companies improved to some extent. In any event the theatrical ambitions of the settlements were a function of their ambitions in adult education. For example the Beechcroft Settlement Players originated from a Shakespeare reading group in the Settlement garden. The Settlement was described as 'only producing the best plays of which it is capable', which included not just Shakespeare, Shaw and Ibsen but Greek drama and Elizabethan comedy. At Maes-yr-haf the first drama group also began with a Shakespeare reading group. At Bensham Grove the Settlement Players had begun in 1920 with reading groups for Shaw. At Spennymoor Farrell reported that reading groups had emerged from a man reading Eugene O'Neill's *The Hairy Ape* to others around the fire, and from this a drama group eventually began. However, the first public performance (*The Cradle Song*) had arisen through miners' wives 'seeking something different and colourful'.[40] As a former student recalled of these sessions, a recollection in this case of the war years but it seems to hold good for the earlier period at Spennymoor too, 'I cannot say we produced many plays but we did them thoroughly and the number of play readings which we held gave all of us the opportunity not only to enlarge our knowledge of plays available but to read plays we couldn't ever possibly produce'.[41]

By the later 1920s the Sheffield Settlement Players had established a reputation for well-acted performances not only of Shaw and Shakespeare but Chekhov, Marlowe, classical Greek dramas, verse plays by Yeats and the first performance in English of Goethe's *Iphigenia*. The local verdict on their programmes was that they represented 'a long list of courageous productions which no others will touch'. This continued through the following decade with performances such as a musical selection from Milton's *Comus*, and Kalidasa's *Shakuntala*, an Indian verse-poem from an ancient text. Their record, as the supportive local press remarked, 'ordinarily would be regarded as far beyond the scope of amateurs'. The Sheffield Settlement maintained their traditional programme of classics through the Second World War.[42] The Manchester University Settlement also seems to have featured highly ambitious productions, certainly in scale, that aimed to meet the traditional settlement objective of bringing residents and neighbours together. Frida Stewart recalled that it was a principle to involve as many people as possible, and so plays frequently included mass participation through crowd scenes. Mary Stocks, historian and management committee member, authored a play about Chartism in Manchester in which local people enacted a mass demonstration with torches, marching through from the back of the hall, and they also made up the crowd scenes in *Julius Caesar*. According to Stewart (and the history of the Settlement by Mary Stocks) the programmes were deliberately varied and those involved were not deterred by practical difficulties over staging. For example, in 1935 they performed the anti-war play *Peace on Earth*, by Albert Maltz and George Sklar, part of the forthcoming wave of American left drama that was to come to Britain that decade. This involved elaborate lighting effects and expert timing during many crowd scenes, and here Stewart sought help from Joan Littlewood and Ewan MacColl's Manchester Theatre of Action. Other ambitious ventures were Purcell's *Fairy Queen* and Gray's *The Beggar's Opera* with their double casts of players and musicians.[43]

Bensham Grove, the Durham House University Settlement and Rock House staged Ibsen's *Peer Gynt*, produced by Eric Barber in a reprise of his success with this piece with the Sheffield Settlement Players in the early 1920s, and always well received. In both these cases the production was open-air and ambitious. At Seaham for example it involved more than one hundred members of the local community as performers, dancers and musicians.[44] The Settlement Community Players in York were also noted for innovative and varied programmes. In the mid-1920s they performed Ernst Toller's Expressionist *Masses and Man* and Karel Čapek's *R.U.R*, which, satirizing factory mass production and social mechanization, introduced the figure of the robot. *R.U.R.* was performed by the Newcastle People's Theatre in 1926 too; this was at the same time that both plays were being taking up by the embryonic Workers' Theatre Movement in London, and suggests that the explicit theatre of the left did not have a monopoly on the new progressive drama during the decade.[45] Later productions in York included, besides Shakespeare, Shaw, Ibsen and Sheridan, some first performances of contemporary Spanish drama, a mass pageant involving all the other local amateur theatre companies, 'variety entertainment' and plays by Eugene O'Neill. At least one local critic though believed that Ibsen was 'the type of social drama in which they have established a reputation'.[46]

Figure 2 Bensham Grove Settlement production of *Peer Gynt*, 1925. Reproduced with the permission of Tyne and Wear Archives Service SX51/16/2.

Adult education and writing

Katherine Dewar's educational principle of encouraging independent thought and action was put into practice with the drama group, so that Harkness House was described as the only settlement drama club in Scotland to perform original plays, in this case written by their own members.[47] The significance of this will be discussed in the next chapter, but it is worth noting that the production of original material, especially written by students, was a departure from mainstream adult education practice at the time. Whereas the 1919 Report recommended that students be encouraged to write 'in their own local language' literature 'made out of the same stuff as the tragedy and comedy of their own surroundings', in practice the priority in adult education was the appreciation of great literature and thus the best of human culture and common values. As the Sheffield tutors expressed it, 'Education, when it expresses itself in the Little Theatre, cannot take the form of any plays except great works of art'. Adult education in the inter-war period, be that of the WEA or the NCLC, rarely included what would later be termed 'creative writing' courses. It may have been part of the expectation of the drama courses that students might enact the plays they were studying, but it was not part of the mission that they should write their own.[48]

One example of a Harkness student who did was John Farnan, an unemployed labourer, who wrote *Sacrifice*, on life among tramps. The most prolific author attending this Settlement was Frank Farnin, a bricklayer from Bellshill who also acted with the group. Having begun with performances for limited audiences at Harkness House the Players progressed to audiences of the wider public. They presented four plays at Bellshill Miners' Institute in 1938: *War Memorial* by Farnin, which will be discussed in the next chapter, and his *Exiles*, about the effect on a family of the Means Test. These were with two comedies by other local authors, one, *The Jumble Sale*, with an all-women cast. On this occasion it was clear that they had established their position with the local community and built an audience for their work.[49] In the two years before the outbreak of the Second World War the Harkness House Players were regular participants in Scottish Community Drama Association festival competitions. The Settlement project closed by the end of 1936 when the funds from the Pilgrim Trust had been exhausted. Dewar was unable to attract funding from the Scottish Council for Social Service, the responsible section of the NCSS. Nevertheless, after the closure of the Settlement and its transition to a community centre the Players continued as an amateur drama group and were still assisted by Katharine Dewar, their Glasgow producer and a local councillor who acted as their business manager.[50] As we have seen they continued to perform locally with their own material.

Some performances in Wales

In Wales there is evidence of a direct engagement with contemporary issues by settlement drama groups. An early performance by the Bargoed Settlement in the Workman's Institute was a four-act play, *The Rising Sun*, by Herman Heijermans, a playwright described as 'the Dutch Ibsen'. This drama concerns a small shopkeeper and his family facing ruin at the hands of large retail competitors and as such it was probably a recognizable issue for small communities; several packed houses were apparently deeply responsive to it.[51] Another Bargoed production in demand in South Wales was *Land of My Fathers* by novelist Jack Jones. He had won an amateur theatre play-writing competition with this piece and it became a play of choice with the amateur societies of Wales, produced both in Welsh and English. Performances by the Bargoed

Settlement Players were particularly successful with audiences in the mining valleys and so it is worth some discussion here.[52] The author's notes in the published text of *Land of My Fathers* state that although it is set in the Rhondda it could be played in the colloquial English of any accent, and Jones believed that it had just as much relevance for the coalfield areas of England and Scotland.[53]

The play has little in the way of a plot as such and the action takes place within one room in a miner's terraced house. The focus is on the interrelationships between the different characters within a family and their neighbours during a prolonged period of unemployment. We see the – well-attested – effects of the Means Test on family life, the poverty and day-to-day struggle to survive it necessitated: the lack of hope and prospects, and also a background of protest. There is humour, some bitter, as when Aunt Marged says of her husband that, 'He never sings "Land of my Fathers" on the road home unless he's half slewed, for it's only then he's able to forget he's a dole man who's got none of the land of his fathers ...'. Some of it though is affectionate and concerns gambler son Lemuel and his greyhound. However, Jack, the communist, is the only character to whom it is difficult to warm. Released from gaol after a protest march he criticizes the local unemployed families for not rallying 'to the only Party which is conscious of the historic mission of the working class'. He himself will leave the land of his fathers ('there's no use going on working with material like that') and join the exodus of young workers to the Midlands and the London area 'where the final struggle will take place'. Nevertheless he is not the cartoon Bolshevik of the right-wing popular press but a plausible if dogmatic militant, eventually on good terms with his family at the double wedding in the final scenes. At the conclusion of the play the national rearmament programme has led to the pit's re-opening but amid uncertainty about how many of the older workers will be taken on.

In terms of the politics of the Rhondda at the time – struggles against unemployment and relations between the dominant political forces, Labour and the communists, rival contenders for working-class support – *Land of My Fathers* was apposite. The themes and issues of the play, as with the earlier *In Time O' Strife*, would have been familiar terrain for local audiences who would have seen their own situations performed back to them by those who had the same experience. They would have identified too with Aunt Marged's assertion that, 'Work, Katie, is the only thing that makes men steady an' decent. Without work to go to they're lost, an' we women can't find 'em ...' The female roles in the play are strong ones to reflect real life roles in maintaining the domestic life and economy under pressure. The Bargoed Settlement performances of Jones's play led to the accolade of 'one of the leading companies of Wales', and 'highly creditable performances' with 'acting of outstanding talent'.[54] The theme of drama like this portraying Welsh life will be continued in a later chapter.

Drama in education

It has been shown that both the 1919 and 1926 Reports on adult education identified drama as a means to attract and teach a wider range of students than could be achieved through conventional course work. The 1926 Report confirmed the belief that drama 'was at its highest as an instrument of education' when the serious study of plays was followed by the production of them by the students.[55] The Beechcroft Settlement provides an example with the open-air Shakespeare pageant it organized in 1921. Male students constructed an Elizabethan village as a setting, period costumes and hand properties were researched, designed and made by women students, 'the work as intense as at the classes in any art or technical school'. The event consisted of scenes and tableaux from three Shakespeare plays, performances of three complete plays, as well as reconstructions of Elizabethan shopping and games researched by students. Nine hundred people visited, and further historical pageants were produced in the same way: on Wat Tyler, a Pageant of Great Women and the History of Birkenhead, which was seen by ten thousand people.[56] This method of student research across a wide spectrum before production was also used by Barber in County Durham when a production of *The Merchant of Venice* involved arranging the venue, a miners' hall, to resemble an Elizabethan theatre.[57]

This use of play-making as a tool for wider education was common practice in the settlements, if often on a smaller scale. As Farrell explained, 'Play rehearsals are not just play rehearsals. They also become times when social and political teaching is possible because it's necessary, often, to know just what a character's social, political and religious background is before one can get to grips with him . . .'[58] This of course is also in line with Gregson's perspective at the Leeds Industrial Theatre in the 1920s where for them play rehearsals necessitated the study of history, literature and what he called 'the manners of other ages'. Similarly in Sheffield drama was interrelated with literature and history courses: studying *Wuthering Heights*, for example, involved, besides the text, studying social history and then dramatizing the story for public performance.[59]

Process and product

In their work with their drama groups some settlement staff followed the educational principle that the process was as important as the product. For example, in 1932 when Lettice Jowitt encouraged a WEA class in a Durham pit village to form a theatre group, she told them that, 'There should be no stars in an association of this kind. I find it a good idea – although this is sadly neglected by local amateur societies – that principals, no matter how excellent their performance, should stand down for someone else in the next production'. She had taken a similar position with the Bensham Grove Players several years earlier when she emphasized that taking part in community play-making was an opportunity for good teamwork. Thus it was reported of Eric Barber's production of Ibsen's *Brand* that 'our teamwork gives us the opportunity of putting into very practical form the fellowship through association in which we believe'. Further, an early press review of the Bensham Grove Players noted that 'no names were on the programme to emphasize that this was a co-operative community effort'.[60] Such co-operative efforts of course demonstrated education for good citizenship too.

The issue of participation but anonymity could be taken seriously where theatre was allied to adult education. The 1926 *Report on the Drama in Adult Education* had noted that 'Many successful companies attributed so much importance to this point that they required their members to observe complete anonymity'; on the other hand, one company from whom it had received evidence printed on the programmes, as a matter of policy, the names of absolutely everyone who had contributed to the production, including the scene-shifters and programme sellers.[61] Similarly, the work of Sheffield Settlement Players was presented as a great communal effort, and there too the names of the cast did not appear on the performance programmes, suggesting that the emphasis on communal effort was a principle that was shared, at least by the university settlement theatre groups.[62] The Beechcroft Players also maintained their casts' anonymity on programmes and publicity. However, this was not necessarily the case with other settlement groups such as the Harkness House Players, Rock House, Mansfield House, the York Settlement Community Players and the Welsh companies.

At Spennymoor among Farrell's Players co-operative effort as a learning process was also an objective. Cast members were expected to perform other tasks as well as or until they were on stage: 'It is the rule of the company that each and every member of it shall be first and foremost a theatre craftsman, and only then a potential actor or actress. The dilettanti, suburban mannequin-parade type of actor is not encouraged.' This is an example of how the co-operative effort valued all the skills and crafts – the painters, carpenters and seamstresses as well as the actors – that contribute to a performance. Besides communal effort and satisfaction there were also cases to foreground of participation in amateur drama giving rise to significant individual development. Farrell later described how a pitman with a seemingly incurable stammer had joined the company, where voice production exercises dealt with his difficulty to such an extent that he was able to take the lead role in their 1939 production of the medieval morality play *Everyman*.[63]

Reception – reviews and the press

This close attention to the process is not to say that the product – a theatrical performance – was neglected. As Nicholson, Holdsworth and Milling observe in their survey of amateur drama, to value the different craft skills involved should also mean appreciating that their creative satisfaction derives ultimately from a successful production. During the Second World War, John Murray, working in a local munitions factory, took part in Spennymoor Settlement productions and recalled rehearsal procedures with Farrell. His account demonstrates how thorough those rehearsals and preparations were:

> We might spend a whole evening on two pages and during that time BF would put us into various situations, moving characters about, giving us the opportunity of acting another part, perhaps leading off into several exercises of how to enter or exit successfully, pausing in the line, throwing one away, becoming various characters. His biggest teaching vehicle was that of priming two actors in several pieces of dialogue and allowing the rest of us to try and guess what relationship they were, what the situation was and then putting it to the actors later that they had got across something and how it had come across. It would be analysed until late in the evening and the rehearsal resumed the following week.[64]

Between the opening of the settlement in 1931 and the outbreak of war in 1939 Spennymoor appears to have fielded fewer dramatic productions than its counterparts elsewhere. As we have seen the first in 1934 was *The Cradle Song*, a three-act comedy by the Spanish playwright Gregorio Martinez Sierra. The second in 1935 was J. M. Synge's *The Playboy of the Western World* and the last in

1939 was *Everyman*. This was the first performance in the Settlement's own Little Theatre. *The Cradle Song* was rehearsed for twelve months before performance; as Farrell reported, 'the play-reading group is clamouring to give a public performance but nothing will be done until definite standards have been reached'.[65]

At the Round House in Manchester Mary Stocks recorded that Frida Stewart's productions may have lacked the detailed finish that an intensely drilled cast can demonstrate, but nevertheless the 'setting, movement and casting amounted to genius', praise endorsed by the *Manchester Guardian*. For example, that paper's review of *The Fairy Queen* in 1935 commented that it was 'not in any sense a unified work of art but it was a rich and splendid and at times beautiful medley of poetry, charming music, dances and fine dresses'. The reviews of plays by the local newspapers of settlement plays were almost invariably supportive. In Sheffield, for example, it was said of the settlement drama group that 'of the quality of their plays the most competent judges in the city and out of it have spoken in the highest terms'.[66] Whether this was a genuine appraisal of the performances or from a local desire to support the aims of the settlements is possibly moot. Local newspapers would tend to support local amateur drama societies almost on principle but they are a useful, indeed often the only, source of evidence about the product on stage. Certainly the favourable reviews in the Welsh press could include detailed explanations for the judgement of each individual acting performance, and this was not uncommon in other parts of Britain. Local reviews of the Beechcroft Players, for example, were supportive of their efforts whilst at the same time identifying unevenness in either acting or staging. Similarly, reviews of the York Settlement Community Players could occasionally be critical of some of the acting or staging but this was never enough to challenge the consensus that they 'made a valuable contribution to dramatic work in York'.[67]

A learning process can be observed with the Settlement group in Bellshill. As we have seen the Harkness House Players began with novice casts performing plays by novice writers; the first local reviews were supportive of shortcomings that were 'due to the inexperience of author and actors'. After a performance of Frank Farnin's *The Three Wise Men* (a Christmas appeal for international co-operation for peace) at a community drama festival the adjudicator illustrated how meaning can be conveyed by gesture and movement on stage as well as dialogue, resulting in the author and cast taking up tuition from him. Almost a year later Farnin's one-act peace play *The War Memorial* was performed to great effect at a League of Nations meeting in Hamilton Town Hall on Armistice Day

1937.[68] The play will be discussed in the next chapter in the context of play-making by unemployed casts and writers.

Social composition – players and audiences

In view of the expressed aims of the educational settlements, and the objectives set out by important voices in the amateur drama movement since 1918, it is important to consider the social diversity of the participants. This is particularly the case with the traditional university settlements and those with an established WEA practice. Courses at Bensham Grove certainly attracted working-class students, as evidenced by the effect of the miners' lockout in 1926, when the annual report described how, 'The condition of the mining industry has made the past session a difficult one for the WEA branch . . . Money has been desperately scarce, and many students have found regular attendance at classes impossible of late, owing to the new arrangement of shifts.' Nevertheless, as we have seen it has been suggested that working-class WEA students such as these favoured economics and industrial studies whereas settlement students were more likely to take up literature and drama. There is also evidence, discussed above, that would query this generalization about preferences. The Bensham and District WEA, who were based in the Settlement there, covered eight villages and 'a large group of Post Office workers from Newcastle and Gateshead' who combined to organize dramatic performances. Efforts were made to attract members of the unemployed club (which the next chapter will discuss) to join study circles and play reading groups, and they gave at least one performance themselves.[69]

As was noted earlier the Manchester Settlement, one of the traditional residential university settlements, mounted large-scale productions with opportunities for local people to participate. One recollection about the casting is particularly interesting. Stanley Heath, remembering 'a religious play' states that, 'There were some local people in the production – in the crowd scenes! They didn't get the plum parts.' The play may have been the Settlement's production of John Masefield's *The Trial of Jesus* in 1938, or of Martinez Sierra's *Holy Night* in 1933, the latter certainly having at least one settlement student in the lead role. It seems from Heath's account at least that the Settlement residents tended to acquire the 'plum parts' for themselves whereas the contributions of local people were confined to crowd scenes and stage carpentry.[70]

As has been discussed this was a potential issue with the workplace drama initiatives of the previous decade. This account points to a class-based division of labour between the working-class settlement members who made the sets and costumes, and the middle-class members who took the leading stage roles. This could have been the case where university settlements had residential students with higher levels of education. Nevertheless, Frida Stewart – whose work at Ancoates was outside the period of Stanley Heath's recollections – refers to an unemployed wire-worker, clearly possessed of great natural talent, taking the lead role in Molière's *The Bourgeois Gentleman*, and another who mastered difficult solos in *The Fairy Queen* as well as any professional. In another example the cast of the Settlement production of Beaumont and Fletcher's *The Knight of the Burning Pestle* in 1936 was made up of 'mostly unemployed members'.[71]

The Sheffield Settlement Players claimed socially diverse casts. According to the Settlement historian 'most of the actors were manual workers in the early years, and people who were out of work'. Not only that but most of a cast in 1926 were 'unemployed people living in extreme poverty who had scarcely been able to speak six consecutive words of English when they started the class in dramatic art a year before'.[72] The public were told – admittedly by supporters in a fundraising appeal – that 'it's student members are mostly poor people, many of them very poor people indeed'. Their publicity stressed that their casts were comprised of 'ordinary people – steelworkers, clerks, teachers and typists', showing how the Settlement was bringing out their acting ability; and that in one of their Shakespeare productions in 1937 the roles of Othello, Iago and Cassio were taken by steelworkers. Also, that an unemployed worker had taken on Lear and another one Hamlet. The Mansfield House Players – the social class range of whose cast in *The Pigeon* had gained the approval of the *John Bull* reviewer – were 'all working men and women'.[73]

At Spennymoor we have seen that both miners and their wives took part in productions and not simply as 'spear-carriers': the opening of the Players' Theatre in 1939 featured a performance of *Everyman*, with a young coalface worker, the man formerly with a speech impediment, in the title role. Similarly the Harkness House Players were drawn from a settlement whose members were principally 'unemployed miners, steelworkers, joiners and their wives'. The unemployed workers were involved not only in the performances but also in the play-writing. In Edinburgh Catherine Orr commented on the enthusiasm of the 'miners, seamen, typists, housewives and unemployed lads with no prospect of work' in the Kirk O' Field drama group.[74]

What can be said of the audiences these theatre groups built? This is more difficult to clarify. Almost invariably reviews focus on the responses of the individual reviewer and rarely deal with the social composition of the audience surrounding the reviewer. Thus the York players were described as attracting 'their usual crowded audiences' at the Co-operative Hall [75] but with no indication of who they were. However, the social composition, and relative isolation, of Welsh and County Durham mining areas, for example, would suggest that the audiences had similar backgrounds to the performers. At the same time the fact that programmes were not those that would be found in the local commercial theatres – theatres which would have been available in the cities at least – meant that some settlements potentially attracted theatre goers from the middle and professional classes as well as the local working class. Settlement theatre certainly avoided exclusion through price. The York Community Players asked for contributions rather than charging admission; Mansfield House offered a subscription system for seats with a wide price range; the Welsh settlement theatre charges were as low as possible, as were those of the Sheffield Little Theatre and the Spennymoor Settlement. The theatres or performance spaces were often either in working-class areas, central venues close to them or others such as Co-operative or miners' halls that would not have been seen as culturally exclusive. The Little Theatre that the Spennymoor Settlement was able to open in 1939 depended in part on local fund-raising and indicates the level of support it had achieved in the impoverished area it had sought to serve.

The educational settlements demonstrated the intersection between adult education and the amateur theatre sector during the inter-war years. In offering those with little formal education opportunities for play-making at every level they democratized cultural participation. At the same time, the belief that their purpose was to introduce students and audiences to quality drama meant that the choice of play was entirely the preserve of the tutors. There seem to have been few opportunities for students to develop play-writing skills of their own. This did of course offer audiences quality drama that the commercial theatre was unlikely to risk, and they were capable of high standards of performance and production even when their choice of material was ambitious. Some established performance spaces in communities where none had existed before and extended the social diversity of the Little Theatre movement. Courses at the settlements provide examples of innovative practice in combining the study of drama texts with their practical performance and their social history.

Some of these settlements arose through the unemployment afflicting areas of Britain. As long-term unemployment became confirmed early in the 1930s the government introduced specific projects to occupy workless people. The next chapter looks in detail at how amateur was included and the issues that emerged.

3

Social Control or Self-Expression?

Amateur Theatre and the Unemployment Crisis

The crisis of 1931: state and voluntary sector responses

The international recession which followed the Wall Street Crash of 1929 generated unprecedented levels of unemployment. In Britain this had reached 20 per cent, almost three million people, by 1932, and it divided the nation. Some parts of the country associated with growth industries such as motor manufacture prospered, whereas the burden of recession fell hardest on the areas dominated by heavy industry, principally the north of England, South Wales, the west of Scotland and industrial Northern Ireland. In a number of localities unemployment persisted at over 50 per cent for years.[1]

Britain had Conservative or Conservative-dominated governments from 1931 until the outbreak of war. Labour had been routed at the General Election of 1931, following the decision of leader Ramsay MacDonald to respond to economic crisis by forming a 'National Government' with the Conservatives. This coalition embarked on an austerity programme which reduced benefits and subjected claimants to an inquisitorial Means Test to determine eligibility for support. The result was persistent political protest, in particular by the Communist Party-led National Unemployed Workers' Movement (NUWM).[2] The Special Areas Act – originally they had been designated 'Distressed Areas' but the government soon modified the title – was passed in 1934. The Act appointed Commissioners in designated areas such as County Durham and Tyneside, South Wales and the west of Scotland to promote their economic regeneration and stem their depopulation as younger people left for work elsewhere. The consensus of historians is that this was a hesitant and ineffective intervention with only a marginal effect on unemployment.[3]

The absence of any sustained government economic policies to combat unemployment was accompanied by a limited response to its social consequences.

The government reaction to the protests and controversies over its austerity programme was not to modify its effects on the unemployed. Instead it was to empower the voluntary sector to alleviate the results of long-term unemployment through part-funding clubs and social centres. This was done after 1932 by channelling funds from government and charitable sources to the National Council for Social Service (NCSS), who co-ordinated and supported the many local initiatives taking place. The result was a national network of what were variously called social service centres, voluntary occupational centres or unemployed clubs. They offered materials and instruction in boot-repair, carpentry and allotment gardening, organized adult education sessions, and organized family holidays and outings. Later when clubs for women – principally the wives and family members of unemployed men – were organized the activities covered clothes making and alteration, quilting, toy-making, family recipes and other means to alleviate household management on the breadline.

By 1935 1,334 clubs had been established around Britain with a total membership of 142,210 men and 15,771 women. The numbers reflect the marginal economic position of women in the areas of heavy industry where they had few opportunities to work outside the home. There was little debate about unemployment amongst women; the issue was the effect on women of the unemployment amongst men.[4]

Much of the British left believed that these initiatives were designed to diffuse the potential for unrest among the unemployed, giving the appearance of action whilst in reality leaving the real problem of worklessness untouched. Suspicions such as these were only reinforced when some of the donors to the clubs, such as the Liverpool Steamship Owners' Association, were also known to have funded organizations to counter-act the influence of the NUWM. The mainstream trade union movement suspected that the workshops could be used to produce goods at below trades union pay rates and thus undermine the conditions of those in work. Throughout their operation most of the social service centres were treated with suspicion by their local labour movements and co-operation was rarely forthcoming. The strength of the political opposition to the clubs was also recorded in the official history of the NCSS.[5]

By 1933 the British Drama League (BDL) had become involved. The League was affiliated to the NCSS and agreed to contribute to alleviating the social effects of long-term unemployment, a problem it saw, accurately enough, as one likely to afflict an entire generation. The proven value of drama in 'giving a means of emotional expression, and of living many lives in the imagination' – might similarly 'help to dispel the terribly humiliating feeling of the unemployed that the earth has no use for them'. The BDL encouraged all affiliated groups and sympathetic professionals to assist where possible, and this could and did include the drama advisors attached to County Councils and other statutory bodies. George Makin worked as a drama advisor in County Durham before moving to the Derbyshire Rural Community Council. He believed that the social service movement should pay special attention to using drama because it demanded teamwork and co-operation, and provided opportunities for a wide range of skills. Further, play-making could enhance self-respect and thus counter the psychological effects of unemployment by developing hitherto unknown abilities. This echoed the assumption, common at the time, that worklessness would engender apathy and listlessness. There were also local voices advocating drama for the unemployed: in Yorkshire Gregson stressed its educational value and role in personal development, just as he had done with the Leeds Industrial Theatre. The BDL and the amateur theatre movement generally were extending the role of drama in adult education, one officially recognized since 1919, to the unemployment crisis. Such an initiative was entirely in line with the principles and objectives of the BDL, but it took place in the context of how the social service centres operated and why they had been established.[6]

Support structures

The support given by the BDL and other national groups built on the infrastructure that had developed during the 1920s. As we have seen the Rural Community Councils (RCCs) in counties like Derbyshire and Nottinghamshire – counties whose villages included colliery villages – had Adult Education Committees arranging drama classes, and Drama Leagues affiliated to the BDL. As the activity of the Nottinghamshire Drama League nurtured amateur groups in the county it apparently had 'a strong appeal' for those out of work. In the early 1930s it was estimated that in three or four of the drama groups a large proportion, more than half in one case, of the membership were unemployed, and later 'the zest with which unemployed workers are taking up dramatic work' was attracting attention.[7] In addition the RCC staff tutor in drama worked with drama groups across a network of social service centres, responding to where an interest in performing lay. Also, the drama group formed from the Nottingham County Association of Unemployed Workers was supported by the University College Nottingham Adult Education Department, just as in Belfast the Queen's University drama society coached groups of unemployed workers in producing plays.[8] In Derbyshire RCC Makin similarly extended his work to include the social service centres, and as we shall see he left an important account of his work with unemployed drama groups.

The educational settlements were a significant element in the amateur theatre and adult education infrastructure. The attachment of social service centre work – carpentry, boot-repairs, allotment gardening and so on – at the older educational settlements such as Bensham Grove and Manchester University brought a new clientele who required a new approach. In the words of a Bensham Grove report they were 'presenting special problems which we could not deal with as part of ordinary Settlement activities'.[9] Or, as Bill Farrell explained:

> Always at the back of their minds is the thought that nothing is worthwhile to them, nobody really cares whether they live or die and so what does it matter whether they do anything or not? And in most cases they are more often hungry than not, always anxious how much longer their clothes will last and always wondering whether a mythical someone will set them on.[10]

They were not the trade unionists seeking self-improvement or advancement through the Workers' Educational Association (WEA) university extension courses; in fact they were unused to formal adult education and it was soon found that a far more informal method of organizing discussions around a topic was necessary. The settlements established in South Wales in the 1920s already had experience of this, and those established elsewhere in response to the unemployment crisis followed that model. The traditional settlements like Manchester, as we have also seen, had some success at involving the unemployed in dramatic work.

By 1936 there were nine music and drama advisors attached to the regional organizations of the NCSS: for example, the Tyneside Council for Social Service, whose advisor functioned as teacher and producer for the unemployed clubs of the region, stimulating play-reading and drama groups where the interest could be found. By 1937 at least half of the thirty-two clubs had established groups giving local performances.[11] In Nottinghamshire the NCSS and the Rural Community Council funded a three-day residential drama course for social service centre members in 1937, and by that time too training days were being held for the centres in Derbyshire. The NCSS, the Community Councils and the national amateur drama organizations were committed to developing the standards of theatrical activity in the centres. Hardwick Hall in north-east England was opened to provide residential training courses for selected club members, and in this it was joined by the existing adult education providers at

Coleg Harlech in Wales, Fircroft College in Birmingham and Newbattle in Scotland. The courses included play production. At the same time non-acting club members were trained in stage carpentry and metalwork, and the equipment they produced became the communal property of all the clubs in a particular area. The Pilgrim Trust survey concluded that the courses at Hardwick Hall had contributed to 'the conspicuous success of the dramatic work in the unemployed clubs of north-east England'.[12]

As will be discussed later, festivals were also seen as an important means to improve dramatic efforts in social service centres just as in the amateur theatre movement as a whole. Wales had a long-established infrastructure for drama festivals in the form of the national and local eisteddfodau. However, the producer of the Blaenau Ffestiniog community performance of *The Pilgrim's Progress* – where the cast was largely made up of unemployed quarrymen – observed that the entry fees for these festivals were such as to exclude all but the more affluent drama societies. Both the BDL and the Scottish Community Drama Association addressed this problem. They undertook to waive their usual membership subscription and festival entry fee for drama groups from the unemployed clubs. They also agreed to meet the travel fares of unemployed casts to a competition together with meeting the authors' royalty payments for performances.[13]

Performance spaces and properties

Buildings for use as social service centres were often lent or donated and the unemployed craftsmen organized to refurbish and adapt them. In Scotland the Clydebank Mutual Services Association, a centre opened with the support of prominent local figures in a town with 53 per cent of the working population unemployed, obtained a former dance-hall with a stage area. This became the Clydebank Little Theatre, hosting performances by the Association Players and other local amateurs. One of Makin's groups at the Derbyshire pit village of Clowne represented a 'both unusual and welcome development' to a festival adjudicator because 'the unemployed men and women actually made with their own hands their Little Theatre'. This had been reclaimed from redundant colliery buildings. In Nottingham too the Unemployed Association built a theatre space in their donated headquarters building. In Hebburn-on-Tyne a disused electricity station had been converted into a social service centre by the unemployed. This, named the Power House, became something of a showpiece centre and the refurbishment included a large stage area. In Lancashire the Dalton Unemployed

Association Drama Society began performing in 1933 and by 1935 the group had the use of the upper floor of a building in the town which they converted into a small 'community theatre for Dalton'. Both the Clowne Centre and the Power House were both hubs for the local social service centre groups in their areas and provided venues for training days and festivals. As with the Little Theatre movement, performance spaces were being established through re-purposing redundant buildings.[14]

Drama groups that by definition had no income relied on ingenuity and the craft skills of their members and their families as regards stage sets, properties and effects. This was a feature of Manchester Settlement productions as has been mentioned, and some commentators believed that this differentiated the unemployed groups from the conventional amateur dramatic societies. On Tyneside, for example, this was noted about a group who made their own sets from anything that came to hand, such as empty biscuit tins for floodlights. The carpenters at another centre made collapsible props which could be carried easily to venues. In Makin's view 'the unemployed man is at a vast advantage over any other type of amateur actor, for he is a professional craftsman, and to him economic necessity is the mother of artistic invention'. For example. one of his productions – possibly O'Neill's *In the Zone* – was performed in a deserted billiard hall, and involved a scene set on board a ship. An ordinary lamp was hung on a spiral spring from the roof of the hall in such a way that it swayed gently from side to side throughout, giving the illusion of the ship's roll. A tin table in one wing (part of the permanent furniture) was continually vibrated by hand to produce a noise 'extraordinarily like the throb of an engine. The cost was precisely nothing but the effect everything you could wish for'.[15] The gender-determined division of labour entrenched in society at the time was similarly entrenched in these drama groups too, although it was also most likely the case in the theatre industry as a whole. Whereas the men's clubs supplied the skilled carpenters, electricians and decorators to refurbish stages, lighting and scenery it was the role of the women's clubs to provide the seamstress work necessary for costume adaptation. This required, given the economic condition of all concerned, recycling and an imaginative use of scrap material.

Casting

The first wave of unemployed clubs were for male workers and reflected the fact that in the coalfields and areas of heavy industry the opportunities for female employment outside the home were strictly limited. Thus worklessness was regarded as a male issue. Therefore until women's clubs were formed in the social service centres the drama groups featured all-male casts. Some dealt with this restriction in repertoire by appealing to the local amateur drama societies for female volunteers ('three or four young ladies') generally recruiting them from the settlement theatre groups. Others used plays with all-male casts. One imaginative example was the group of unemployed men coached by the Queen's University Drama Society in Belfast: they performed *Philoctetes* by the Greek tragedian Sophocles, which involved no female parts but a wide scope for actors and chorus.[16]

The membership of the women's clubs at the centres was drawn largely from the wives and families of unemployed men. Besides providing the performers for female parts they also formed their own groups: the Clay Cross Social Services Centre Women's Group Players in Derbyshire, the Jarrow Women's Welfare Players on Tyneside are examples. The latter group, echoing the practice of the Women's Institutes, performed plays such as J. M. Synge's *Riders to the Sea*, where the sole male part was supplied by the husband of one of the members. Plays with mainly female casts such as Ida Gandy's *In the House of Despair* could also be mounted once the women's clubs were involved. All-women groups were formed, for example at three of the scattered social service centres in Nottinghamshire, where it had proved 'impracticable to join up with the men's section'. At the Spennymoor Settlement the women's group, all new to drama, was the first to begin rehearsing a play and later involved the men. Maggie Farrell recorded the women's talent and enthusiasm, and explained that she had chosen a Phillip Johnson one-acter for them because it was 'one of the very few plays for women of any real theatrical or literary value'. As will be discussed in due course, some writers for the amateur theatre responded during the decade to the shortage of plays with all-women casts.[17]

Gordon Lea, producer with networks of unemployed clubs on Tyneside, stressed how the nature of the groups determined the choice of plays. Those with very few characters demanded a great deal of work, and experience, from the players; those with very many were beyond the reach of a small group; plays which placed all the weight on one or two characters could leave the rest of the group with too little to do. He also involved experienced local amateur players, having found that with a new group the amateurs could carry the weight of difficult characters or take at least one principal role, thus allowing the others to develop their confidence and grow into more demanding roles. This practice was also followed at least in their early days by the Merthyr Settlement Players.[18] The fact that the men at least in these groups were looking for work – and would leave immediately if they found it – did have implications for casting. Frida Stewart recalled that occasionally a man would get a job on the night of the dress rehearsal, 'an occasion for rejoicing' but not one that made her job any easier. Gordon Lea on Tyneside recommended 'doubling' wherever possible. This meant training two performers for the same role so that if one left the group the part was covered.[19] As regards production methods one particular initiative in unemployed theatre stands out, and it leads to a discussion about how some producers approached the task and the contribution they made to British actor training in general.

'Unemployed Dramatists' and commedia dell'arte

Professional actress Kathleen Edwards was a drama instructor at unemployed clubs across London, and she initiated a theatre project out of her work with them. In 1934 she hired a London theatre for a week and her students performed 'a burlesque of a nineteenth century melodrama' devised by one of their number. This was the genesis of the 'Unemployed Dramatists': a company she took on tour of South Wales and the West Country in 1934, and during 1935 and 1936 to the north of England.[20]

On each of these tours the families of the almost all-male casts lived on money loaned until benefits were paid when the claimants returned. Acting as the benefits advisor and claimant advocate for the company was one of Edwards's tasks. The purpose of the tours, according to a cast member, was to encourage the unemployed to write and act plays from their own experience and to prove to them that this was possible 'without sets, costumes or even written dialogue'. Another was to encourage the users of the unemployed clubs to form their own drama groups or to revive ones that were struggling. Often on tour there were no formal scripts, dialogue was impromptu and changed according to circumstances and the audiences. This approach had been set out by Edwards, who recommended that having agreed a 'producer' for the group they should then decide on a plot:

> your own experiences, comic or tragic, which could be acted by your members; don't worry about dialogue, have your characters coming on or off to fit the plot and let them say what they like. The producer will decide what is 'unsuitable'. Once the play had been performed before several audiences and the actors begin

to repeat the same sentences then write those words down. This is the time to begin a new play.[21]

The approach was derived from the commedia dell'arte tradition and Farrell had noted its use – 'a very old Italian method' as he put it – by unemployed drama groups a few years earlier. Nora Ratcliff also made comparisons between such forms of improvisation and the interpolations of the medieval English mumming plays. These tours echo too those of Jacques Copeau's in France during the 1920s.[22] For example, in some villages Edwards's group performed a comedy after a plot had been roughly arranged and the dialogue developed by the characters as the action developed. Always, members of the audience were induced to take part and improvise a role with reportedly good results.[23]

An Unemployed Dramatists member described two types of plays on tour, one comic and using songs and recitations, the other type 'portrayed unemployment or had definite propaganda value'. An example perhaps of 'propaganda value' appeared in a sympathetic report of their work in *Drama*. This mentioned a performance of the opening scene from *Coriolanus* where a senator confronts a group of hungry, angry citizens and solves the problem by sending them to war. Other scenes of the group's own devising included *Down and Out*, in which two unemployed men approach a 'toff' on London's Embankment, and *Who's Next*, concerning two job applicants and a supercilious employer. They also developed a contemporary skit on the biblical text that a labourer is worthy of his hire.[24] The press reviewers were intrigued by this form of commedia dell'arte and were complimentary about the performers. In Wales in particular, where the Unemployed Dramatists visited NCSS holiday camps for the unemployed on the coast as well as unemployed centres in the mining valleys, they attracted large audiences, supportive press coverage – including praise for the performance of the audience participants – and endorsement from the Mayor of Cardiff. Edwards had aspirations for a permanent centre for unemployed drama in London. This did not materialize, but as we will see unemployed drama groups in South Wales became part of the amateur performance landscape during the decade. Edwards's project may well have helped this development.[25]

Spontaneity and improvisation

One of the drama teachers and theatre professionals working with the unemployed clubs developed a theory and practice of stage improvisation.

Robert G. Newton was a BDL Drama Adviser in the East Midlands Region that included the Nottinghamshire coalfield. He has been credited with being the first writer in English to systematically set out the value of improvisation for actor training.[26] At the time Michel Saint-Denis (a one-time visiting lecturer at Merthyr Tydfil Settlement) was offering improvisation in his London Theatre Studio, which opened in 1936, but it appears to be the case that with this exception it was not part of mainstream actor training in Britain. Newton drew on his drama classes with unemployed groups for what became a standard work on acting and improvisation. He emphasized the value of improvisation for teaching players – any players – to think of their material in terms of theatre as well as everyday life, helping to train the imagination and feel for the theatrical moment, what he called 'the right thing done in the right way at precisely the right time'. Newton was explicit that it had been his work with the unemployed drama groups that had been the genesis of his approach – he quoted the comment of an unemployed miner that you only had to watch children playing to see that they were 'the best improvisers in the world'. Moreover, he stressed of his account that 'not one word would have been written but for the assistance of amateur actors – particularly groups of unemployed people'.[27] There are other examples too. Makin, who had worked with unemployed clubs in the coalfields of County Durham and Derbyshire, stressed how 'recorded improvisation' at rehearsal was important to really capture the drama that was not only being acted and produced but made by club members, as here were the potential new plays.[28]

A matter of education?

One reason Newton gave for developing improvisation was that learning parts and lines was 'too much of a mental effort' for 'a large proportion of the population whose education ceased at fourteen and whose only culture is gleaned from the Sunday papers and the cinema. Yet it would be wrong to debar such people from the imaginative development that comes from putting on a show'. Makin's account tallied with this to some extent, adding of his casts that years of unemployment had had 'a very deadening effect on their whole mental equipment'. According to him though the women in the colliery areas were 'very much more alert'; this he attributed to them needing all their mental resources in daily struggles to make ends meet. Nonetheless his own practice did not rely on improvisation although he clearly put it to use.[29]

Other producers working with unemployed or working-class performers contested these reports, in one case directly. Nora Ratcliff produced amateur plays in Yorkshire villages during the 1930s. In an otherwise enthusiastic endorsement of Newton's approach she stated that in her experience actors with little formal education could find issues with reading out the printed page, an activity they were unused to, but never with memorizing. Likewise the producers with an unemployed drama group in Leeds found that the difficulty was not with learning parts but that many simply had no experience of reading out loud. However, this was straightforward to resolve through practice. Similarly Frida Stewart in Ancoates recalled extraordinarily intelligent cast members among the unemployed, able to learn lines and grasp the essence of a character at great speed. Farrell in Spennymoor also reported that no real difficulties had been experienced in these areas. In Nottinghamshire the drama tutor with the social service centres reported that memorizing lines and movement 'at first presents great difficulty' but it 'is interesting to watch standards and interest improve as the work progresses'. Kathleen Edwards, the exponent of commedia dell'arte improvisation with the Unemployed Dramatists, had used improvisation in response, not to any lack of education among her casts, but because London was more fortunately placed regarding employment. As men found work the casts 'were continually changing, and to meet this difficulty we have no script. The players are told the point and what they have to do, and they make up the words to suit the situation.'[30]

Therefore among these producers at least there was no consensus that improvisation was a response to the lack of formal education among their casts. Clearly though it encouraged inventiveness and developed talent among casts unused to a printed text. Improvisation had emerged as an innovative topic for discussion in actor training in Britain largely through play-making with the unemployed groups in the 1930s.

Plays and performances

Henry Mess, in a later account of the unemployed centres, concluded that their dramatic groups did well wherever there was a skilful instructor. In such cases not only was a good deal of latent talent discovered but 'the performances were creditable and nor was there any need to choose plays of poor quality'. In contrast John Allen of the Left Book Club Theatre Guild noted, in 1937, the 'fairly considerable amount of activity' associated with NCSS drama work, although he found it 'depressing that the plays on which so many of these groups have been working are outworn West-end successes'.[31] Both commentators had an agenda: Mess to validate the drama groups and thus the work of the NCSS; Allen to do the opposite.

The dramatic programmes were mixed but the balance of evidence lies more with Mess than with Allen. The Bensham Grove Unemployed Club certainly had a concert party, described by J. B. Priestley in his *English Journey*, but the same club had a drama group performing *The Bishop's Candlesticks*. The Aberdare Settlement produced *Show Boat*, a Broadway and West End hit of the 1920s which was an innovative combination of music, song, drama and action. The Settlement performances in 1938 involved most of the membership and were a community effort: with an unemployed miner as musical director (and, presumably, a 'blacked-up' cast) they attracted a total local audience of around six thousand. As Claire Cochrane comments about Welsh amateur drama at this time – and the point will hold good for elsewhere in Britain – when the glamorous products of the professional theatre were both geographically and financially inaccessible to most people the amateur movement was one way to gain access to them.[32]

Comedies and human interest were reported by drama advisers to be popular themes, and Gordon Lea recommended plays with action and a social message as ones the groups would respond to readily. An example was Galsworthy's *The Escape*, a play popular with Tyneside unemployed groups and with the early reading groups at the Merthyr Tydfil Settlement. The drama unfolds through a number of short scenes and has small parts in sufficient numbers to provide roles for novice actors. The plot concerns a convict, gaoled in circumstances that draw our sympathy, who escapes from Dartmoor prison. The large number of short scenes are episodes in which he encounters, before recapture, a range of different people and situations, providing moral dilemmas for all involved.[33] *The Escape* had been a popular film at the time and this probably recommended it to the group members.

Other accounts of performances reflect the emphasis on quality drama that the adult education sphere promoted, even though they do not match the ambition of the university settlement theatre in which the unemployed participated. On Tyneside, for example, Shaw and Shakespeare appear, with open-air performances of the latter performed by casts drawn from several centres. Similarly the Power House Players, again drawn from different centres, performed John Masefield's passion play *Good Friday* to appreciative audiences each Easter from 1935. The Nottingham group's first performance was Eugene

O'Neill's *In the Zone*, his psychological drama set in an ammunition ship during the First World War. The lists also reflect the one-act plays that became popular with the amateur theatre of the 1930s: the Nottinghamshire groups' performances included *The Bishop's Candlesticks* and *The Fourth Proposal*; in Derbyshire the Clay Cross Social Service Centre Women's Section also toured Co-op halls with comedies.[34]

The social service centre drama groups, and the settlements which set out to include unemployed people, also performed works in their own dialects, related to their own circumstances and by local authors, as has been shown in the case of Harkness House. In Derbyshire the Clowne Centre entered Elsie Entwistle's *Life's Day* at a local drama festival, a one-act play published after its entry in a Village Drama Society play-writing competition in 1934. It is a domestic drama set in one cottage room and chiefly centres on a miner and his wife, a part-time cotton worker. We learn that the miner is estranged from his step-daughter and her husband, and thus also their new baby. When the miner is laid off his wife emerges as the protagonist, calculating how they will get by and achieving a family reconciliation that ensures both a cordial relationship and a rent income from their new lodgers.[35]

Clydebank Little Theatre premiered *Fog*, a first play by a local man, Richard Francis. This apparently melodramatic piece involves a long-term unemployed man driven to crime, a seriously ill child needing help the family cannot afford, and the resilient and principled wife. Despite the melodramatic element reviewers found it 'remarkably well constructed' and with exceptional dialogue.[36] Harry West in Nottingham wrote two plays and at least one was performed by unemployed drama group members. The first, *Green Grass*, followed a shipyard worker and his family as they endured unemployment and then rediscovered physical and mental well-being through activity at a social service centre. This propaganda for the cause of the centres was followed by *Circling Mists*: this one-act play concerned a pit explosion and it was intended that unemployed miners would take the main roles. Plays about colliery disasters, such as *Below Ground* by Harold Brighouse and John Totheroh's *The Great Dark*, also featured in entries by social service centre drama groups in County Durham.[37]

In Lancashire the Dalton Unemployed Association Drama Society began performing in 1933 and a year later were finalists at the Barrow and District Drama Festival. Their play was *A Lodging for the Night*, a comedy of two tramps taking up residence in a barn. The author, John Bewaldeth, was a local contributor to the amateur stage who also wrote the one-act play that the Dalton group entered for the early rounds of the Barrow Festival in 1935. This was *The Yard*, set in a ship-repair yard with a cast of eight workers and their foreman, the action largely being the men at work. Bewaldeth has a good ear for factory banter and it comprises a good part of the dialogue, along with spontaneous satirical songs about their foreman, Adams. One man, Whelan, is amiably nicknamed 'comrade' by the others; he is the workshop socialist, and given to political commentaries on their situation:

> Who makes the wealth of this firm? We do! Who makes the success of the Directors possible? We do! And what say have we in the running of the firm? Damn all! ... Which of us knows the moment when we may get his cards and begin the round of the Burroo and the Means Test for the rest of his natural days? Do you? Or you? Any of you?[38]

Such interventions cut little ice with his workmates, who ignore visions of socialism in favour of more mundane concerns – 'give me regular work and a chance to feed my kids, with enough for a glass of beer at week-ends, and I don't ask nothing more'. Their job insecurity is brought home to them by their own actions. Charlie, the youngest and quietest, is goaded by continual banter about his new girlfriend into attacking one of his tormentors. The fight broken up by the foreman who threatens them all: 'We can get plenty to fill your places – got that?' Despite the efforts of Charlie's target to plead on his behalf the young man is summarily dismissed. *The Yard* offered the unemployed men the opportunity to perform in their own dialect situations they would have been familiar with, and although not 'political' drama in the conventional sense the realities of job insecurity at a time of high unemployment are brought home.[39]

Groups also performed material that would not be politically contentious. In Northern Ireland the Bangor Unemployed Men's Club took first place at the Northern Fries with the Irish play *Going West*. Two soldiers from Northern Ireland celebrate their survival after a battle in Flanders, only to discover that they are from the mutually hostile republican and unionist traditions. They fight, only to unite again against their common German enemy. The Barnsley Social Services Centres Drama Group won the first round of the town's first drama festival in 1939, and reached the semi-finals of the BDL's Northern Area competition the same year. Both appearances had been encouraged by the labour-exchange manager who also chaired the festival committee. Their entry was an abridged version of the first act of John Davison's *Shadows of Strife*, which concerned a working-class Yorkshire family on the eve of the General Strike in 1926. They also presented this as part of a programme of amateur drama at the Barnsley Theatre Royal, drawing praise for the 'completely naturalistic acting' of the women cast members in particular. As Steve Nicholson points out, *Shadows of Strife* was first performed in 1926, the year of the General Strike and the miners' lockout. It portrays the strike as the work of Bolshevik agitators, the Conservative-supporting, aspirational brother as the voice of reason and the other brother, the socialist, as loutish and violent. Thus whereas the cast were playing people like themselves on stage their theme conformed to conservative political narratives. Nevertheless the group were also reported to be rehearsing *Firedamp*, a play by one of their own members and which presumably concerned a mining explosion.[40] In contrast to Davison's work *The Pitman's Pay* by Ruth Dodds appeared in the Tyneside social service centres' repertoire. Again this is politically noteworthy in the sense that the play, as we have seen, has a focus on optimism and the regeneration of working-class strength and collective self-confidence.[41] Another contrast in County Durham was George Makin's production, using a composite cast of twenty from different centres, of *The Path to Glory*, an anti-war satire popular with the peace movement.[42]

It is unclear how far, if at all, the club members were involved in the choice of plays, as also seems to have been the case with the educational settlements. It is also unclear whether this was contentious. The influx of unemployed workers into the Sheffield Settlement may have been behind the performance of *The Ragged-Trousered Philanthropists* there in 1928 – the tutors' statement about 'great works of art' as the function of the Little Theatre, quoted in the previous chapter, was a response to the students' statement in favour of art as propaganda.[43] As regards the Sheffield programme this performance was certainly not typical. In general there is evidence that some groups performed plays which were ambitious, could reflect on their own circumstances, and were in some cases written by their unemployed members. There were also doubtless 'worn-out West End successes' too but as a generalization about performances that is not accurate.

Authorship and the unemployed

In the only historical critique of the unemployed clubs to make reference to the drama groups, Richard Flanagan highlights a 1938 report to the NCSS from Lionel Millard, a onetime County Drama Advisor. In this Millard states that the purpose of the social service drama groups was to develop taste and judgement in the appreciation of plays rather than to help and encourage play-writing.

Flanagan points, in contrast, to the working-class novelists of the 1930s who used their experiences of unemployment in their work, some enduring examples being Walter Brierley's *Means Test Man, We Live* by Lewis Jones and Walter Greenwood's *Love on the Dole*. If the NCSS centres were effectively steering the unemployed away from expressing their lived experiences through writing plays about them, argues Flanagan, then this can be seen to be potentially defusing a political awareness among the service users. Thus the drama projects tended to reinforce what he believes was essentially a project of political containment, distracting the workless from their situation.[44]

It is possible that Millard was simply re-stating what was, as noted in the previous chapter, an orthodoxy of adult education rather than a formal NCSS policy: literary appreciation was best gained through exposure to great works. The educational settlements for example did not promote authorship as a route to dramatic appreciation even before their involvement with unemployed clubs. Nevertheless some social service centre drama groups did write their own plays and they were assisted by the drama advisors. It is clear that Edwards supported those in her group in London to create their own work based on their experiences of unemployment. Makin was enthusiastic about these groups performing plays written by their own members: he cited an example, which will be noted in a later chapter, of a Durham miner, a member of such a group who had a play on mining conditions accepted by a Left Book Club Theatre Guild. It was 'best of all, from the point of view of the Social Service clubs' that plays were not only acted and produced but written by their own members. One of his Derbyshire groups, the women's section of the Social Service Centre Drama group at Clay Cross, performed *Courtin a Collier* written by one of their members, Elsie Moody. The entire group were miners' wives and the theme of the play was the local Markham Colliery disaster of 1938. Besides those in Clay Cross, Makin arranged for performances in other villages. At least one of the plays performed by the Nottingham Unemployed Workers' Association concerned the effects of long-term unemployment, even if simultaneously promoting the work of the social service centres.[45]

As has been discussed the Harkness House players produced plays by their own members, such as *Exiles*, which concerned the effects of the Means Test on families. Frank Farnin's *The War Memorial* is one surviving text which demonstrates a political engagement with the contemporary issue of war preparations. On Christmas Eve an old serviceman sits by the town's war memorial, a sculpture of a soldier in full kit. He learns that the statue can speak on this one night of the year, drawing on the spirit of the dead sculptor who wished to commemorate 'the innocent lads he saw slaughtered'. The old soldier converses with a passing county councillor; in response to the unemployed veteran's observation that 'it's nice enough to see that the town hasn't forgotten it's dead, although it does seem absent minded about the living', the councillor assures him that recovery is around the corner: a munitions factory could be built soon. A response from the statue causes him to run away in a panic when he realizes the stone can speak. Next two young women ('flappers in full war paint') pass by, discussing the prospect of a future war. One looks forward to earning good wages in a munitions factory while the other fantasizes about nursing, and marrying, a wounded officer. Either way there will be some excitement at least. The statute sighs: 'Poor misguided youth, living in an atmosphere of distrust and rearmament, reading the daily press with its headlines of war clouds and war prophecies. No wonder they talk so.'

Two young men on their way past are engrossed in a political discussion, one blaming capitalism for creating war and holding that only revolution can change that, and the other simply believes that war is human nature. Once again, the statue despairs: 'One believes in imperialist war, the other his cry is class war, and never for all the time I've stood here, do I hear a word of peace – the joy and happiness it brings. Always I hear WAR, WAR, and RUMOURS OF WAR.' Finally, the statute returns to his silence as the bells chime, having declared that 'the world needs to cultivate a peace mind'; before wandering off the old soldier watches a woman leave a red rose on the memorial to show that at least the names there have not been forgotten.

The play articulates the disillusionment of the First World War veterans who subsequently found themselves unemployed, a situation that would have been familiar to the members of Harkness House. It expresses an ambivalence over the function of the war memorial, the hypocrisy of respecting the fallen whilst having no apparent concerns over the rising threat of another conflict even worse than the last. The use of a ghost-type figure in an anti-war play was common in the mainstream theatre at the time and so *The War Memorial*, written by a working-class amateur, contributed to the genre. According to a press review the audience of two thousand in Hamilton Town Hall were 'carried away by the high quality of the acting and the gripping theme of the play'. This suggests that the piece certainly had an impact, and also that both author and cast had seriously engaged with the critical help they had secured from the community drama festival adjudicator.[46]

Elsewhere in Scotland the Clydebank Mutual Services Association were described in 1933 as 'making their own plays' in the local vernacular. There do not

BLACKLEG   ORCHARD AND STOCKS   1937

Figure 3 Manchester University Settlement performance of *Blackleg*, 1937. Copyright of the University of Manchester MUS/5/1/13. Reproduced with permission of the University of Manchester.

seem to be any reports of performances although by the end of the decade they were touring one-act plays around venues in the area. Frida Stewart at Ancoates singled out *Blackleg*, written by unemployed wire-worker Jack Orchard with assistance from Mary Stocks. This was performed at the Round House in 1937 and subsequently broadcast by the BBC Northern region in 1939. According to Stewart the play was drawn from Orchard's own experience and showed an unemployed man torn between a desperate need for work and a revulsion to blacklegging. It included effective scenes and dialogue with his family and strikers at the factory gate, but apparently the BBC broadcast version removed tendentious passages.[47]

Some of these examples are from projects receiving funding and oversight from the NCSS, others from the Pilgrim Trust, and some most likely from both. They suggest that it is unlikely that there was any formal policy of discouraging dramatic writing by the unemployed themselves. Allen suspected that because the NCSS depended on government funding it would prevent its affiliated groups from freely expressing social discontent.[48] This may have been an inhibitory factor but the evidence shows that some independent spaces could be and were opened for social criticism through performance.

Scale and impact

As the 1930s drew to an end some newspaper commentators around the country agreed that the social service centre drama groups had had a positive effect. As regards amateur drama in Durham for example 'much of the real interest and enthusiasm in the County arose with the advent of the social service centres'. Similarly in South Wales 'the increasing interest in the dramatic art is due mainly to the drama groups which have been formed in the unemployed clubs'. The evidence for that increasing interest was the formation in 1938 of the Rhymney Valley League to further the interests of the dramatic societies in the Bargoed district. The instigator was Ambrose Evans from the Bargoed Settlement who co-ordinated the drama groups across the unemployed clubs. By 1939, across the Rhondda as a whole, there were twenty-nine unemployed clubs servicing both men and women and out of these there were twenty-five drama groups. Elsewhere in Wales the Aberdare Valley Educational Settlement, like the others functioning as a hub for the area's unemployed clubs, reported that 'the demand for drama groups has called for the construction of a stage, complete with effects and lighting, in Ynysboeth and the Settlement'. As was generally the case with all unemployed drama clubs these stages and effects were built by the craftsmen among the membership.[49]

Some theatre advocates working in the Special Areas and the Rural Development Areas believed that their work could revitalize the theatre as a whole. Farrell in Spennymoor, for example, told the Durham Historical Society in 1936 that whereas the commercial theatre was 'a deplorable example of decadence' it was being countered in the numerous 'derelict villages' where the unemployed were producing plays. This was the beginning of a 'great national revival'. Makin's drama work with unemployed clubs led him to argue that alongside their sociological function lay a cultural one in that, through participation, they were making closer bonds between the drama and the people. This was in line with the theatrical revival along democratic lines that the founders of the British Drama League had envisioned.[50]

A critique

Ellen Wilkinson, the MP for Jarrow on Tyneside and a national figure on the Labour left, published a seminal account of the effects of unemployment in her constituency. Her book *The Town That Was Murdered* included a critique of the social service centres and it was published in the same year, 1939, as Makin's account of his drama work with them. In several respects Makin, at least from the perspective of the theatre work, responds in effect to Wilkinson's general criticisms without apparently being aware of them. Wilkinson does not deal with the unemployed clubs' drama groups as such but her general points are relevant to a discussion of them.

She argued that the social service movement was the outcome of an attack of conscience among the more socially minded of the affluent classes. Conscience about the effects of unemployment but with no understanding of the need to address structural inequalities through political action. In her view some of the problems with social service centres arose from the feeling that the unemployed were some sort of class apart, needing to be assisted and provided for by others. She was particularly angry at middle-class people assuming they were entitled to organize activities for older men; men who, as in her Jarrow constituency, were highly skilled with proud craft traditions, independent and used to taking responsibility. Further, there could be real problems with activities that effectively segregated the employed from those out of work. Unemployed men had commented to her 'so bitterly' about this being the case at the Power House Centre at Hebburn, where as has been shown the drama group was something of a showpiece. If the membership of such clubs were to be limited to the unemployed, either actually or in effect, the consequence would be stigma and isolation. Wilkinson believed that the future of successful social service centres would be on the community centre model: providing activity for all and controlled by the service users themselves, which as she recognized was already best practice with some of them.[51]

Makin's account was a mixture of his own experience of producing plays at the unemployed clubs and his own recommendations about how this work should go forward. Like Wilkinson, he believed that the only real solution to unemployment was work. Like Wilkinson, he was scathing about the patronizing behaviour of the well-meaning middle classes towards the unemployed. In contrast he explained that his approach to stimulating an interest in making plays was based on respect, respect for the skills of the people he was working alongside. They were skilled men who respected craftsmanship, and so he always began by demonstrating theatre skills. This included using make-up to transform a young person into an old person, movement, voice projection and the use of the stage. He opposed anything that segregated the unemployed and 'reduced them, culturally or in any other way, to the status of a community within a community'. Therefore he disagreed with special festivals for unemployed drama groups, and advocated their entry to BDL or other festivals 'on terms of complete equality with all comers'. He also, like Wilkinson, believed in the transformation of the social service centres into community centres open to everyone.[52] This shows that at least some experienced producers in amateur theatre were alert to the social class realities of the environment they entered into and responded to them through their own practice.

Competitions and audiences

Drama festivals or competitions were an important feature of the amateur theatre during the inter-war years and the unemployed drama groups were no exception. As we have seen a number participated in their local festivals and BDL competitions around the country. As was the case with all other amateur groups these events were an opportunity to see the work of others and to receive constructive evaluation from an independent adjudicator. As the Nottinghamshire RCC staff drama tutor recorded, the invitation to the groups to take part in the RCC drama festival 'proved a tremendous impetus' and the encouragement of the adjudicator 'will go a long way towards further efforts'. It also meant reaching a wider audience than one made up of the 'friends and well-wishers' who attended the first performances of the Nottingham group for example. As Makin recorded 'our plays are performed not only by, but chiefly for, the unemployed'. The wider festivals provided the opportunity for others outside their communities to see their performances.[53]

The NCSS, most often through its local Councils for Social Service, organized drama festivals specifically for the unemployed groups. This was pioneered by the Tyneside Council of Social Service from at least 1935. These non-competitive festivals of one-act plays 'for teams of unemployed men and women' aimed to 'sum up and crown the unemployed drama work for the year' and to give the various groups the opportunity to learn from each other. By 1939 over 200 players on Tyneside were taking part.[54]

Such initiatives raise the issue of the identity of these groups and the relations between that identity, the wider community, and the amateur theatre movement as a whole. On the one hand concerns were voiced about regarding the unemployed as a separate community within society. Lettice Jowitt at Seaham, for example, argued that unemployed people were 'sickened' by being treated as unemployed, meaning being regarded as outcasts and unable to contribute to the ordinary life of the community. The WEA Secretary in South Wales expressed outrage at references to the unemployed 'as if they were a race apart'. Makin of course disagreed with the whole idea of special festivals for unemployed groups and believed that the concept of separate festivals should be abandoned. There was a similar perspective in some official circles, at least in Scotland, where temporary clubs were envisaged as transmuting into permanent centres for the whole community. Thus when what had been the Harkness House project was re-modelled in the new Carfin Hall it was presented as an adult education and community centre. Similarly the Pilgrim Trust, an important sponsor, supported the 'desirability of not separating the employed and unemployed into two distinct camps' and of providing permanent facilities for all.[55]

As unemployment eased in the later part of the decade the NCSS itself was taking the view that the activity in the social service centres was now less to do with the unemployed as such. It was reported that those who had obtained work continued in many cases to use the networks they had made during unemployment. The Tyneside Council for Voluntary Service stated, for example, that it was 'significant' that members of the unemployed drama groups in the area who obtained work still continued to be active members of their groups. This strengthened the argument for a policy shift towards community centres, and by 1935 the Pilgrim Trust was reporting that the concept of special clubs for the unemployed was 'slowly fading away', diluting the initial image of social service centres as unemployed projects. A formal transition was under consideration by the outbreak of war in 1939.[56]

Nevertheless, the discussion does illustrate the status the drama groups of the social service centres may have had within the amateur movement as a whole. In some cases the very names of the groups could be explicit, and not just Edwards's 'Unemployed Dramatists': North Shields Unemployed Men's Drama Group, Dalton Unemployed Association Drama Society and Nottingham Association of Unemployed Workers Drama Group were others. It is quite likely that even an attachment to a social service centre – Clay Cross Social Service Centre Women's Section Drama Group, or South Shields Social Service Centre Drama Club – would announce that the casts were drawn largely from the unemployed and their families. This would have been far less explicit of course with the settlement drama groups. A number of these had been established years before the NCSS project. Also, the names of some groups such as the Power House Players or the Clydebank Mutual Services Association Little Theatre suggested simply an amateur drama society. Nevertheless the fact that, for example, the Power House Players were drawn from the different social service centres on Tyneside was known to press reviewers and the local area. This social identification through nomenclature was at its most obvious through the social service centre drama festivals confined to the unemployed groups alone. The treatment of the unemployed as a distinct social category of their own, at a distance from the rest of the community, could have been reinforced, something that the adult education and some drama commentators wished to avoid.

The social service centres aroused political suspicion as to their purpose. However, Leeworthy goes as far as to conclude that the settlement unemployed centres in South Wales functioned as 'significant centres of resistance to government policy' regarding the unemployed. This may be overstating the case but it does identify, as historians like Flanagan do not, the levels of discussion of economics and politics that were enabled by the classes in these centres alongside the carpentry, holidays and boot-repairs. Certainly the unemployed clubs attached to the educational settlements or following their model hosted discussion-based classes that encompassed 'economic problems, international affairs, and social problems in the main', as well as literature, languages and music. If the purpose of the social service centres was to dilute political awareness then in South Wales at least they were remarkably ineffective. As Harris notes, there were more unemployed clubs there than anywhere else in the 'Special Areas' yet it was here that the protest against the cuts of the1934 Unemployment Act achieved unprecedented community mobilization.[57]

There remains much for social historians to discuss about the social service centres but the drama clubs took amateur play-making into the most disadvantaged communities in the country. The passing comment of Alyce Von Rothkirch that the unemployed centres of Wales 'ran drama clubs to give their members a meaningful hobby' does a disservice to what was achieved both there and elsewhere in Britain.[58] Obviously much depended on the expertise and personality of the instructor or producer and it is unlikely that they were all as skilful as George Makin, Frida Stewart or Kathleen Edwards. The unemployed clubs drama project originated with some prominent elements in the adult education and amateur theatre spheres and not from the unemployed themselves. Nevertheless despite these imbalances in the power relationships between the unemployed and the drama advisors it is not plausible that club members would give their best efforts to produce plays unless they were motivated to do so. Easy generalisations that the plays were necessarily trivial or politically safe are not supported by evidence. Some opportunities to create space for independent perspectives were taken.

The performance, especially to an outside audience, was itself an intrinsic part of the perceived social value of the activity. All taking part – not just the stage casts but the carpenters, painters, seamstresses and scene shifters – knew that their own individual contribution was essential for the success of the project; it was a 'co-operative community effort'. Thus it offered a sense of being valuable to those whose industrial employment, the source of structure and meaning in life hitherto, had been withdrawn to leave them at risk of believing themselves socially superfluous.

A report about the women's clubs serviced by the Merthyr Tydfil Settlement believed that, 'It is certain that the clubs for women meet a need for self-expression and for relief from the strain of domestic management on the income of an unemployed man'. In County Durham the miners' wives who pioneered the Spennymoor Settlement Players were said to have been seeking some colour in their drab lives. The drama teacher with the Nottinghamshire Social Service Centres reported that the members believed that 'the greatest benefit is derived from getting away from the monotonous round, and finding one of the rare chances for self-expression . . .'.[59] Any such relief or benefit could only be strictly temporary and the British Drama League, the WEA and the Councils of Social Service statements did not pretend otherwise. Forms of escape would always be sought and through drama the escape was entirely by the imaginative and intellectual resources of the unemployed themselves. For drama advisors like Makin this was theatre with a purpose.

These groups did make a contribution to community life and potentially a significant contribution to the cultural resources that were available. Little Theatre and performance spaces were established, regular performances given and networks of amateur drama groups nurtured. It was noted in both South Wales and north-east England at the time that the social service centre theatre initiatives were providing a stimulus for the amateur drama movement as a whole in their areas. These projects led to early efforts to formalize improvisation into British actor training for the first time through the work of Robert G. Newton. To what extent were these projects purely palliative? Were they, in providing opportunities for unemployed men and their families also providing a distraction from the cause of their problems? Frida Stewart recalled struggling with the idea that she was involved simply in palliative measures. Shortly after the event and from the standpoint of a political activist she reflected on her experience with mixed feelings:

> after the players had drifted home and the lights were out and the stage lay empty and dead, I used to wonder what was the good of it all. We'd taken the men and their wives and children out of their grim, hopeless lives for a few hours; we'd given them a glimpse of a different world, and they had avidly seized it and made

the most of it – but that world of colour and light and – yes, though it seems an overworked word – of beauty; that world evaporated as soon as the curtain fell, and the hard facts of life were all that was left. Facts of the Unemployment Assistance Board, of damp and dry rot, of hungry children, of the eternal battle against dirt and soot, of queues at 'the Labour', of life on the dole.[60]

Nevertheless, Stewart sought a further post as an NCSS Drama Advisor working with unemployed groups; she suspected though that the NCSS denied her this post because of productions like *Peace on Earth* and her contact with the Communist Theatre of Action in Manchester. Some members of the group at the Spennymoor social science class found their way to a conception of drama according to which, as Farrell recorded, theatre has a function other than entertainment and could be a form wherein 'the hopes, desires, aspirations, sorrows and joys of the people can be expressed'.[61] In any event this chapter has argued that play-making with the unemployed groups deserves serious attention and not dismissal.

It is clear from the account so far that festivals and competitions were an important element of the British amateur theatre movement during the inter-war years. This was not without discussion and controversy at the time. The next chapter will explore this, and examine the effect competition had on amateur play-making and the opportunities it opened to present plays on the issues of the day.

4

Competitions, Festivals, Politics

Competitions and festivals

The drama festival, or competition, was ubiquitous throughout the amateur theatre movement in Britain during the inter-war years, and this continued through the Second World War and into the post-war period. Besides amateur theatre groups adult education drama classes, Women's Institutes, County Drama Leagues, social service centres – all regarded the festival experience as an important milestone in their activities. Entry for a festival provided an incentive, a goal and a performance where audience and cast were unknown to each other. Regular competitive festivals gave all entrants an opportunity to showcase their work, observe the work of others and hear comments about them from an independent adjudicator. As Claire Cochrane states, 'the competitive dimension to amateur performance was taken up with great enthusiasm' at the time,[1] but it must be added that a 'competition' could be a different event from a 'festival', although the two terms were often used interchangeably.

In all such events amateur drama groups performed and received an assessment from an independent expert adjudicator. The groups mentioned earlier might take part in festivals where the purpose was simply for the benefit of the assessment and to observe the work of their peers. Otherwise in competitive festivals the assessment concluded with the participating groups ranked in order of merit with a declared winner, and there could be a trophy awarded or a cash prize alongside the attendant publicity in the local press. There were no firm demarcation lines: groups from social service centres and the Women's Institute (WI) could and did enter competitive festivals and their producers considered it to be an important stage in their progress that they could do so.

A competitive festival might be organized by a County Drama Association such as Derbyshire or Nottinghamshire or a network of Welsh chapel drama groups. Another example were the town drama festivals, annual events often arranged to coincide with the holiday season, or to attract visitors, or to display the cultural activities of the area. The number of entries determined the length of the festival and it could easily last for a week. Generally at these events the different drama groups performed on the same stage and comments came from the same adjudicator.

A theme in this chapter is the National Festival of Community Drama organized by the British Drama League and the Scottish Community Drama Association. The participants were amateur drama groups affiliated to those organizations. These festivals began in 1926 but had obviously been preceded by the National Eisteddfod in Wales, even though drama was a subsidiary element in that event. The British Drama League (BDL) and Scottish Community Drama Association (SCDA) national festivals were essentially knockout competitions. Britain was divided into five areas: Eastern, Western and Northern England, and one area each for Scotland and Wales. In turn there were many local divisions within each of the areas; they organized the competitions in their localities, with the winners going forward to an area final, usually in a city theatre, and then the area winners would compete in the national final held at the Old Vic Theatre in London. The national winner was awarded the de Walden Cup, named in honour of the President of the BDL. During their progress through the competition groups would have to perform on different stages – different rounds were held in different locations – and be assessed by different adjudicators, in contrast to most of the independent festivals.

One metric for the growth of the amateur movement can be taken from the entries to the BDL and SCDA annual festivals. It is recorded that the first contest in spring 1926 attracted seven entries whereas in the autumn of that year they rose to 150. The combined entries reached a peak of 1,133 in 1936 before stabilizing at 1,005 a year later and remaining at around that level until the outbreak of war.[2] This metric was reflected at local levels too, as we have seen in the case of the Nottinghamshire Drama League. However, it was observed at the time that some of the best-known amateur companies in the country did not participate in festivals; for others the travelling costs were an obstacle and could necessitate community fund raising to meet the expense of the finals. On the other hand some local groups were very active participants indeed, with one in Wales attending no less than thirteen competitions during 1936.[3] In any event the press publicity given to the regional and national competitions of the BDL meant that the organization's other work was overshadowed by the competitive festival. In 1946 it could be claimed that, 'Possibly the greatest achievement of the amateur theatre is expressed in the Drama Festival'. Initiated by the BDL with the purpose of raising standards of production and performance in amateur theatre, abundant anecdotal evidence appeared to confirm that this was indeed being achieved. There was also an element of educating the audience, as Patrick Carleton, himself an adjudicator, explained:

> With the remarks of the adjudicator, these festivals really amount to courses of lectures upon technical aspects of the drama, profusely illustrated ... my experience has been that the audience, in every case, took the very liveliest interest in everything the adjudicator had to say, fully understood the points made ... a more understanding attitude towards the theatre is being created.[4]

Carleton and others in the BDL believed that the adjudicators' comments were helping to build an audience educated in drama, one which was appreciative and not hostile to innovation. In turn the aspiration was that, having been made aware that such audiences were available, the professional theatre could be persuaded that quality drama was commercially feasible. Thus the amateur stage would contribute to the theatre in general by growing the audience for it; this obviously met a key objective of the League.[5]

This chapter examines the reservations which developed over the amateur festival phenomenon, such as its effect on play-writing and, in particular, the

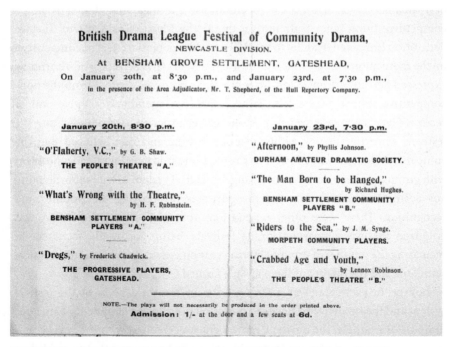

Figure 4 Programme for British Drama League Festival in Gateshead, 1928. Reproduced with the permission of Tyne and Wear Archives Service SX51/6/2.

one-act play format which often dominated. It discusses how some writers sought to develop the form and how this could also be a means to give expression to some issues of the time. It discusses too how play-writing for competitions contributed to dramas of life in Scotland and Wales, and how far the regular festivals of the BDL and SCDA were opportunities for socially engaged work.

The festival effect and the market

At the end of the 1930s two accounts appeared, one by Sydney Box and the other by John Bourne, which assessed the strengths and the weaknesses of the drama festival model.[6] Both authors were playwrights for the amateur stage and both too were experienced festival adjudicators. These separate accounts took similar positions regarding the issues arising from festivals and competitions. One key point lay in the differences implied in the terms – a 'festival' or a 'competition'. The competitive aspect was always open to criticism. Eric Barber, adjudicating in Edinburgh, cited the experience of Workers' Educational Association (WEA) class groups in England to suggest that performances might be drawn from the best amateur casts in an area, 'to emphasise the idea that drama is not a competitive thing but a truly festival thing'. The Merseyside Amateur Theatre Federation expressed disquiet to the BDL over 'the potential effect of competition on the motivation' behind amateur theatre. Ten years later actress Sybil Thorndike expressed her 'utter distaste' for the competitive events as distinct from the non-competitive festival where the teams entered co-operatively, to give and to receive. Her views were probably based on her experience of adjudicating WI festivals since the 1920s.[7] Although both Bourne and Box believed that the competitive element was effective in raising standards they identified a problem with groups, or their producers, working the festival system to win, subordinating any aesthetic considerations for the purposes of securing the trophies and recognition. There were other reservations too. In Scotland the SCDA was criticized in several quarters for its festivals, being apparently focussed on increasing the number of groups entering year on year at the expense of technical standards and the quality of the plays performed.[8]

Bourne in particular was a strong critic of certain aspects of the festival system and the influence he believed it exerted over the development of amateur drama. For example, the amateur movement was credited with the revival and spread of the one-act play as a form, with at least 300 new one-act plays published in acting editions between 1937 and 1938.[9] This was almost entirely due to authors identifying a space in the market created by the amateur movement: when it came to festivals and competitions time pressures meant limitations on what could be performed, and so they featured one-act plays or only extracts from longer ones. Bourne pointed out that this eruption of one-act plays onto the market was purely a product of the needs of festival entrants and not because writers needed to express themselves in that way. As we have seen, in the 1920s and 1930s the one-act play had a poor reputation in critical and adult education circles. It was assumed in Derbyshire, to take one example, that 'one-act plays are hardly likely to be satisfactory from the Drama Committee's point of view, which is that villages desired bigger work in dramatic art'. Critics and adjudicators too could describe 'the modern spate of one-act plays as mainly rubbish'.[10] In Britain the one-act play has never achieved the critical status of its literary counterpart, the short story, and possibly the inter-war suspicion of the genre is a factor behind both this and the subsequent academic neglect of amateur theatre – the assumption that the frequent reliance on one-act plays meant reliance on inferior material.

The market responded to the demand, not just for one-act plays, but to the lack of dramatically competent one-act plays for all-female casts. Flora Robson estimated in 1934 that women actively interested in drama, presumably meaning acting, outnumbered the men by ten to one. It remained the case that many published scripts did not respond to this well-known aspect of amateur theatre, although Sydney and Muriel Box wrote two anthologies, their motive for doing so not 'out of any pronounced feminist convictions' but simply to address a well-known gap in the market. Their target was also the amateur drama festival and their play anthologies, containing a variety of genres such as comedies, more tragic pieces and serious plays, eschewed ambitious sets and scenery and required teamwork from casts as distinct from roles for stand-out individuals. As we have seen in relation to the Women's Institutes Nora Ratcliff had predicted that if the demand from amateur companies for plays with female casts was there it would be filled.[11]

Some commentators believed that the festival system would have no sustainable effect on the quality of modern drama unless it could nurture the three-act format. Similarly Linda Mackenney observes that Joe Corrie, the miner and political playwright, could only develop his themes for the amateur movement as far as the one-act format permitted, ruling out more plays on the scale of his *In Time O' Strife*.[12] Further, writers for this market had to tailor their plays to suit the festival rules – no more than forty minutes' duration – and what the adjudicators wished to see. Thus to meet typical adjudication criteria five or six characters should be involved as opposed to a duologue; too many scene and lighting changes would overburden stage staff.

Another important issue was the making system, one which was essentially the same for any type of festival. The largest group of marks, 85 per cent, were technical ones relating to acting, production and stage management, whereas the smallest categories of marks related to 'enterprise' and the choice of play. This reflected the fact that festivals had been developed as a means to improve the standards of acting and production in amateur theatre.[13] For Bourne this was serving to thwart the emergence of innovative productions, of new and experimental drama, by placing too much emphasis on performance standards and not enough on the dramatic merit of the material performed. Bourne and Box were not the only commentators concerned about a potential 'festival effect'. The amateur movement was unconstrained by the professional theatre's dependence on financial success, and therefore it had the opportunity to present plays that were experimental, or of artistic but not commercial value. This was recognized as important for the survival, growth and popular availability of good drama. Thus James Gregson, acting as an adjudicator for a festival in Yorkshire, criticized the productions for 'playing it safe instead of making experiments'; the national BDL competitions were likely to 'crush out the spirit of enterprise' when they should be fostering it.[14]

Developing the one-act format

If there was a mass of poor one-act plays available to amateurs there were those in the movement who sought to improve the range and innovate within the form. Milling, Holdsworth and Nicholson observe that theatre history over-concentrates on the radical and the innovative at the expense of the bedrock,[15] the regular programmes that built an audience's appreciation of different dramatic forms. At the risk of perpetuating this it should be remembered that at the time the one-act play was disparaged in literary and educational circles. Therefore these attempts to innovate it for the amateur stage are of interest.

Muriel and Sydney Box are best known for their contributions to the post-war British film industry, Muriel in particular being belatedly celebrated as one of the pioneering women directors. However both, whether writing separately or jointly, were also significant contributors to the pre-war amateur theatre. By 1939 they had published 'upwards of fifty plays' and for a period in the mid-1930s they were amongst the most performed playwrights on the British amateur circuit.[16] John Bourne used the work of Sydney Box as an example of what he termed 'the episodic, short play' as a potential way forward for the one-act format. Besides being a playwright Box was also a screenwriter with a British film studio. This experience prompted him to advocate adopting cinematic techniques for the stage, not for their own sake but to support and extend narrative possibilities: short episodes punctuated by spotlights and blackouts; also the end of reliance on the 'fourth wall' between the stage and audience. He was aware of the American Federal Theatre Project and workers' theatre methods, themselves adopted from the early Soviet stage. As will be discussed later these methods were gaining currency in Britain at the time through the left theatre movement.[17] This is an example of how the British amateur movement was open to international influence, probably coupled too with the experience Box had gained in the film industry. The next section will examine how Sydney and Muriel Box attempted to move the one-act play form in a different direction whilst at the same time responding to the political atmosphere of the period.

Fantastic Flight, written by Sydney Box in 1935, was performed by a number of amateur groups. In this a millionaire arms manufacturer realizes that the world, largely through the actions of men like himself and the weapons they have unleashed, is doomed. As the final war begins a hundred of the world's best and brightest are assembled in helicopters to plan a new civilization whilst below them the old one is consumed in poison gas. The play was innovative in technique, using silhouette projections and with three different areas of the stage alternately lit or blacked out by way of scene changes. This was the cinema-influenced technique he was later to advocate in his account in 1939.[18] Two further examples of one-act plays by Sydney Box are worth examining in more detail. This is because both of them were popular items on the festival circuit and both of them show an engagement with contemporary issues. These plays were published under the pseudonym Cedric Mount because, according to his biographer, by 1936 Box feared that his name was becoming over-exposed in the amateur play market.[19]

Twentieth-Century Lullaby opens with a mother singing a lullaby to her sleeping child. He is named Peter Ulrich Smith, and his mother's hopes for his future are a good education, a secure career, a nice church wedding and comfortable family life. In a series of pointed scenes these dreams are contrasted with a likely reality: the school curriculum is rigid and old-fashioned; unemployment is high and business success demands unethical advertising and financial practices. His marriage is unhappy and ends in divorce, which loses him his job. These scenes feature the appearance of a Schoolmaster, a Businessman, a Clergyman and a Politician, and include an off-stage voice of the 'Announcer', who provides ironic commentaries with statistics about unemployment, the decline of church marriages and divorce rates. These offer a background to the episodes in Peter Smith's life events and climax with news of a declaration of war:

Politician   Peter Ulrich Smith, your king and country need you.

Announcer   Peter Ulrich Smith, your king and country need you.

Politician   For the glorious destiny of your nation –

Schoolmaster   For the honour of the old school –

Clergyman   For the carrying out of God's immutable purpose –

Businessman   for the sake of the profit-and-loss account –

All   Your king and country need *you*.[20]

At this point the mother angrily calls a halt and refuses that future just as the baby wakes and cries. Then a figure of the Madonna appears to offer reassurance in a quasi-religious framework: every baby is a potential leader and saviour of mankind, a force for change, 'all motherhood is hope'. Thus although the mother's dreams for the future are interrupted by potential and plausible clashes with contemporary reality, and strong displays of cynicism and bitterness, the proposed resolution is one of hope. Sydney Box described this play in a discussion about the techniques of the one-act play without revealing that he was in fact its author. He pointed out that the staging is experimental, with episodic scenes, the use of an off-stage announcer as a narrator and the mixing of realism with fantasy.[21]

Twentieth-Century Lullaby was credited with more performances than any other play during the British Drama League's National Festival in 1936. For example, the Treharris Amateur Drama Club – which included some unemployed miners – had won the Welsh final with a production of it that year and went on to the national final in London.[22] As was noted in a previous chapter, the spread of drama clubs for unemployed miners in South Wales had stimulated interest and participation in amateur theatre generally, encouraging a social diversity in the groups. The play was performed for local Peace Week and Peace Council events by amateur dramatic societies – for example, the Hull Electricity Board Drama Group and Bingley Workers' Educational Association – as well as by left and Peace Pledge Union theatre groups. In a political context too Wolverhampton

Left Book Club Theatre Guild played it to local trade union audiences in November 1937. It was translated for performances in Welsh in 1936, the year in which it was the winning play at the Welsh BDL final, and it was broadcast on the Welsh radio service two years later.[23] Performances were not confined to drama competitions. It was staged as part of the entertainment programme for hospital fund-raisers and by League of Nations Youth Groups; a variety of organizations saw their amateur dramatic clubs perform *Lullaby*, indicating perhaps that the final spirit of idealism displayed at the end could outweigh the cynical portrayal of business practice and the manipulation of patriotism shown earlier. This seems to have widened its appeal considerably – for example, the drama group of a Presbyterian church in Belfast played it to a Unionist Women's Association there.[24]

His play *Dirge Without Dole* was a piece about unemployment and also about an amateur drama competition. The opening scene shows a haggard, unemployed man, and his wife and two children around an iron bed. Represented on other different stage areas are a bishop, a black-shirted fascist, a scientist and a businessman. The unemployed man addresses the audience, explaining that he is long-term unemployed, one of two million living outside the theatre building. Encouraged by the other figures the family tell their story: mill work, early marriage, and then unemployment, the Means Test and a gradual loss of hope for the future. The role of speaker alternates between the man and wife with the children providing a form of chorus, and speech is in the form of short statements always addressed to the audience:

Man   I've tramped the streets to look for work

Wife   He's queued and fought and begged for work

Children   (together) Written and 'phoned and asked for work

Man   But the answer is always –

Wife   Nothing doing

First Child   Nothing –

Second Child   – doing![25]

The symbolic figures put forward their solutions. The 'bishop' advises trust in God, the 'businessman' offers the hope of work when rearmament begins followed by service in the army when another war breaks out; the fascist urges action against Jews; and the 'scientist' suggests a diet people on the dole can afford and survive on ... possibly. Finally, a caricature communist urges revolution and the scene disintegrates into confusion, but leaving the family intoning, 'Can nobody hear our SOS?'

At this point a dinner-jacketed figure appears and we discover that he is an adjudicator and the scene that has just been played was actually an entry for a local drama competition. In one performance at least during a real festival this left an audience believing that the character actually *was* the adjudicator delivering judgement.[26] The verdict is damning – 'no company which chooses a play of this type can hope to succeed in a drama festival' – and the adjudicator goes on to attack the play politically and artistically: the theatre 'should be a place of escape from the cares of life' and so the prize is given to another 'entrancing little piece of work at which no one could possibly take offence'.

After the adjudication most of the cast are unsurprised that this 'propaganda play' has crashed and are only concerned with the potential public reactions to them personally. Only the two playing the man and wife characters defend the play and spurn the celebrations with the cast of the winning entry: 'Two million people are sitting in their dingy, overcrowded rooms, without food, without fire, without jobs, without hope. Doesn't it *do* something to you?' Finally as they too disperse an excerpt from the first scene is repeated:

Man   Can nobody hear our SOS?
  Hour after hour we are crying for help
  Hour after hour we are standing and waiting

Wife and Children (together)
  Hour after hour after hour
  Hour after hour after hour

All   Can nobody hear our SOS?[27]

Dirge Without Dole therefore satirizes a stereotype of middle-class amateur dramatics and BDL competitions, as well as contradicting the audience's expectations about what is being performed in front of them. It raises queries about the value of social drama and reminds the audience that unemployment remains a serious human issue. Despite this a political criticism could be made that the unemployed family have no agency of their own, they are dependent on the agency of others, and there is no suggestion of adopting any collective political response.

Its first performance was given at the Dunlop Works Drama Festival in Birmingham by one of the factory teams, apparently to an 'enthusiastic reception'.

Other workplace theatre groups entered festival competitions with it – for example, the Littlewoods Dramatic Group in Liverpool and the Hull Electricity Board Recreation Club in Yorkshire.[28] Amateur dramatic societies all over the country had some success in the later 1930s with *Dirge* as their entry: the Preston Drama Festival, the Doncaster Drama League Competition and the Flintshire Drama Festival are examples, as well as in Leicester and Scotland. The Bedford Left Book Club Theatre Guild won first prize in their category at the Bedford Music Festival with it in 1939.[29]

Both Box and Bourne were advocates of 'progressive and experimental' drama. Bourne's definition of experimental was 'a little ahead of current tastes in either form or content'. An example he used was Box's work, and similarly the adjudicators at the Glasgow and the Warwickshire Drama Festivals in 1939, reacting to performances of *Dirge*, welcomed 'this essay in experimental theatre' and hoped it would lead to 'more experimental drama by groups in the Association'.[30] In these examples the one-act form was being developed in more innovative ways to express socially engaged themes.

Amateur theatre, class and nation in Scotland and Wales

Among the aspirations for the amateur stage were its potential role in supporting a national theatre in Scotland and Wales, in the sense of promoting plays about Scottish and Welsh life. The amateur environment, free from commercial pressures, would be key, and festivals would obviously be a means of promoting a culture of specifically national drama. This was certainly the aim of the Scottish National Players, formed in 1921, and of the leaders of the Scottish Community Drama Association during the inter-war years. According to historians of Scottish theatre, however, the prime movers in both the National Players and the SCDA were drawn from a middle-class milieu, and conservative in both politics and art. Thus they promoted a dramatic narrative of Scotland that was restricted to rural Highland life and romantic episodes from history. They actively discouraged plays about urban living and working-class conditions, and effectively therefore a drama of contemporary social comment and politics. Their reaction to the working-class dramatist Joe Corrie is thus a point for discussion, and a comparison with work on the amateur theatre and national narratives in Wales during the same period is useful.[31]

Linda Mackenney argues that productions of Corrie plays often faced discrimination by festival adjudicators on political grounds, and attempts were made to discourage the performance of his or similar plays of contemporary social comment. Nonetheless she also points out that his plays were in great demand for one-act play competitions in Scotland; further, they won the annual finals there in 1933, 1935, 1936 and 1937. It was the Glasgow Corporation Transport Players' production of *And So to War* and the miners in the cast of *Hewers of Coal* by the Newbattle Burns Dramatic Society, who won in 1936 and 1937. In the first work, a satire, a dictator faces down calls for war from industrialists, clergy, financiers and bribed trades union leaders. He announces that only wealthy men aged over fifty will be called up to fight. *Hewers of Coal* concerns a team of miners entombed after an explosion, their interaction and issues of profit versus safety underground. It was noted at the time though that: 'It is apparent to the most haphazard student of amateur drama that, probably resulting on his success, there is an anti-Corrie bias in some parts of Scotland.'[32] Corrie's work also appeared in England: performances of *Hewers of Coal* and *Children of Darkness* were praised at festivals in different parts of the country.[33] Corrie's serious plays do explore Scottish national life but they do so in terms of class and power.

In Wales the absence of plays of Welsh life in the amateur movement drew comment at the time, for example by Bourne. When he adjudicated a festival in 1935, one with more than fifty entries, he commented on how little material about Wales had been performed. A survey by Alyce Von Rothkirch (strictly limited in the years covered and confined to one newspaper, as she readily admits) of Welsh amateur repertoires suggests that they relied on the thrillers and comedies traditionally associated with amateur dramatics, and largely by English authors.[34] A wider focus, related to earlier chapters, can show examples of the Welsh amateur movement attempting to deal with working-class life in industrial Wales, and especially unemployment.

As we have seen, Jack Jones's *Land of My Fathers* was originally written for the amateur stage and widely produced by Welsh amateur companies. It was performed in several Little Theatres, and at the Maesteg, Pontypridd and Barry Drama Festivals, and it was also taken up by Welsh diaspora communities in English industrial cities, communities that had formed there to escape the unemployment the play described.[35] The author stated his awareness that the points it made were equally applicable to other parts of Britain, particularly mining areas experiencing similar social devastation. Thus his 'play of Welsh life' as it was recognized by his coalfield audiences made connections with the class experience of coalfield Britain.

When Jones came to dramatize his 1934 novel *Rhondda Roundabout* he gave first performance rights to the amateur Garrick Players of mid-Rhondda. It was premiered at Maesteg Town Hall where, now that the state rearmament programme has ensured that 'so many people are engaged on night work at the collieries', matinee performances were arranged. This play is an interaction between familiar Valleys characters such as the preacher, the bookie, the communist, the miner, a shell-shocked veteran and the housewives whose strength sustains the community. The twelve scenes do not provide a narrative but, to the confusion of some critics, aim to create a unity of impression, one which expresses an indomitable resilience.[36] Jack Jones's plays had successful commercial productions in London which, as Rebecca D'Monte comments, shows that theatre managers may have been more open to such subject matter than has been assumed. It also shows, alongside some of the work of the unemployed clubs and settlements, that the amateur movement in Wales could take on more serious themes as well as the thrillers and comedies.[37]

Another 'true picture of Welsh life in the mining valleys' which one press review believed was 'probably the most discussed play of recent years' was *Cold Coal* by Evan Eynon Evans.[38] The author, a corporation bus driver in Caerphilly, had had previous successes with one-act play competitions for the amateur stage. These were comedies; his *Prize Onions*, about rival allotment gardeners, reached the final of the 1939 BDL national competition when performed by Tonyfelin Amateur Dramatic Society. Another was *The Affairs of Bryngoleu*, described as a 'welcome departure' for Welsh drama in that 'there is neither a deacon nor a Nonconformist minister to attack' – apparently thus avoiding two stereotypes of the genre.[39] Like *Land of My Fathers, Cold Coal* concerns a mining family and the effects of mass unemployment. It too began as an entry to an amateur play-writing competition, and was performed by amateur societies across South Wales; it too had 'a setting familiar to everyone in the audience'. Familiar to the players of the Tonyfelin cast also, made up as they were of 'schoolteachers, insurance agents, miners and shop assistants'.[40] It was taken up by other Welsh amateur drama groups and the Pontyeymmer society in particular gave repeat performances owing to its popularity.[41]

Once again the drama takes place in the living room of a miner's cottage, the home of the Llewelyn family and visited by their close friends. Sons Arthur and David are among the long-term unemployed ('fed up with the hunting and the hoping, the creeping and the cringing') and the father's job is at risk. Both have fiancées but cannot afford to marry, both worry about being a financial handicap to their working brother, and there is talk of migrating for work in England. Despite this there is humour, both of the black variety ('it takes a year or two to learn how to loaf successfully – it requires certain negative qualities that dad hasn't developed yet'), and through the resilience of mother Ann, and through the son Wensley. His appearances function as a relief from the serious scenes with humour and comic verses about life in the colliery village. The play is, though, a tragedy. Young couples become impatient, and in a scene where we expect the unmarried Mair to announce that she is expecting Arthur's baby there is in fact another serious assault on community values: desperate to afford a marriage, Arthur is strike-breaking at a nearby colliery. In this he is later joined by David. Although the parents robustly condemn this action – 'you're the enemy of your own people' – the condemnation is actually nuanced. The sons are described as seeking bitter revenge against circumstances, unable to see the harm they are doing to others because they have been blinded by the harm done to them.

In the final scenes David and Arthur seek refuge in the house when being chased by an angry crowd of striking miners and their families; this dangerous situation ends, and the crowds dispersed, as the dead body of Wensley is carried home following a pit accident. John Llewelyn, his father, concludes the play not with a political statement but with a prayer against the greed for gold, the lust for power and all the forces that have made his family's tragedies possible.

These plays are Anglo-Welsh dramas since although they had some performances in Welsh – and *Land of My Fathers* was performed at the 1938 Eisteddfod – these were translations from the authors' original English. They explored a British class experience in a Welsh context rather than an affirmation of a distinctively Welsh culture. These plays celebrate the resilience of communities under intense pressure and, like Corrie, Jones and Evans wrote about such communities from their own experience. Unlike Corrie the other two had incomes, albeit precarious ones, independent of their writing and so they were also independent of the one-act play market. Their contributions could be three-act pieces. Again unlike Corrie, Jones and Evans do not seem to have attracted the hostility of the cultural establishment in Wales. Possibly this reflects, as we have seen, the community-wide resistance to the Means Test and cuts to benefits which characterized Welsh society between the wars.

Thus far the discussion has identified some examples of socially engaged drama on the amateur stage. This begs the question of how far it was present in festival and competition. Given that these were a significant activity in the amateur sphere it is legitimate to examine how far festival plays related to the issues of the day.

Progressive drama and the BDL: plays and performances

Joe Corrie believed that plays should be concerned with 'the problems that beset the people', and 'if possible offer a glimmer of hope to them' rather than 'do nothing to disturb the peace of the well-to-do'. In these circumstances 'the festival is the one hope of the author with a purpose' because festivals offered local drama groups a freedom of choice and independence over what they could perform. They were not tied, as he believed was often the case in rural areas, to familiar material calculated to simply divert rather than challenge an audience attending performances to support local charities. In contrast to the critics who saw festivals in terms of their limitations, so far as he was concerned they were an opportunity.[42] If he was correct to urge amateurs to 'use the freedom of the festival' as an opening for challenging drama, how far was this opportunity taken?

In May 1939 five plays were presented at the BDL Annual Community Theatre Festival, the last before the outbreak of war in September. The left-wing London Unity Theatre took the first prize with their *Plant in the Sun*, an American play about trade union organization which it had premiered the previous year. Stirling Amateur Dramatic Club were placed second with *Shells*, an anti-war play set in a Flanders trench. Another finalist was the Hereford Young Men's Christian Association (YMCA) Players with *This Earth Is Ours*, concerning an American farmer's struggle against a powerful utility company and a corrupt sheriff's department. This play featured short, episodic scenes separated by blackout and not curtain movement, an example of the techniques used by the American left theatre and recommended by Box. Thus three out of the five finalists were presenting political material although two, unlike Unity Theatre, had no connections with left political movements. Unity's magazine noted with approval the number of finalists 'definitely dealing with social problems'.[43]

The left cultural critic and actress Barbara Nixon observed in 1935 that BDL events were 'showing a noticeable decrease in the number of trivial works produced in favour of more serious plays . . .'. In her opinion many amateur groups had reached a high technical standard through the festival experience; however, they were still suffering from 'a lack of interesting plays'. Two years later John Allen commented that the prize winners in recent BDL Festivals represented 'an encouraging sign that there is a definite swing in favour of plays with subjects that matter'. Both critics were espousing the popular front political strategy and its implications for cultural practice at the time, an issue that will be discussed in the next chapter. It is possible, then, that both were looking for evidence to support their existing views but at the same time the festivals do indicate a more diverse choice of play than might be assumed.[44] Allen's comment was responding to the finals of the BDL competitions of 1936 and 1937. In the first of these the joint second place among the five finalists was given to two anti-war pieces: the Glasgow Corporation Transport Players for *And So to War*, the satire by Joe Corrie in which a benevolent dictator sends the war-mongering over fifty-year-olds into battle while the youth is kept safely at home; and *The Last War*, by Neil Grant, performed by Shrewsbury Amateur Dramatic Society, in which a cast of animals representing the creatures of the earth celebrate when humans destroy themselves through warfare. Another finalist was the Treharris Amateur Drama Club with *Twentieth Century-Lullaby*. As some press reviews commented three out of these five plays in the finals had an anti-war theme.[45]

In 1937 the winning entry was the Newcastle Central Young Women's Christian Association (YWCA) production of *The Willing Spirit*, by local author Esther McCracken, in which a man who has been unemployed for three years finally gets a job but is too weakened by undernourishment to be able to take it. This was accompanied by the Newbattle Burns Dramatic Society's presentation of *Hewers of Coal*, again by Joe Corrie, which as we have seen follows the relationships between five miners before and after a colliery explosion caused by management neglect.[46]

These were examples of amateur companies with no links to the organized left staging productions that engaged with the politics of the day: the consequences of long-term unemployment, the rise of fascism, European dictatorships and the threat of war. Further, in some examples the dramatic techniques used were by no means conventional ones. Evidence of amateur theatre societies staging political plays is not confined to the national finals. In 1938 the Vaughan College Players from Leicester reached the Western Area Final with that classic of 1930s political theatre *Waiting for Lefty*, by Clifford Odets. The other finalists in the Western Area included the Plymouth Co-op Players with Joe Corrie's *Hewers of Coal* and a Walsall group with *The Hat Trick*, a Neil Grant satire on dictatorships. The following year they reached it again with *Dirge Without Dole*. On that occasion they came second to Hereford YMCA's production of *This Earth Is Ours*, who then as we have seen proceeded with it to the national final in London. Earlier in 1939, and away from the competition circuit, the Vaughan Players had performed Stephen Spender's anti-fascist verse play *The Trial of a Judge*, and Spender gave a talk about the play on the night. This was the first appearance of the play outside London after its performances by the Group Theatre.[47]

The observations by Allen and Nixon were not the only ones on the appearance of socially engaged drama in BDL festivals, although others were more cautious about the implications. It was noticed in 1936 that Corrie's serious plays reached the finals of festivals but his most performed works on the amateur stage were the country comedies. Similarly, although four out of the five finalists at the London final in 1939 were indeed examples of 'social drama' this did not reflect the festival as a whole, 'which was not concerned with serious plays'.[48] The noticeable presence of political and socially conscious amateur theatre in local, regional and national finals should not be assumed to be a representative sample. Nevertheless the presence was there and it attracted comment. Given that the festival marking system was angled towards acting and production as distinct from the choice of play, a conclusion could be that these substantial works were demanding more from producers and casts, and thus impressing the adjudicators. Alternatively, the adjudicators may have been reacting positively to entries which were beyond the ordinary. As one put it, 'Anything that is different comes as a very welcome relief. No adjudicator no matter how honest and experienced he or she may be can fail to be struck by anything that is unusual.'[49] Whatever the explanation the results go towards vindicating Joe Corrie's position that festivals presented an opportunity to present more challenging material.

Peace festivals and plays

Amateur theatre had a routine presence at other festivals besides those celebrating drama. The presence of peace plays at drama festivals, and the popularity of *Twentieth Century Lullaby*, illustrates the presence of anti-war sentiment as a social movement, one which gained momentum during the inter-war years. The Peace Festival, or Peace Week, was a common event around Britain at this time. Both their numbers and their scale grew as the 1930s wore on and the international situation deteriorated. A Peace Week would usually be organized by a committee comprising League of Nations Union branch members, local authorities, schools, churches, and other organizations wishing to remind communities about the destruction of war and to promote international co-operation for peace and security. Usually amateur drama performances were included. As an example the Maesteg local authority organized 'the most elaborate peace festival ever witnessed in South Wales' in 1939. The three-day outdoor event involved mass choirs, tree-planting, exhibitions and public meetings; the Garth Social Services Club performed 'a satirical tableau' and an amateur group gave a performance of Priestley's *I Have Been Here Before*. Peace plays themselves were performed outside formal peace festivals, such as at meetings organized by local branches of the League of Nations Union, one example being productions by the Trecynon Players at the Aberdare Little Theatre in 1937.[50]

In Scotland two examples are the Peace Weeks held in the neighbouring industrial towns of Airdrie and Coatbridge. Airdrie saw 400 performers and seventeen tableaux in their Peace Pageant of 1937. Local amateurs performed Joe Corrie's *And So to War*, which along with his *Martha* – concerning a widow who loses her son at the end of the 1914–18 war – had also been performed by the Mutual Service Association Players in Coatbridge. *And So to War* was particularly popular at such events and as the decade wore on 'watched with mixed emotions by an audience mindful of contemporary events'.[51] The Pax Players – amateur theatre groups associated with the churches and affiliated to the International Pax Players – were prominent in local Peace Festivals around the country. The Edinburgh group performed at Airdrie in 1937 and also a year later when their production of *The Path to Glory* was particularly praised. This play by a significant figure in the amateur movement, Lawrence du Garde Peach of Derbyshire, was a three-act satire whose BBC broadcast had drawn complaints from army officers who thought the portrayal of the army command in the play was 'overly cynical'. *Moloch* was another frequent choice for the Pax Players, a three-act tragedy by Winifred Carter in which, on the outbreak of a world war, a mother poisons her son to spare him what her eldest son endured during the Great War.[52]

The promotion of peace in the inter-war years could take different political forms and this is reflected not only in the peace plays of the time but their contexts and the reaction to them. Participation could be drawn from across the religious and political spectrum, with all that that could involve. For example, the Bootle Peace Week Committee in Lancashire included Conservative Party representation and expected their views on how to promote peace to be respected. Therefore when Merseyside Left Theatre performed left plays by Corrie and others during Peace Week the local press ran critical letters about them for some time.[53]

The all-women dramas written by Muriel and Sydney Box have been mentioned; worth noting too is that a recurring theme in several of them was opposition to war. One, *Bring Me My Bow*, attracted hostility from the Lord Chamberlain's Office in 1937 when a Women's Institute drama group applied for a licence for public performance, as distinct from one solely for its own members.

A proposal to refuse a licence – and thus to ban the play – was overruled by the Home Secretary. Nevertheless, as the historian of British theatre censorship points out, the episode revealed an official anxiety about the possible political effects of the peace plays that emerged during the decade. *Bring Me My Bow* is set in a girls' public school on speech-day where the guest speaker, the wife of the Minister of War, announces that scholarships for university places have been drastically cut in order to fund the rearmament programme. The one remaining scholarship will be awarded to the author of the best essay on the theme of rearmament as the most effective means to secure peace. However, the most able student, whose father was killed in the Great War, refuses to write on such a theme, and in a dream sequence a chorus reinforces her stance with a series of anti-war verses. The play was performed by amateur groups and appeared in both the Midland and Northern Area finals of the BDL annual competition in 1939, a significant year in which to deal with these issues on stage given the Munich crisis and the eventual declaration of war.[54]

Another of their one-act plays in the same genre was the prophetically titled – as Prime Minister Neville Chamberlain's Munich conference with Hitler was to prove – *Peace in Our Time*.[55] The play opens in the country house garden of Lady Crosby, the wife of an MP, who is hosting League of Nations delegates from Japan, Britain, the Soviet Union and the USA. Of the two Crosby daughters one is married to a pilot and believes in armed deterrence, whereas the other has a pacifist belief in disarmament. A credible rumour of war, introduced by a figure of death, reveals that the League delegates are more committed to their own countries success at fighting it than to avoiding it. The pacifist daughter declares that we have 'glimpsed the reality behind our shams' and that peace will be unachievable whilst 'our whole scheme of life is founded on conflict, and the survival of the strongest'. Can this change in time to save the future?

Although there were one or two exceptions, the plays for female casts the Boxes published for the drama festival market were set in decidedly genteel social milieux. The communities of women represented were likely to be situated in an exclusive school, affluent home or a country house, with working-class women appearing as the servants. Despite the anti-war messages some of the plays contained they relied, as Hope Dodds had explained in the 1920s, 'upon analogies and references to a certain way of living and thinking' that were those of the comfortably placed. An interesting exception was a contribution by Muriel Box herself, *Angels of War*, a three-act play on the fortunes of eight women ambulance drivers on the Western Front during the First World War.

The drivers are drawn from diverse backgrounds and cope with long hours of draining and sometimes dangerous work – one is killed by shrapnel – together with cold and squalid living conditions. They are very much a collective with no character in a lead role. One theme, something of a common one in the genre, is the erosion of a young recruit's uncritical patriotism by the realities of what the women are dealing with. Tensions arise between them, caused basically by the exigencies of their work and the need for relief from it, but these are suspended when comradeship requires a common front against authority: their authoritarian commandant and her aide, 'Creeping Lizzie'. The dialogue has a bawdy humour together with language that must have been just within the acceptable boundaries at the time. In the final scene the drivers discuss their forthcoming demobilization at the end of the war and how their lives and expectations have changed. One of them is convinced that:

> there can never be another war after this ... It can never happen again. I feel I can look forward ten, twenty years to 1938 and hear people saying 'No, that generation gave up everything it held dear in life so that there should never be another war as long as the world lasts. They did that for us ... They didn't let us down and we mustn't let them down.

> **Moaner**   But if they do ...?

> **Vic**   If they do, then we've been through it all for nothing. But they won't, will they?

> **Moaner**   (musingly) I wonder ...[56]

Angels was performed by women's amateur groups in the 1930s, including WI companies, suggesting that at least some of these groups were willing to present material dealing with a critical political issue of time. During the possible censorship controversy a civil servant had commented of *Bring Me My Bow* that he 'could not understand Women's Institutes performing this sort of rubbish'. In fact the WI had a commitment to inclusivity that involved, in deference to Quaker members, eschewing any approval of militarism. The autonomy enjoyed by local branches meant that some too participated in anti-war activities.[57] It can be added that these women's drama groups could stage other comparatively progressive material as well as peace plays. In 1939 the drama group from the Duns branch of the Scottish Women's Rural Institute went through the knockout stages to win the final of a SCDA festival organized for the SWRI. Their play was *Dirge Without Dole*, a choice for which they were complimented for originality.[58]

Other anti-war plays featured in the amateur repertoire. *The Pen Is Mightier* was a stage satire by Robert Victor and very similar to, if not actually the same, as his radio play *Tin Soldiers*, broadcast in September 1937.[59] Two generals of opposing armies (one of which seems British) agree between each other to stage advances and counter advances by their forces, but only on the map. The purpose is simply to generate dispatches to meet their respective governments' propaganda needs whist avoiding bloodshed. Unfortunately a visiting War Minister discovers the truth, but, fittingly, he sacrifices himself by arranging his own death at the front in order to protect his political legacy. *The Pen Is Mightier* was performed in BDL area competitions in Liverpool and the Midlands during 1938 and 1939. Away from the competition circuit it was staged by several other amateur societies and a League of Nations Youth Group during much the same period.[60]

Another example is *Shells* by Lawrence du Garde Peach, of the Derbyshire amateur theatre, and author of *The Path to Glory*. His play *Shells* centres on two cockney private soldiers in a Flanders trench alert to the occasional shellfire. We are introduced to their hopes, fears, attitudes and domestic circumstances through blackly humorous dialogue. One of them can't help but speculate where people go after death, something he tries to discuss with a passing padre. Then the two privates are shelled but appear to recover, and are staring at two bodies; as an officer and sergeant inspect the two corpses the privates speak to them only to discover, in a dramatic twist, that it is they who are dead and the bodies are their own. Stirling Amateur Dramatic Club (having changed the dialogue from cockney to Scots) gained second place at the 1939 national finals with this, as we have seen; this was following their first place with it at the SCDA competition final in March that year. In 1938 a British Legion drama club had won first place with *Shells* at the Fraserburgh Festival, so the play was known in Scottish amateur circles.[61] Although *The Path to Glory* was broadcast du Garde Peach's subsequent *Patriotism Ltd* – a satirical farce about politicians and arms manufacturers – was banned by the BBC in 1937. It was performed nonetheless by the 'farmers, shopkeepers, dairymaids and labourers' of the Great Hucknall Village Players before adoption by repertory companies.[62]

The performances of peace plays, both within and outside the drama festival circuit, demonstrate that there was an interest in such material in the pre-war amateur theatre movement, reacting both to the experiences of the First World War and the prospect of a Second. It also suggests that the market responded to the interest in such plays as it had for those with mainly female casts. The varying politics of the peace play of the time, and the forms used to express different ideas about those politics, will be discussed further in the next chapter.

The BDL and politics

Linda Mackenney considers that the British Drama League was a 'highly conventional amateur drama organisation' and so it is worth considering the reactions to the presence of political theatre amongst its activities. There is some evidence of a variety of personally held political stances among SCDA adjudicators, and more to the point these emerged in some of their festival judgements. In one Glasgow competition the official noted that two clubs had presented plays, one *Our Place on Earth*, dealing with the 'tragic position of Jewish people in Europe'. He believed it was 'praiseworthy' that clubs should put on plays dealing with such contemporary events. However at the next stage of the competition the following month a different adjudicator (despite praising the historical play *The Jews of Hodus* entered by the Glasgow Jewish Institute Players) took a very different view. Although there was 'sincerity in the production' of *Our Place* it was 'really a piece of dramatised journalism and definitely propaganda of a one-sided view of Germany'. This was hardly likely to encourage groups to enter this kind of material.[63] Unsurprisingly, then, despite Corrie's success in using the SCDA to present some radical material, the left theatre movement in Scotland came to consider the organization to be right-wing, resisting proposals to participate in a SCDA festival for that reason, and joining other groups in promoting their own festivals outside the SCDA circuit.[64]

Although the evidence is mixed there is enough to qualify Mackenney's generalization. Elements in the BDL were clearly sympathetic to left theatre. Robert Mitchell, for example, was a festival adjudicator with the BDL who produced Unity Theatre's famous satirical pantomime *Babes in the Wood* in 1939. Another prominent figure in the BDL and the amateur movement assisted local left theatre: Nora Ratcliff, as has been mentioned, was a prolific playwright and producer for the amateur stage whose achievements in the inter-war years were notable. She won awards for her own plays on occasion and for several years was a producer with the Bradfield Village Players in Yorkshire; her 1938 book *Rude Mechanicals: A Short Review of Village Drama* was considered one of the key texts on the subject. She also contributed a long-standing series of articles about village theatre in diary form for *The Amateur Theatre and Playwrights' Journal*, and her own dramatic work was used by amateur groups in BDL and SCDA festival competitions.[65] Her contribution to the Left Book Club Theatre Guild, the national network of theatre groups with left progressive politics, will be considered in the next chapter. Another village drama stalwart, du Garde

Peach, authored as we have seen anti-war plays satirizing the armaments industry and its relationship to politicians.

Under Bourne's editorship *The Amateur Theatre and Playwrights' Journal* published several progressive one-act plays, gave favourable reviews to Unity productions, and to published collections of leftist plays, and carried articles such as William Kozlenko's praise for the 'unparalleled social achievement' of the Federal Theatre Project in the USA. Raymond Birt, another BDL adjudicator, contributed a highly sympathetic account of the Left Book Club Theatre Guild, the subject of the next chapter.[66] There is no suggestion that BDL figures such as Bourne, Birt or Mitchell favoured progressive plays when they adjudicated competitions but their careers also suggest that they would not be biased against them. In Scotland, however, the position seems to have been different. Therefore although there were certainly sympathisers and even active assistance for left theatre among the prominent figures of the British amateur network this cannot be claimed to be consistent. Indeed, it may be interesting that Mount/Box portrayed the adjudicator in *Dirge Without Dole* as so hostile to the idea of any socially engaged drama.

Did the centrality of the one-act play in competitions inhibit the development of amateur drama, as some feared? There were certainly significant attempts to innovate within the form and to make use of cinematic production techniques, showing an openness to international influence. These innovations were developed through attempted engagement with the social issues of the day, and this widening of the narrative shows that the production of this drama by the amateur theatre extended beyond the activities of the groups established for political theatre. This weakens any assumed binary opposition between political and mainstream amateur theatre between the wars.

There was of course far more to amateur performance than the annual festivals, which, as was pointed out at the time, were not necessarily so characterized by serious drama as the successful plays might suggest. Certain other questions are likely to remain unanswered. An obvious one is why and by whom particular plays were selected by the amateur dramatic groups concerned. Was the choice of play an attempt to influence an audience politically or simply to do well in competition by presenting material that was different from the predictable repertoire? *Dirge Without Dole* is clearly a case in point, with its guying of a stereotypical adjudicator and competition. Some groups, such as the Vaughn Players, the Hull Electricity Board Drama Group, the Glasgow Corporation Transport Players and the Newbattle Burns Group, did perform progressive plays more than once. This suggests that some of the well-regarded groups did have socio-political as well as dramatic purposes, as well as a wish to succeed.

Another question concerns the audiences. The contemporary reports and reviews, as is so often the case, generally centre on the reactions of the individual critic or adjudicator rather than the collective responses of the audience they were amongst. Possibly the 'enthusiastic reception' and 'was well received' in the reports may simply describe audiences seeing members of their own communities or workplace colleagues performing successfully rather than responses to the messages of the plays. Nevertheless it is also possible that these audiences, unlike, for example, those attending a meeting, were not so predisposed to sympathy with the political aims of the plays. In that respect the ideas may have been able to reach a wider constituency than might have been the case with audiences attending a political event. The frequent appearance of peace plays among the amateurs also suggests engagement with a social movement around a key issue of the time.

At the end of the decade at least two figures associated with the BDL– Bourne and Birt – were welcoming the prospect of the Left Book Club Theatre Guild, the Sheffield branch of which had attracted Nora Ratcliff as a producer. Birt had expressed hopes for the Guild in *The Amateur Theatre and Playwrights' Journal* when it was formed and Bourne had gone further. He believed that in the amateur movement working-class perspectives tended to be voiced through sympathetic middle-class writers whose awareness came from the imagination and not from experience. As a contrast his example was Joe Corrie whom he described as 'the only working-class playwright of note in Britain'; certainly, no other was as well known throughout the amateur movement as Corrie. For Bourne the Left Book Club Theatre Guild was a significant development because 'the working-classes are being drawn into the amateur movement and are being encouraged to create one-act plays of their own'. Although 'at the moment there exist only half a dozen or so native products that are worth more than a minute or two of consideration', here was a real potential to develop the one-act play outside the competitive festival circuit.[67]

The next chapter examines the Guild and the extent to which it met the expectations expressed for it. It also examines this attempt at a formal link between the amateur movement as a whole and a specifically political theatre initiative.

5

'The terribly urgent struggle'

The Left Book Club Theatre Guild, 1936–9

The popular front

The Left Book Club Theatre Guild for which Bourne expressed such hopes must be understood in its political context. Whereas the crises of the early 1930s were domestic ones around unemployment, later in the decade the crises shifted from the domestic to the international. Hitler's assumption of power in 1933 was followed a year later by Mussolini's invasion of Abyssinia; in 1936 the elected government of Republican Spain was attacked by a military coup, beginning the three years of the Spanish Civil War. One year later Japan invaded China in the first phase of an imperial expansion. In 1937 too the first gas-mask factories opened in Britain and air-raid testing began. The international situation deteriorated rapidly as Hitler annexed Austria in 1938, and during the Munich crisis of that year British Prime Minister Neville Chamberlain conceded Hitler's plan to annex the Sudetenland. The rest of Czechoslovakia became a German 'protectorate' in 1939.

In many quarters there was a feeling of bewilderment and anger over British policy and this was articulated most clearly over the situation in Spain. Under a policy of 'Non-Intervention' the British government refused to allow Republican Spain to buy arms for its own defence, whilst simultaneously ignoring the flagrant breaches of the policy by Hitler and Mussolini. The British approach was to become notorious as 'appeasement', whereby Britain and France avoided confronting fascist territorial ambitions until a world war was inevitable.

By 1935 and in order to resist this advance of fascism in Europe and Japan, communists began to move towards trying to build a 'popular front' of all working-class organizations and progressive opinion against fascism, war, and in Britain against the National Government and its conduct of appeasement in foreign policy. The British left largely responded by pressing for the policy of 'collective security'. According to this the two remaining European democracies should agree a pact with the Soviet Union for mutual assistance against aggression by Germany and Italy. Although this proposal originated with the Soviet Union and so was obviously pushed by the Communist Party, it had a resonance too with those who were not pro-Soviet but who believed that such a collective stand would deter further fascist expansion. However, the British government never showed any real interest in pursuing it.[1]

A popular front was rejected by the Labour Party leadership but it found support among those who were impatient with what they saw as Labour's caution, and lack of urgency, over the threats of fascism and war. An important expression of this came through the Left Book Club, established in 1936 and with 57,000 members by 1939 – a larger membership than any of the political parties at the time. It was both a book club and a political force, conceived by the publisher Victor Gollancz as a means to provide information and education 'to help in the terribly urgent struggle for world peace and to build a better social and economic order against fascism'. Members received a book of the month and a newsletter, *Left News*, for their subscription; the books, on international or domestic political themes, were chosen by Gollancz, Harold Laski from the Labour left and John Strachey, a Marxist close to the Communist Party. The choices included exemplary accounts of social conditions in the inter-war years: George Orwell's *The Road to Wigan Pier*, Ellen Wilkinson's *The Town That Was Murdered* and Wal Hannington's *The Problem of the Distressed Areas*. Altogether millions of books were circulated. Local branches of the Club arranged public meetings and discussion groups around the themes of the books and the Club also organized mass rallies addressed by well-known Labour left and communist politicians.[2] The purpose was to unite all progressive opinion to pressure the National Government and the rallies were amongst the largest of the decade.

The Labour leadership officially rejected a common front with the communists and some important Labour figures also rejected the Club, correctly identifying that it never produced material critical of the Soviet Union even during the purges and trials in Moscow. It also suspected communists of manipulating local clubs and whereas this has been confirmed in some cases it cannot be assumed to have been the norm.[3] In any event both the Left Book Club and its Theatre Guild appealed to the wide constituency of those willing to campaign both against the spread of fascism in Europe and the inexorable drift towards war, aims which did not appear as contradictory at the time as hindsight suggests they were.

The Left Book Club Theatre Guild

The Unity Theatre was formed in London in 1936 by a number of people with previous experience in left political theatre together with some new sympathisers. The Left Book Club Theatre Guild (LBCTG) came about during the following year due to the appreciable number of local Club groups, interested in amateur drama, who were approaching Unity Theatre for advice about plays they could perform. Earlier in Manchester, Bristol and Glasgow, for example, others interested in developing political theatre beyond agitprop were establishing their own drama groups. The Left Book Club offered links with local trade union and progressive parties and an opportunity for a national theatre movement alongside the local Clubs.

At its peak before the outbreak of war in 1939 the Guild claimed to have nearly 250 affiliated theatre groups, approximately one for every four local Left Book Clubs. They varied widely in their activity and duration: an internal questionnaire survey in 1939 – albeit one with a low response rate – found that half the groups responding were 'energetic' and the rest 'erratic' or had ceased altogether.[4] Some groups such as those in Newcastle or Sheffield were named Left Book Club Theatre Guilds but others, although affiliated to the Guild and often sharing repertoires, had locally chosen names: Bristol Unity Players, the Glasgow Workers' Theatre Group, Manchester Theatre of Action or the Merseyside Left Theatre. Activities were reported in *Left News* and the short-lived *Theatre for the People* until the outbreak of war in 1939.

Statements of intent

This theatre expressed its purpose with explicit statements: the Glasgow Workers' Theatre Group intended to build a theatre 'which exists to reflect the lives of the workers, to expose and explain the evils of the society in which we live and to further the cause of social justice'. In Bristol the Unity Players aimed for 'new plays with new technique' which would return to the tradition of a theatre which was 'a social voice and a social force'. Merseyside Left Theatre saw itself as 'performing on a political platform not on a theatre stage', playing to working-class audiences probably new to theatre attendance, and dealing with 'the most urgent political issues of the day'. Dave Ross, a railwayman in Newcastle, was clear that a class perspective was important to his group: 'We claimed to be a theatre with a purpose in life. It wasn't to depict the idle buggers who'd never done a hand's turn, you know, like in the Noel Coward shows, we wanted to show real plays with social significance, something that affected the working class'.[5]

Colin Chambers observes that despite the close links with the Unity Theatre in London there was no centralized authority over the LBCTG affiliates from that quarter. The observation can be widened, because there is evidence of suspicion over anything resembling attempts at control. At the first meeting of the LBCTG National Committee it was agreed that the Guild's Play Department 'has been greatly under the jurisdiction of Unity Theatre, this acting to the detriment of the guild nationally and it was decided to change this by plays being submitted to the national committee, criticisms to be sent to the organisers'. It was recommended that play reading clinics be organized in each district to strengthen local initiatives and not rely on London. Further, 'should any new theatre journal be published by Unity the Guild will request representation on the board'. There are glimpses too of the need for declarations of independence, such as when the Bristol secretary clarified in 1943 that her group 'was in being before London Unity Theatre and was not set up as a branch of it, although London Unity thought so'.[6] These groups, albeit seeing themselves as part of a national movement, were a loose network and several were clearly confident and self-reliant.

Class and participation

Some historians describe the Left Book Club as having been largely middle-class in membership. This is because there was a geographical preponderance of Clubs in suburban London and the comparatively prosperous areas of south-east England. In addition, where Club networks were organized around occupational groups they were generally professional and not manual ones.[7] Exceptions can be made to this generalization about membership and this is demonstrated by some LBCTG activists.

The Guild itself did make some effort to ascertain the social basis of its affiliates. The 1939 questionnaire survey suggested, from the small returns, that 40 per cent of them 'were working class'. Other evidence, from recollections and the occasional press report, is sporadic but tends to bear out social class diversity. Dave Ross, the railwayman in the Newcastle LBCTG, recalled its composition as 'a number of school teachers, a number of unemployed, a clerk and a labourer at Swan Hunter's shipyard, a postman, an electrician and a clerk on the Quayside ...'. In 1939 ten members of the Merseyside Left Theatre Group were prosecuted for attempting to perform material at the Chester Drama Competition that had not been licensed by the Lord Chamberlain. Their occupations were described, variously, as three unemployed, two teachers, a typist, a shop assistant, a dental mechanic, a rent collector and an insurance agent. One of the unemployed was the merchant seaman and writer George Garrett, whose stories were admired by George Orwell.[8] The founding statements of Bristol Unity Players described members as 'workers in industry, clerks, teachers, shop assistants and in the distributive trades . . .'; the Glasgow group included an electrician, a bookbinder, a dressmaker, unemployed men and a former merchant seaman, and also a Glasgow School of Art graduate. According to participant Maurice Ridley his company in County Durham were miners and their wives, students and unemployed – 'all having a whale of a time putting over left-wing stuff and plays like *Waiting for Lefty*'.[9]

An important point, perhaps, about the social diversity of these groups is an observation about Bristol. This is that 'members working long hours on the factory floor, with distances to travel and homes to mind tended to be ready only for occasional shows and infrequent rehearsals'. Therefore much of the administration was in the hands of those 'whose time was more their own'. This certainly describes some of the successful LBCTG producers of whom several already had theatre experience. In Bristol producer Joan Tuckett was well known in local amateur theatre as was Nora Ratcliff in Sheffield; in Newcastle Sophie Learner was a schoolteacher as was Jerry Dawson in Liverpool. Monmouthshire and South Wales relied on Norman Draper and Stanley Jones, the first a local government officer and the second an engineering lecturer. In Glasgow producer Lawrie Lawson was a Co-operative grocer. The principal factor in the success and duration of local groups must have been the availability of committed producers able to develop confidence and talent amongst amateurs.[10]

Symmetry with the BDL

As was discussed in the previous chapter the critic Barbara Nixon had noted, as had John Allen, a trend towards more serious plays in British Drama League (BDL) events, and how amateur groups had raised their technical standards through participation in the festivals. Also, that 'such co-ordination and opportunities for mutual learning' was a model the left theatres should adopt.[11] The Guild functioned for affiliated theatre groups in a similar way to the BDL, and it is not implausible to claim that the League may have been a model, since the positive effects of its work were clearly being acknowledged. The Guild too circulated suitable material and its pamphlet *List of Plays Recommended by the Left Book Club Theatre Guild for Production by Left-Wing Amateur Groups*. As with the BDL play library scripts could be borrowed. It advised on scripts and provided a 'clinic' service for new playwrights, and made recommendations for group organisation – including, importantly, meeting the requirements of the Lord Chamberlain's office for licensing productions. The Guild alongside Unity Theatre promoted regional and national training schools. The BDL as we have seen facilitated theatre professionals, including well-known figures such as Edith Craig, to develop acting and production skills amongst amateur companies. This too as the case with the LBCTG: professionals such as the Unity producer Herbert Marshall and composer Alan Bush were involved in weekend schools and national conferences, while classes held in London by Unity Theatre included contributions from Flora Robson, Sybil Thorndike and Michel Saint-Denis, the latter a contributor to adult education classes in South Wales as we have seen.[12]

Local training events were supported, again with contributions from experienced figures. A weekend school at Matlock, for example, involved Ratcliff, a producer with Sheffield LBC; a conference in north-east England, for example, heard a 'long and comprehensive account' on the Stanislavsky approach to acting from Farrell of the Spennymoor Settlement. As we have seen some of his students developed interests in political theatre and had become involved in the local LBCTG. Thus in this case there was an intersection between amateur theatre whose purpose was educational and that where it was political. In a context where classes were discussing international affairs in the later 1930s this is unsurprising. The intersection was not always welcomed, however. At the Sheffield Settlement warden Arnold Freeman was concerned about a leftwards drift of some of his students towards the LBC and its theatre.[13] Recognizing that some groups would not have the services of an experienced producer *Theatre for the People* re-published *Outline for an Elementary Course in Acting*, by the American Federal Theatre Project veteran John E. Bonn. This came complete with exercises derived from Stanislavsky.[14] In Newcastle schoolteacher Sophie Learner trained members with such exercises, as Dave Ross recalled:

> If a new member came in we'd sit in a circle with the new one in the middle, feeling very ill at ease about this. The Sophie would say, 'I'm throwing an imaginary box, catch it' and the person would respond and make to catch it. Then Sophie would continue, 'What's in the box, what shape is it, what colour is it' and so on. You'd see the self-consciousness peel away from them.[15]

Similarly members were encouraged to watch people when they were out, how their expressions changed when they did different things, how this could be learnt and used to help convey to an audience that the actors were 'doing whatever it was they were supposed to be doing'. In Glasgow training was taken seriously, with young actors encouraged to join local acting and dance classes and even to take walk-on parts with touring professional companies in order to study them. Similarly Tuckett in Bristol recommended attendance at local amateur shows to appreciate the standards required. Joan Littlewood and Ewan MacColl formed their own acting school for the Manchester Theatre of Action, featuring movement, and acting methods derived from Stanislavski. As with the National Council for Social Service project at Hardwick Hall for unemployed drama schemes, the LBCTG also ran schools aimed at producers so that they could return to their groups with enhanced skills.[16]

Engaging with the amateur movement

Leading figures in the LBCTG, besides, arguably, following the BDL model, always stressed the necessity for local groups to engage with their local amateur dramatic societies. This was a new development; the revolutionary politics which had motivated the Workers' Theatre Movement were abandoned in favour of anti-fascism, and abandoned too was their dismissive attitude to the mainstream and amateur theatre. Partly of course this was the influence of the popular front strategy – Allen explained that it was far easier to attract actors on an anti-fascist basis than on a socialist one – but it was also a recognition, like the emphasis on training, that attention had to be paid to the quality of dramatic material and production. As the Guild repeatedly stressed to affiliates, 'the theatre to be effective is an art to be mastered'. At the same time Guild officers saw their theatre as a potential means to attract new recruits to the progressive movement whose primary interest was in drama.[17]

The advent of popular front politics – and the accompanying move away from the agitprop reliance on dramatizing slogans – certainly did attract some producers who were already experienced in amateur drama before they were involved in the Guild. Ratcliff in Sheffield, Tuckett in Bristol, and Margaret Leona in Devon are examples, following in the earlier footsteps of Frida Stewart in Manchester. The Belfast Guild had Douglas Praunsmandel, a professional actor and producer from London. South Wales was supported by Norman Draper and Marjorie Phillips from the local amateur societies. Ratcliff was part of a BDL delegation – along with Stewart – visiting Soviet theatres in 1934 and returned impressed: she gave lectures on her visit to audiences in Sheffield, praising the importance she claimed the Soviet system gave to theatre and its role in the lives of the people.[18] By 1938 if not before her work encompassed the Sheffield LBCTG as well as the mainstream amateur movement. Examples can be found too of others moving from the amateur movement to the left theatre. The play *Girls in Uniform*, based on an earlier German film, was popular with those amateur companies able to assemble the large female cast required. The analogies between the repressive institution portrayed and life in Hitler's Germany were not lost on Celia Baker, who cited her role in it as the background to her involvement with left theatre.[19] There was a practical reason for encouraging this engagement besides improving the quality of dramatic productions: the lament from groups that 'they have not enough members and the ones they have are so occupied with political activities that they have little time for their theatrical work'.[20] Thus the view was encouraged that new people could be attracted to the progressive movement through their interest in the theatre.

At this point it is useful to examine a cross-section of the plays performed by this movement. This is done by discussing their ant-fascist material, then the productions around the threat of war, and then finally the plays aimed at trade union members.

Spain and anti-fascism

One of the mostly widely performed pieces by the LBCTG was *On Guard for Spain*, a 'mass declamation', a poem designed to be performed by speakers and chorus. Written by the Australian-born communist Jack Lindsay it both reflected and contributed to the extraordinary passions generated by solidarity campaigns with the Spanish Republic.[21] It is a long and somewhat uneven poem, rich and rhythmic and with lines such as 'the sun tied ribbons in all the trees' and 'the moon smelled of oranges'; but at the other end of the scale melodramatic ones like 'I rose from the bed of my wife's young body/at the call of Liberty;/ oh feed with my blood our flag's red flame/Comrades, remember me'. A contemporary emphasized the profound effect a performance could have; writing during the Second World War, he recalled how audiences were moved by the roll-call of the names of Spanish cities because they knew the atrocities that had occurred there. In his own case it meant the difference between supporting a cause not only intellectually but emotionally too. He explained that before the performance he already had a knowledge of the Spanish situation, but such intellectually acquired conviction was likely to be 'shallow unless it is quickened by feeling'.[22]

In such examples both the performers and most of the audience were involved to varying degrees in support for the Spanish Republic, already in an emotional rapport which the performance could strengthen. Typically the verses would be broken down into sections for particular points or experiences, and for solo or group voices. One voice took up a line, two would strengthen it, and then more moving on to the climaxes whilst maintaining the rhythmic qualities. At the same time they would move as much as the performance space allowed; marching, standing in parallel lines, forming apexes with individual speakers stepping forward to emphasis particular lines. Any props were required to be portable, such as a bandage to show a head wound, wooden staves to represent rifles, a red lamp adapted to resemble a brazier. Dave Atkinson was a young post office worker and a cast member when Newcastle LBCTG performed the piece:

> It was a very popular thing. What I found amazing was that a poem like that, which was so rich in metaphor and symbolism could really go down well with people who you wouldn't expect to appreciate it … you didn't expect the rapt attention which we used to get from almost every audience we played to. We weren't particularly skilled for a start. It was the poetry itself which carried the message.[23]

Figure 5 Bristol Unity Players rehearsing *On Guard for Spain*, 1938. Reproduced with the permission of University of Warwick Modern Records Centre MSS 212/X/2/5.

The Newcastle group gave around thirty performances of *On Guard* over three years, just one example of how the declamation was a prominent feature of Guild repertoire around the country. Again, initiative was used to reach new audiences, as Atkinson recalled:

> At that time when you went to the cinema very often they had turns on in between the films. Sometimes they had kids on, competitions with little prizes, things like that, and we slotted into this. They'd have been watching some rubbish or other and then they'd get this. And they listened and they appreciated it. We got good reactions from political meetings and good reactions from cinema crowds who wouldn't have gone anywhere near a political meeting.[24]

These performances were connecting with a public sympathy for the Spanish Republic that extended beyond political circles; the newsreels that those cinema audiences would have seen carried images, harrowing at the time, of the aerial bombing of civilians and waves of refugees. The admission that 'we weren't particularly skilled' perhaps suggests that *On Guard* was a suitable piece for a new group. Rehearsing this was an introduction to voice projection, memorizing a piece whose language was not easy, and also to the effects that could be achieved through group movement.

Lindsay was a classics scholar and *On Guard*, composed of performed verses with narrator and chorus, shows the influence of Greek drama. In a similar vein the LBCTG in Plymouth – new, but with 'prominent local amateurs in the company' – performed a sequence from *The Trojan Women* by Euripides. It was produced by Margaret Leona, a professional involved with London Unity Theatre, whose aim was for the production to have 'contemporary resonances and emotional connections' with the situation of European refugees. Her interpretation drew on the author's exposure of the hollow glory of war and the attendant human suffering. The performances were at meetings held to press the government for a more liberal policy towards admitting refugees from fascism, and the staging focussed on contemporary relevance. Reviews noted how the production 'dressed the Greeks in uniforms reminiscent of the Black shirts, with modified swastikas on their arms, and dressed the Trojan women in clothes that could not fail to recall Czechoslovakia . . .'. The chorus of Trojan refugees created a tense atmosphere and was used to great effect.[25]

As we have seen in Nottinghamshire, Makin was producing drama by Czech refugees at this time. Refugees from fascism were the theme too of a one-act play written and produced by Enid Windsor for Croydon LBCTG. *Crossing the Frontier* was, as the local reviewer stated, 'topical and alive' given the news coverage of the attempts by German and Czech Jews to escape persecution. The play is set in a railway station on the border between two European countries and the reactions of Catherine, a naïve but well-intentioned British tourist, to the fate of a Jewish family seeking to cross the border to safety. Fascist border guards elicit bribes from the family, and hint at help in return for sexual favours; finally this leads to the arrest of the family and the shooting of the mother as they attempt to flee. This provokes a declaration from a railway worker who has befriended Catherine:

Hans   Brave men and women are working underground. I've been a coward. I didn't realise. God, it was awful. I've never actually seen it happen before . . . They shan't get away with it for ever.[26]

True to the conventional, for the genre, positive ending in the face of defeat, both Hans and Catherine resolve that 'unity is strength, they always say that and now I believe it'. As the reviewer described, the play has flaws, including lapses into stilted dialogue, but some well-drawn characters and the quality of the performances was praised. Refugees from the Nazis were arriving in increasing numbers and this play was recommended for performance to refugee support groups who were approaching local LBCTGs for help with fund-raising and campaigning.[27]

Clifford Odets's anti-fascist drama *Till the Day I Die*, performed by many LBCTG groups, was dramatically conventional but still presented challenges for amateur performers. Set in Berlin it portrays the underground resistance to the Nazis and the activity in it of two lovers, Ernst and Tilly. They know the odds are against them but as Tilly reveals her pregnancy news arrives of the Popular Front Government in France; this juxtaposition of two new beginnings, personal and political, after 'we have been steeled in a terrible fire', symbolize hope for the future. This is one positive point to take from the play in which hero Ernst eventually commits suicide rather than live as a Gestapo informer after capture. Reflecting the strains of illegal and dangerous work the seven scenes contain almost unremitting tension and demand much of the cast to sustain the emotional intensity, and the tempo of the action through the set changes. According to press reviews this was achieved, at least on some occasions: praise for the acting and production of the Belfast Guild encouraged them to tour Northern Ireland with the play in 1939, at the same time as the Edinburgh group impressed critics when they performed it during trades union May Day events. Probably the first British performance had been two years earlier at Bedlinog Workmens' Hall, when the Monmouthshire group played to 'a typical South Wales mining community audience of about 350' with similar stage success – the atmosphere was said to be 'electric' and the 'response was spontaneous' from the audience.[28]

Peace plays from the left

As we have seen 'peace plays' featured in the repertoire of a growing number of amateur companies during the inter-war period, both reflecting and contributing to the political concerns and campaigns of the time. Publishers responded to the demand with, for example, the collection *Ten Peace Plays* in 1938. This interest was also a recommended point of contact between LBCTG groups and their local amateur companies. Allen suggested that they persuade them to produce a peace play in connection with a local Peace Council, the alliance of different organizations opposing the drift to war.[29]

In fact progressive theatre groups could actually be invited to participate in the Peace Weeks and Festivals organized around the country and described in the previous chapter. Manchester Theatre of Action was approached by the local Peace Pledge Union to perform *Miracle at Verdun*, a production which attracted useful future contacts for the group. Bristol Unity Players were similarly invited in 1936 and contributed their own piece, *Passing Unnoticed*, which like Farnin's play in Motherwell was centred on a war memorial. It led to fruitful and lasting relationship with the Bristol Co-operative movement. Liverpool approached local Peace Week organizers and performed material such as Corrie's *And So to War*, but as we have seen causing controversy amongst those hostile to its message.[30] Such was the politically diverse nature of inter-war peace events. The critic Barbara Nixon noted that material that instilled a fear of war but did not contain 'a constructive plan to avoid the danger' would 'not only be ineffectual but dangerous'; simple pacifism or appeasement might be assumed as a response to fear. She recognized that to present some 'constructive plan' in the format of the conventional one-act play would risk a dramatically weak climax, sacrificing theatrical impact for the sake of a political conclusion. Her proposal was that peace plays should avoid naturalistic representation in favour of verse drama, fantasy or a documentary format.[31] Variations on fantasy had been a part of Box/Mount's *Twentieth Century Lullaby*, and to an extent also in Farnin's *War Memorial* as we have seen. Irwin Shaw's *Bury the Dead* was an American play with fantasy that went further in meeting the political criteria and offered a challenging drama for both cast and audience. Set, as the directions said, in 'the second year of the war that is to begin tomorrow night' it certainly fit the atmosphere of urgency.

On a stage littered with sandbags six dead soldiers, complete with blood and filth, rise up from their still-open graves and engage with their burial parties. News of the dead refusing to be buried panics the general staff whilst ordinary soldiers muse on the waste of war. Having failed to convince the dead that it is their patriotic duty to be buried – how else can the war continue? – a general enlists their wives to persuade them. There follows six separate duologues between 'corpse' and wife, six incisive social statements, as the truths the dead now understand are explained. In a final series of short and cinematic scenes military and business establishments panic, living soldiers make common cause with the dead, along with their wives – 'Tell 'em all to stand up!' – leaving a stricken general with no one left to continue the war. *Bury the Dead* combines conventional and dialogue-driven theatrical scenes with cinematic techniques of montage, flashback and spotlights to cut between them. It asks *whose* war exactly is going to be fought – 'a man can die happy and be contentedly buried only when he dies for a cause that is his own and not Pharaoh or Caesar's'. Thus it invites reflection on just causes for war rather than pacifism as such. Some Guild productions clearly rose to the occasion. Bristol, who re-wrote the script to suit their own production and resources, were praised for their use of lighting and movement, the use of scenes to relieve tension and 'the rising from the grave was impressively thrilling'. Liverpool performances were judged to have 'jumped at one bound to the front rank of the season's amateur achievement . . . a team effort of high achievement'. Topicality was also achieved, with Hitler occupying Czechoslovakia between two Liverpool performances and Sheffield's planned staging was curtailed by the actual declaration of war.[32]

The political controversies over Air Raid Precautions (ARP) near the end of the decade – and the public concern over the possibility of air-raids – were another opportunity for theatrical intervention. London Unity Theatre produced a 'living newspaper' on the issue – a form of drama-documentary incorporating statistics, human drama, voice-over announcements and narration and songs. It attacked the perceived inadequacies of government air-raid precautions and the absence of mass shelters, particularly in working-class areas. The form was an adaptation from a major element of the American Federal Theatre Project, which in turn had adapted it from that used during the extraordinary phase of creativity in Russia in the early stages of the revolution.[33] Sheffield LBCTG's version, *The Ballad of ARP*, was produced by Ratcliff at the end of 1938 and featured the loud and impersonal voices of government spokesmen, recitations on the effects of aerial bombardment gleaned from the war in Spain and the reactions of ordinary people. The lack of evacuation planning for industrial areas was satirized in the performance as when, sung to the tune of *Keep the Home Fires Burning*, the audience was exhorted to:

Keep the big wheels turning,
Though the towns are burning,

Though the bombs drop right and left and smash your home;
Don't let phosgene scare you,
You've got gas masks to wear, you
Keep the big wheels turning round till you're all blown home.[34]

The Bristol Unity Players were invited to contribute to the Co-operative May Day pageant in 1939, an event attracting crowds of around ten thousand people. Part of this made use of a narrator and massed children's choir as chorus, appealing for unity to halt the advance of fascism and danger of war. The Co-operative Society agreed a resolution 'recognising the gravity and menace of another world war' and called upon co-operators to 'mobilise their force as citizens in defence of freedom, justice, human rights and the maintenance of peace'. As with *Bury the Dead* in drama, satirical and forceful choral works and declamations were intended to stimulate or reinforce audiences into political activity to thwart the approach of war. The form that activity took of course was the province of the other, sponsoring organizations.[35]

Trade union plays

The revival of employment after the middle of the 1930s also revived some trade union issues, to which the left theatre responded. For example, the Gateshead Progressive Players (who stood apart from the LBCTG) revived *The Pitman's Pay* in 1937 to coincide with balloting in the National Union of Mineworkers over strike action against company unionism. Similarly Sheffield LBCTG staged a Jack Lindsay mass declamation, *Night of Harworth*, at demonstrations and a rally in Sheffield City Hall. This was in support of Mick Kane, a union militant gaoled after a successful strike against company unionism in Nottinghamshire. Again this piece was a lengthy verse broken down into separate parts for several speakers, with the use of movement and voices in unison for additional effect:

Through the streets of Harworth
The chain-gang goes.
Through the streets of Harworth
The scabs slouch to the mine.
Through the streets of Harworth
Again and yet again
The angry whisper blows:
RELEASE MICK KANE![36]

One-act plays tended to be favoured because their length was suitable for accompanying political meetings or similar events. The most popular choice around Britain was the famous *Waiting for Lefty* by Clifford Odets, a play that had emerged from American trade union struggles early in the decade. It presents an American cab drivers' union meeting and the need for rank and file solidarity in the face of both management threats and corrupt union officialdom. Performances demanded short, fast-moving scenes connected by spotlights on different parts of the hall rather than curtain closures on stage. The piece took less than an hour with casts using minimal props and fast changes of symbolic items of costume to change character. This was cinema applied to theatre for audiences more used to film than theatrical conventions. As we have seen, screenwriter Sydney Box had already been incorporating cinematic techniques into one-act plays for the amateur stage, and so this approach was not completely new, but *Waiting for Lefty* took it further. What had most impact on audiences was their sense of involvement in the action. Actors were placed in and around the audience, apparently members of it, and actors entered and left through the body of the hall, so that the entire room was the performance space. The play met several criteria for the left theatre at the time. It was short enough to combine with a meeting and within the capacities of amateurs. Although there were slogans they were plausible within the structure of the drama. The Lord Chamberlain believed that the politics of the play would be ineffective with a British audience because it was 'intensely American'. Thus he missed the point: the target audiences were far more familiar with American idioms through Hollywood films than they were with British theatrical conventions. It was not just the stage techniques of plays like *Lefty* that represented something different in Britain. In a theatre where, traditionally, working-class people were either rogues, servants or comic figures the vernacular speech and characterization in the play as well as the subject matter also made it a popular piece.[37]

Other American left plays which local groups performed included Ben Bengal's *Plant in the Sun*, which London Unity had premiered, with Paul Robeson in the lead in an early example of colour-blind casting. The play concerns a factory packing department where a worker is summarily dismissed; his colleagues respond by forming a union to secure his reinstatement and other demands, culminating in a sit-down strike. According to a contemporary review the play consists of a representation of a few hours in the workplace and the practical necessities of organization. The action is the overcoming of internal feuds and the growth of their sense of group unity. Although the strike is defeated the end is on a positive note, as under the pressure of injustice solidarity and the capacity for organization and action can grow 'like a plant in the sun'.[38]

Another Ratcliff production for the Sheffield LBCTG was *Clogs*, a three-act play by local mineworker George Fullard which was performed in early December 1938. *Clogs* opens with Tom Briggs leading a miners' delegation to a meeting with the colliery management. They are told that due to the company's financial position the men must accept a 12.5 per cent wage cut. Briggs has a counter-proposal to increase productivity through investment in an infrastructure that has been neglected to the point of danger. An implicit point is that the workforce has the practical experience to manage the colliery themselves.

During a scene where management is blaming the colliery deputies (responsible for safety) for falls in production the news of an underground collapse arrives and this introduces a tense scene in which rescue fails. The Coroner's Court investigates the accident and the courtroom scene gives Briggs, the miners' advocate, the opportunity to inform the audience about neglected safety issues in the mining industry. This is done through dialogue, as the witness evidence and cross-examination about the background to the accident supplies the audience with information in a dramatically plausible way. Fullard himself was an unemployed colliery deputy and thus had his own experience and technical knowledge to bring to bear. Nevertheless, accidental death is the verdict, the cuts are imposed, a long strike ensues and with it strike-breaking and confrontations with the police.

The action moves to another court, the Assize Court, where charges are heard against the miners' leaders following clashes between miners and the police who have occupied the villages. Briggs and his colleague Adams are sentenced to two years' hard labour for seditious assembly, but the final speech is the positive tone often customary in left drama:

> **Briggs** We shall return from prison with a renewed determination to continue the struggle. We remain unrepentant, disobedient and rebellious to an authority we consider unjust. The present is yours; the future is ours.[39]

Local reviews were positive about how Fullard had cleverly managed the Coroner's Court scene and avoided excessive 'agony' over the disaster. What sets *Cloggs* apart from some of the other mining accident plays on the amateur theatre circuit – such as *Cold Coal* or Harold Brighouse's *The Price of Coal* – is the dramatically integrated analysis of safety and the politics of cost-cutting.[40]

Both *Lefty* and *Plant in the Sun* lacked substantial female parts, something equally true of *Cloggs*. This was remedied by *Union Button*, performed by Bristol

Unity Players. This was their own adaptation of *Union Label*, an American one-act play staged by several other LBCTG companies. Like the other American trade union plays it is on a growth of trade union consciousness theme. The seven female characters are machinists in a garment factory where the action takes place. As in *The Yard*, by the Dalton Unemployed Group, much of the dialogue is authentic workplace banter between all the women: quarrels, worries about children, romances and ambitions for a better life through the football pools. It is clear that they work long hours to earn a living from low piece-work rates. The male supervisor announces compulsory overtime as from that day, despite the effects this will have on domestic responsibilities. When a persistent complainer is peremptorily sacked one worker, Janet, who has been talking about the need for a union to negotiate improvements, leads a walkout to sign up at the local union office.[41]

Audiences and performance spaces

Where possible active groups, like the local Left Book Clubs, sought to embed themselves in the labour movement. *Clogs* is recalled as having 'confirmed the acceptance' of Sheffield LBCTG by the local movement due to the bookings it attracted from trade union and Labour Party branches and co-operative societies; at least one performance 'gripped the attention' of a mining audience. Glasgow were not alone in becoming a feature of May Day rallies, and they also performed *Waiting for Lefty* to an audience of striking cab drivers in the city. Consecutive stagings of *Lefty* (with *Twentieth Century Lullaby* as a curtain raiser) were performed 'to the evident delight of the audience' by Wolverhampton LBCTG, who had distributed tickets through their trade union contacts. Newcastle, as we shall see, performed a labour history pageant at the invitation of the Durham Miners' Association.[42]

In Bristol the closest relationship built by the Unity Players was with the Co-operative Societies. They supplied the free use of a hall as rehearsal space in return for a number of performances each year. Their anti-war material was particularly appreciated by Co-operative Women's Guilds who consistently maintained a pacifist stance and who launched the white poppy symbol in 1933. In all of these examples there is a close relationship between the perspectives of performers and audiences. There are parallels too with what Baz Kershaw has identified, in another context: that the attitudinal effects on an audience can be felt within the community networks in which audience members participate.

Audiences at LBCTG performances who were members or supporters of a movement, however nominally, could be reinforced in taking their support into their workplace or other communities, and thus the effect of the play could have a wider resonance.[43] In this respect their plays were an opportunity to influence the political landscape.

It is too difficult to generalize, following Raphael Samuel's implication, that the post-agitprop left theatre of the 1930s represents a retreat back into theatre buildings. Certainly, as with the Little Theatres, some groups believed that it was important to secure their own performance building, to confirm their presence in their areas or to establish a local people's theatre. Sheffield and Leeds had done so by the outbreak of war. Nevertheless many Guild groups performed wherever an audience could be found, in any type of hall or platform where a meeting was held or indeed anywhere at all. This was the case as we have seen with *On Guard*: Glasgow performed this on the back of lorries, Bristol at open-air rallies, Newcastle in cinemas and Merseyside were called a 'Left Theatre' but had been active for a year before they performed in an actual theatre.

American influences

It is clear that the American progressive theatre, supported as it often was by the Federal Theatre Project, had a profound influence on its British counterpart. The Glasgow Workers Theatre Group, for example, has been described as being formed by enthusiastic readers of *Proletarian Literature in the USA*, along with others anxious to produce *Lefty* once they had performed work by O'Neill and Dreiser. Angela Tuckett, whose sister Joan was the producer for Bristol Unity Players, lived in the USA between 1937 and 1939 and supplied them with a wide range of plays, musicals and comedies from the Federal Theatre Project and the American labour movement. American speakers on left theatre at LBCTG conferences were given prominence and it is clear that they were held in high esteem. Will Lee visited several groups including Glasgow in 1938, a meeting where Leeds Unity Theatre members were also involved, to speak on the history of workers' theatre in the USA, and John E. Bonn's article on actor training was re-published in *Theatre for the People*.[44]

In terms of short contemporary drama in a demotic idiom the American theatre was markedly more advanced than the British, who did not have native plays of the same calibre. There were no British plays about trade unionism that could stand alongside the American material, and this did not go unnoticed at the time. A festival adjudicator in 1939 commented that 'it was a pity that left theatre clubs had to go to America for their plays', and a press reviewer continued that there was a danger that 'a movement that is vigorous but still finding its artistic feet' could 'stultify itself' by not concentrating on its own social conditions.[45] Possibly the ready availability of the American plays inhibited the development of British contributions. However, the political atmosphere for many at the time was one of urgency, and so using the good American material readily to hand may have been a better option than taking time over developing their own.

Own material

Notwithstanding the centrality of the American drama the LBCTG demonstrated its own creativity. Andrew Davies concludes that once the Guild groups had presented the two or three standards like *On Guard* and *Lefty* 'the cupboard was largely bare' as regards anything else.[46] This underestimates their work. Glasgow's poetic declamations were not confined to *On Guard*: they deployed a range of poets, including Mayakovsky; they performed several masques with song, dance and mime, including *The Masque of India*, a critique of British rule written with Indian students studying in Glasgow. They also produced graphic mimes attacking the Italian invasion of Abyssinia and the Japanese attack on China.[47] Groups were able to adapt inadequate material to be effective in local situations. For example, Newcastle supported rent strikers in Sunderland with a street performance of a sketch, *Enough of All This*. Apparently this was a weak script which the group successfully transformed through using the players in the audience technique popularized in progressive theatre by *Lefty*. As cast member Vince Waddington, then a young electrician, recalled:

> I was standing in the crowd, they didn't know who I was and I was dressed just like them, and it was my part to heckle during the rent strike meeting scene. Well, the people in the crowd around me thought I was a real heckler and they were turning ugly, I thought I was going to get thumped, when there's a line in the play where the chairman of the meeting says to the audience 'let that man have his say', which is what the man playing the chairman did, and so the audience left me alone. That's how involved they were in the action.[48]

One feature of the popular front approach was the encouragement to identify with the progressive elements within the national cultural heritage. This was the political essence of the historical pageants, some on a mass scale and others much smaller, initiated by the communist left and also local left theatre groups. They were appropriating a form of event previously associated with celebrations of Empire and aristocratic ownership. For example, in 1931 Newcastle Conservatives were instrumental in organizing 'The Pageant of the North', a traditional kings, battles and treaties account of the region's history designed to promote pride in 'the achievements of Empire'. The LBCTG in contrast played 'The Pageant of the Militant North' to a mass audience at the Durham Miners' Gala in 1939, featuring speeches and references to the radical figures and struggles in local history and concluding with 'Rise like lions from slumber' from Shelley's *The Mask of Anarchy*.[49]

In 1939 Bourne's judgement of Guild plays was that there were 'only half a dozen or so native products that are worth more than a minute or two of consideration', but he also saw potential. There are reports of performances local groups were planning but thwarted by the outbreak of war that should also be considered. A group in Durham, probably connected with the Spennymoor Settlement as we have seen, had a play about local mining conditions ready for rehearsal. This again could be the one mentioned by Makin as it was reportedly written by one of their own members. Other reports of plays in progress include 'a left-wing Pierrot show', living newspapers on mining conditions in Rotherham, on unemployment in Glasgow, and Manchester. Plays exposing the records of Tory MPs were planned for the expected, but of course postponed, general election of 1939.[50] As war broke out Sheffield were rehearsing two of their own plays: Ratcliff's *Roman Holiday*, a satire on fascism, together with *Symphony in Awakening*, dealing with unemployment and described as using 'cinematic techniques'.[51]

Class and writing

Bourne predicted that the LBCTG could be a means for working-class people to develop one-act plays about their own lives. Similarly Allen, speaking at an LBCTG conference organized by the Glasgow Workers' Theatre Group in 1938, praised 'the vividness of the dialogue in American drama' and asked if 'something similar could come out of Glasgow?'[52] In fact it was not until the Second World War and after that it did. The Guild encouraged local groups to develop their own plays about local issues and encouraged submissions to the Play Clinic at London Unity, from whom 'helpful criticism and advice could be obtained'. Few if any seem to have actually emerged from the Clinic: as one of those involved later recalled, 'We were for a working-class drama which did not then exist ... plays that portrayed working-class life but they still had to have the right message'. Similarly in the literary field the communist-orientated *Left Review* held short-story competitions about working lives to encourage new writers. Eventually this was abandoned as too many entries, apparently 'individualising social problems', did not meet desired political criteria. In both cases there is no information about the rejected scripts, whether the authors were encouraged to continue, or whether indeed any of them did. As we have seen from the LBCTG conference of 1938 there was dissension over the role Unity Theatre had with the Play Clinic, but no details about the issues.[53]

The amateur theatre movement in its various manifestations between the wars did produce some working-class playwrights but not in the numbers to form a significant genre. This is not surprising. Set against any support play clinics may have offered there were structural obstacles to working-class writing: the long hours of manual work, and the overcrowded housing that left little individual privacy and space. Leisure, like work, was gendered, particularly in the coalfields. The three-shift systems so inimical to adult education thwarted any women's participation due to their domestic responsibilities, particularly where there were several workers in the house on different shifts.[54] Nor, as we have seen, was the enforced leisure of unemployment conducive to authorship since it entailed the financial and psychological stress of poverty. The LBCTG certainly offered the infrastructure of advice, support, and patronage that were essential to a new playwright: the writing clinics, contact with producers, publication and circulation that could nurture and present their work. For example, Fullard apparently wrote *Cloggs* four years before the Sheffield group performed it, so presumably he required the support it offered for staging to be possible. However, as with the amateur movement as a whole the debut play did necessarily herald further productions.

Drama festivals

By 1938 if not before leading figures in the Left Book Club Theatre Guild and Unity Theatre were encouraging local groups to engage with amateur dramatic societies, and an obvious route was through the BDL and the different drama festivals. Unity Theatre affiliated to the BDL in 1938, the LBCTG followed, and encouraged its branches to take part in local BDL competitions. In accordance with the popular front strategy the view was that people involved in amateur theatre, including those from the professional and middle class, could be attracted to progressive plays by their vitality and relevance to the contemporary world. As a contemporary article put it, 'It is imperative that we do not shut ourselves away inside a Left amateur theatre movement, but that we maintain the liveliest interest in what is happening in the amateur theatre up and down the country'. Local LBC groups 'must be part and parcel of the amateur theatre movement' which meant that they 'should immediately consider' affiliation to the BDL, with which London Unity had always had friendly relations.[55]

Therefore success by LBCTG groups in festival competitions, besides their contributions to political events, were recorded approvingly in *Left News*. For example 'Bedford Theatre Guild won first prize at the Bedford Music Festival, defeating the local Dramatic Club which was far older and more experienced than themselves ... It was the Guild's first appearance on the public stage and their play was *Dirge Without Dole*.' The Willesden Group entered for the Welwyn Garden City Dramatic Festival with *On Guard for Spain* and came seventh out of over twenty entries. The Rugby group did well with *Waiting for Lefty* at the Warwickshire County Drama Association Festival, and the Newcastle group came second with *Plant in the Sun* at their local BDL Festival.[56] When Sheffield reached the semi-final of the Northern Area BDL competition in 1939 they were among four out of 181 entries. At the start of the year they had won a local competition with *Waiting for Lefty*, and received their prize from a Tory MP.[57] These achievements at festival competitions show that some LBCTG groups at least were reaching a good level of performance standard given that, as we have seen, the originality of a play was not an assessment priority for adjudicators.

Raphael Samuel notes the attention paid by Unity Theatre to BDL competitions with an implication that this was a departure from the legitimate purposes of a socialist theatre movement. As he points out, in line with the binary opposition mentioned initially, the Workers' Theatre Movement of the early 1930s had confined its competitive efforts to the festivals of revolutionary theatre groups in Moscow. In contrast the Merseyside group wished to take any and every opportunity to 'express working-class experience' and seek new members. Similar groups wished to show that they were as good if not better than the conventional amateur companies. Joe Corrie at this time, as was discussed in the previous chapter, was also keen that the message of his political plays was taken to as wide an audience as possible and 'show one half how the other half lives'. He believed that the 'freedom of the festival' was the means through which his own serious plays, at one time dismissed as 'propaganda', were now meeting success at

Scottish Community Drama Association (SCDA) competitions.[58] Exhortations from the centre were by no means mandatory of course; as we have seen at least one Scottish group, the Glasgow Workers' Theatre, eschewed SCDA festivals in the belief that the organisation was politically prejudiced against them. Festivals could be culturally conservative events that did not welcome interventions from the left. When the manager of the Chester Arts Festival brought the curtain down on the Merseyside group it was ostensibly over the licence issue, but the crucial motive was the objection by prestigious audience members to the politics in the performance.[59]

Some LBCTG producers with a profile in the mainstream amateur theatre – and Ratcliff was nationally known – may have wished to register the new progressive groups as a force in the established movement. Success at competitive festivals was an obvious point of entry. For example, Joan Tuckett argued that 'we need to show our audiences in Bristol that we can meet other amateur groups in matters of interpretation on their own ground'.[60] As well as securing a presence in the area they were validating the political activity in artistic terms, and demonstrating the quality of their work through festival commendation.

The left press set great store by success at BDL events. As we have seen its commentators identified a shift towards plays 'with subjects that matter' in the festivals, and most likely believed that it vindicated the popular front strategy. As was discussed in the previous chapter, it is unclear whether 'plays with subjects that matter' were a feature of the festivals or simply confined to the finals, and whether the various successes of left groups owed more to the production style or novelty of the plays they were performing. Nevertheless LBCTG organizers believed that it vindicated their perspective on theatre and society. The Guild was 'the beginning of the indispensable popular basis for a real revival of drama in Great Britain'. It was accepted that the amateur theatre had done much to revive the theatre but inevitably it reflected 'the futility and superficiality' of society, and to this the left theatre, grounded in social realities, provided an alternative, its own version of a theatrical revival on democratic lines.[61]

Theatre and society

The LBCTG perspective on theatre society had parallels with those of the mainstream amateur drama movement. Some key perspectives were common to both progressive groups and their contemporaries in the amateur theatre, at least those where a social purpose was declared. Mary Kelly's history of village theatre traced the origins of the 'divorce between the players and the people' as did Ratcliff's book *Rude Mechanicals*. The 1926 Report on *Drama in Adult Education* had, as background, identified historical periods when theatre was a popular form. A major difference of course was that the explanation of 'the divorce' from LBCTG writers involved capitalism, whereas for others it was mostly associated with industrialisation and mass production. Present in all such projects was the aim of returning quality drama to the people. In the same way the LBCTG referenced historical phases in which theatrical performances of social significance were part of popular culture, and later the decline of theatre as a popular and often participatory activity in England. The *Notes on Forming Left-Wing Theatre Groups* included a brief account of this, invoking the medieval craft guilds and the Elizabethan stage; like the progressive element of people's history, the *Notes* claimed that popular, socially engaged drama was 'something as deep as socialism itself'. Also, 'theatre being in its origins and in the nature of its composition a popular, a people's and in that respect a socialist art'.[62]

There was symmetry too in developing opportunities for self-expression. Allen believed that capitalism had appropriated culture to the extent that the possibilities for artistic self-expression were the exclusive property of the middle and upper classes. The LBCTG in contrast had the potential to offer such means of self-expression to the factory worker. As with some of the educational settlement drama groups the names of casts and producers in LBCTG performances did not appear in programmes and publicity. This was to underline what some settlements called the 'co-operative community effort' the play represented and to the LBCTG it confirmed that collective endeavour was more important than individual achievement. According to Allen the amount of co-operation needed among all those concerned in putting on a play was 'in itself a splendid lesson in practical socialism'. There was also some symmetry with the sphere of adult education. It had been accepted from the *1919 Report* onwards that drama could attract those who might otherwise be deterred by conventional classes. Similarly Allen stated that theatre could present left ideas and exert influence on those 'who would never think of attending a political meeting'.[63]

The outbreak of war in September 1939 (and most especially the vacillating attitude of the Communist movement towards it) brought the campaigning role of the Left Book Club to an end. At first British communists had supported a war against fascism, but the Nazi–Soviet Pact demanded of communists that they oppose the war as an 'imperialist' venture. Active opposition to fascism combined with support for the Soviet Union was no longer possible, at least not until two years later when Nazi Germany attacked Russia. The Club functioned as a political book club until 1948 but after 1939 the campaigning activity evaporated.[64] *Left News* carried no reports about progressive theatre groups, although several were to reorganize or re-form during the war. The LBCTG, over the course of its three years, gave a political expression to some of the original spirit of the BDL, and gave theatrical expression to social movements against fascism and war. It arguably had some influence on British amateur theatre through providing opportunities for actors and producers to perform politically engaged material and take it to local and national festivals. In the course of the war new conditions and dynamics created some new opportunities for amateur theatre with a purpose.

6

'A remarkable revival in dramatic work and interest'

Amateur Theatre during the Second World War

'The needs of the nation at war'

The outbreak of war in September 1939 achieved one of the earliest objectives of the British Drama League: state support for theatre. This was done through the Council for the Encouragement of Music and the Arts (CEMA), and, as the forerunner of the Arts Council of Great Britain, CEMA has a central place in historical accounts of British cultural life during the Second World War. This focus on CEMA in both academic and popular history[1] denies proper recognition of the role of amateur theatre during the conflict. In contrast this chapter will examine how the purpose of the movement was seen as both sustaining morale and cultural values, and how it reached new audiences and encouraged participation in drama. Finally, it discusses how amateur theatre contributed to expressing popular aspirations for the shape of post-war Britain.

CEMA as an infrastructure to promote wartime cultural initiatives was the product of networking by leading figures in the Board of Education, the Pilgrim Trust and the British Institute of Adult Education. The organization was distinct from the Entertainments National Service Association (ENSA) which recruited or conscripted professionals to provide light entertainment for the forces and for munitions workers. In the twelve months until December 1941 CEMA was also an official supporter of amateur theatre. The original terms of reference spoke of preserving the highest standards of the arts in wartime, as a feature of the civilization the war was a struggle to defend; ensuring the widespread provision of opportunities to enjoy the arts, and also 'the encouragement of music-making and play-acting by the people themselves'. Funds from the Treasury and the Pilgrim Trust guaranteed approved events against loss. The importance of amateur drama was recognized at this stage by appointing Lawrence du Garde Peach of the Hucklow Players as honorary national adviser for amateur theatre. He supervised drama advisers in each of four English regions, with Wales constituting a region itself while Scottish amateur theatre was placed under the Scottish Community Drama Association (SCDA). This arrangement was formally established with the co-operation of the National Council for Social Service in January 1940. Du Garde Peach envisaged the role of his team to include advising on the choice of plays 'with real entertainment value' and 'calculated to take people's minds off the war' whilst not being 'frivolous drivel'.[2]

Thus to some extent the early days of CEMA were a continuation of pre-war initiatives in the new circumstances. Here the focus was on those areas with no access to theatre, and, as with the Durham coalfield in the 1930s, it included the temporary employment of drama professionals to stimulate play-making and leave a legacy of active amateur groups. A BBC broadcast about CEMA acknowledged that 'music and plays will both have their place in dispelling the clouds of boredom, and especially plays produced by the people themselves'.[3] The active participation in cultural activity represented by the amateur drama movement had received official endorsement.

The Ministry of Information enlisted the British Drama League (BDL) to use its affiliates to 'maintain the morale, courage, spirits and good humour of the people'. Whereas ENSA would provide entertainment for the services there were other groups – evacuated and refugee families, civil defence and munitions workers – who would need similar support. To this end Geoffrey Whitworth toured the Ministry of Information and Civil Defence regions to address convened meetings of the local amateur dramatic societies. He explained that, to meet the aims of the Ministry, in the circumstances of war 'purely artistic aims would have to take second place to those of service'. Amateurs who had pursued quality drama were now, for the sake of the war effort, encouraged to embrace popular entertainment for the forces. By the end of 1940 the BDL had gained representation on the Central Committee of ENSA, the Advisory Council for Education in HM Forces and the Consultative Council of the Ministry of Labour, this last regarding munitions workers. Thus the amateur theatre had 'close relations with the various movements which have been inaugurated, both officially and unofficially, to utilize the drama as an asset in meeting the needs of the nation at war'.[4]

Nevertheless the genesis of the BDL during the first world conflict had included a conviction that there was a latent appreciation for quality drama amongst the public, one that could not be met by the commercial theatre. Thus

Whitworth also pointed out that the war would present 'a new audience which was waiting and hungry for some form of cultural life'. There were new audiences to be reached, amateur drama would prosper but that it would function 'far outside the radius of the professional theatre, and its field of operation will be the munitions factory, the rural areas and the schools'. The BDL would also serve the nation through promoting 'the self-entertainment of the people'. Lena Ashwell, speaking from her own experience during the first war, stressed that the appetite of troops for serious work should not be underestimated. Touring could bring drama to thousands who had never seen a play acted, and if that meant that only rudimentary sets could be transported that was far less important than good standards of acting.[5]

Therefore at the outbreak of war the amateur movement envisaged different purposes. One would be to provide popular entertainment for service personnel, particularly small units in remoter locations where it would not be cost-effective for ENSA to perform. Another would be to aim to produce quality drama, and to take it to the new audiences which would as before come about during the conflict. Progressive activists in the amateur movement such as Farrell at the Spennymoor Settlement had a further objective derived from their pre-war thinking:

> Many years ago, the theatre belonged to the people, it was both a temple and a forum. It can become so again. It may come as a result of this war. It should be ready, prepared to do its true job, to act as a social force in the inevitable rebuilding of our social structure when the armies return.[6]

The chapter will discuss how these different if interlocking purposes were pursued. At the same time it is important to consider the context in which that often took place.

Blackout, conscription, war work and continuity

The conditions imposed by the outbreak of war did not bode well for amateur theatre. Conscription – as Ratcliff put it, male actors 'saying goodbye to amateur drama in order to take up strange and unrehearsed roles elsewhere' obviously had an impact. It could include conscription for work at a distant munitions factory, and this included women as well as men. People who knew they were likely to be conscripted were reluctant to make long-term commitments to their local drama clubs. The blackout in city and town centre areas and the threat of air raids inhibited performance, as did the official commandeering of halls previously used for rehearsal. Petrol rationing ensured that transport was a problem. Cast members in war industries worked hours of overtime, others were required for fire-watching and civil defence duties; there was also a wide range of wartime voluntary organizations in which participation was expected. In these circumstances regular rehearsal and performance could be a challenge. The return of full employment generated by the war accelerated the transition of the settlement and other unemployed clubs into community centres. Here too the effects of war were felt, for example, at the Bargoed Settlement:

> Despite many difficulties such as severe weather, blackout, care of evacuee children, several male members of the family working on different shifts, and a large number of club members working at full pressure in armament factories, the Women's Clubs are making valiant efforts to carry on in these difficult times.[7]

In Liverpool the first drama company in the city to perform after the war began was Merseyside Left Theatre in November 1939. They presented the Odets anti-fascist play *Till the Day I Die* 'with a courage that in the circumstances was considerable' since the venue was 'an outlying suburban hall on a filthy pitch-black night'. The hall was filled to capacity for two nights. In the same month Sheffield Left Book Club Theatre Guild (LBCTG) were performing three one-act plays including their own *Roman Holiday* and *Symphony in Awakening*, and as in Liverpool the city-centre blackout moved their shows to halls in outlying areas. These two groups formerly aligned with the LBCTG were supporting the war at this stage, albeit with warnings against fascism that had been overtaken by events. Producer Nora Ratcliff, writing before her own conscription, reported that they had been invited to these community and social centres. Like Ashwell, she stressed that the rudimentary props that were all that could be carried on public transport would be accepted by audiences provided that the acting itself was convincing. Therefore amateur groups must maintain their acting at 'festival standard'.[8]

Despite the problems the amateur movement made a strong response to the events of 1940 and 1941. The Carfin Hall Dramatic Club, the successor as we have seen to the Harkness House Players, presented four one-act plays at the Miners' Welfare Hall in March 1940, the programme including works by Joe Corrie, and Muriel Box. In December they organized a school for local amateur groups led by tutors from the SCDA. Two years later the group presented one-act plays at their local theatre, having 'carried on the work of the movement under conditions that are not conducive to enthusiasm'.[9] Other existing groups such as the Bargoed Settlement Players 'produced plays in very difficult circumstances in many parts of the valley'; this experience was paralleled around the country, for example on Tyneside where the Hebburn Power House group were attracting capacity audiences. Rural areas had been included in the new or revised national organizational arrangements. The NCSS re-constituted a Joint Committee for Drama and this encouraged Rural Community Councils (RCCs) and the various County Drama Committees to continue to promote drama. As Mick Wallis records, in 1940 the Yorkshire RCC selected amateur players from the York area to tour small villages with performances of Shakespeare and Shaw.[10]

The annual BDL Festival of Community Drama with its final in London was suspended during the war but local festivals continued and the amateur movement considered this essential. Participation in a festival was a recognized motivator to maintain standards but now their status as a vital cultural asset was affirmed by the BDL. Activists like Farrell stated that the theatre arts were part of civilization, and that 'we must not in the fight to save civilization leave the things we are fighting for to starve'. Thus drama festivals – both competitive and non-competitive – flourished around the country throughout the war, frequently to raise funds for the multitude of war-time charities. There was none of the earlier debate about their value or effect on play writing. Du Garde Peach reported that in the first six months of CEMA support the English advisers had assisted with twenty-two local drama festivals and adjudicated at half of them. They had also assisted in 400 amateur productions, organized twenty-six conferences for groups and an additional twenty-six schools on dramatic production. The guarantees against loss had proved unnecessary.[11]

The Durham County Drama Association had been formed shortly before the outbreak of war to organize county-wide festivals of one-act plays, and this it did during 1940 and 1941. As Farrell observed, 'The record would have been creditable even in times of peace, but in view of the extraordinary circumstances prevailing during the winter of 1939–40, when everything militated against dramatic activities, it was a magnificent record of which the constituent bodies can be proud'. South Wales in particular maintained a reputation for well-attended amateur festivals: Drama Weeks at Ferndale or Treorchy attracted total audiences of over a thousand to the Workmen's Halls for full-length and one-act plays in both Welsh and English.[12]

In 1942 CEMA took the strategic decision to focus solely on the professional arts sector as representing the highest expression of the national cultural achievement. This excluded the amateur and effectively assigned it an inferior status. The drama advisor posts were withdrawn although the Carnegie Trust

UK funded advisor posts with the RCCs and local authority education committees. In this context a symbolic event was when CEMA refurbished and took over management of the Theatre Royal in Bristol, following a local campaign to save the building. As part of its mission to present good drama for the whole nation CEMA began a programme of the classics there in 1943. A year later the Bristol Guild of Players, representing the local amateur societies, requested the venue for an amateur drama festival. Despite being a proposal for a festival of three-act plays by established companies this was firmly refused. Joan Tuckett reported that it took determined lobbying by the Guild of Players to reverse the decision. The refusal of state support to the amateur sector was to characterize post-war policy.[13]

Audiences and participation

The amateur sector took on venues where it would not be practical for ENSA to tour: the innumerable small, often isolated outposts of anti-aircraft sites, searchlight batteries, field ambulance and signals units. The regional army commands organized transport for what in practice were often all-female companies. There are recollections of a company assembling when they had finished work, changing and making up in the backs of lorries and performing in village halls, tents and aircraft hangers. The BDL published *Variety Entertainments in War-Time: Learning How to Do It*, and toured short courses for groups wishing to present variety programmes in small halls where no stage or proper hall was available. It was reported that drama societies were 'readily turning to light entertainment' and are 'offering it to their own normal townsfolk audiences, evacuees, refugees, and to the troops quartered in their districts' as a contribution towards the war effort.[14] Such performances were generally the musical and variety shows that the evidence indicated were the preference of the services. For example, early in the war welfare officers in the forces consistently reported that variety shows were the most popular entertainment for the troops, and that any music was more popular than straight drama. This was confirmed by occasional reports from officers that tired men were soon bored by plays, particularly those that were poorly presented.[15]

Although variety entertainment was popular it was by no means the whole story; straight drama was presented and participation in play-making encouraged. Between the Dunkirk evacuation and the invasion of Normandy many inactive troops were stationed in camps at home. Therefore the BDL encouraged its affiliates to contact local army welfare and education officers and ask them to identify soldiers interested in amateur drama. As Michael Dobson observes, the size of the pre-war amateur movement was such that this army had more practised actors, technicians and producers than ever before. In 1941 over 200 military and aircraft units were borrowing play texts from the BDL library, and by 1944 over 700 forces drama groups were BDL affiliates. Involving troops in local amateur drama could bring its own problems, such as when rehearsals at the Spennymoor Settlement theatre were abandoned after the male cast members, soldiers, were posted away at short notice.[16] In Norfolk several local amateurs toured with shows for the troops and performed in venues ranging from camp theatres, village halls or in the open air. One reported playing to service audiences amounting to around 25,000 over a year, with a hundred productions of three full-length plays. Makeshift staging was a necessity but had not proved an obstacle to a successful performance. Forces drama groups were encouraged, as were those from fire service and civil defence units, to enter local drama festivals. At the Surrey and District Drama Festival in 1941, for example, several teams from neighbouring camps took part and the audiences were largely drawn from the camps also.[17]

Drama for schools and evacuated families

Rebecca D'Monte has noted how the war developed nascent forms of theatre in education as drama companies were organized to perform in schools, with plays both for evacuated children and their classmates. This account can be broadened to acknowledge that the amateur movement introduced not only performances for children but drama as a teaching medium for conventional school subjects. As soon as the evacuation of children began in 1939 Robert G. Newton advocated 'informal drama' with schoolchildren, particularly where evacuations had swollen class sizes to up to a hundred. He believed this would be a popular way to relieve teachers alongside the educational value, and the classroom problem was in fact an opportunity to develop children's theatre.[18]

A good example is Derbyshire where the RCC, like many in the same position, committed itself to 'carrying out music and drama work as fully as possible' in response to the influx of troops and evacuated children into the rural areas. The numbers of evacuees joining the local children had necessitated schooling on a half-day system that left many children under-occupied. Some of the time was filled by using historical plays by du Garde Peach for readings accompanied by movement, gesture and expression, although short of a production. A commentator noted that this would be useful in breaking down the opposition of conservative teachers; play-production as an extra-curricular activity was accepted, but this use of drama as a pedagogic tool in general learning was innovatory. Du Garde Peach had obtained funding from the Carnegie Trust UK to train teachers at the Great Hucklow village theatre for the purpose, and later funding for a schools drama advisor was secured. In January 1940 it was reported that the scheme was fully operational and it was anticipated that by April fifty-eight schools would be involved.[19]

The experience of the pre-war amateur movement was evident in the strategies for participation employed in rural areas with, for example, mothers evacuated to the villages. Mick Wallis has noted how Mary Kelly's war role was with the University College of the South West's Rural Extension Scheme in Devon. She organized weekly classes in the villages (using teachers with drama experience who had come with the evacuees) to promote the integration of evacuated families and host communities through theatre activity. She later reported that thirty classes around the county were studying acting, speech, mime, movement and production. Improvisation was the basis for group play-making, with festivals organized to showcase their work.[20] As we have seen, improvisation as a method with those completely unused to play-making had been developed with unemployed people before the war. The use of adjudicated but non-competitive festivals for them to showcase their work parallels that used, for example, with the women's groups in the Nottinghamshire social service centres.

Theatre for the shelters and civil defence

Resisting the blitzkrieg bombing of cities, using the London underground stations as air-raid shelters, the work of the fire and civil defence services; these are central to the British narrative of wartime resilience. By the summer of 1941 open-air theatre had emerged in the bombed areas of London, involving amateur groups alongside professional companies like the St Pancras Theatre. In the case of the West Ham Open-Air Theatre ('in a corner of battered dockland') this grew from performances given by air-raid shelterers to other shelterers, so that a year later they were playing Shaw, Goldsmith and the comedies of A. A. Milne to local audiences. Some of these initiatives came through official channels, such as the shelter welfare officers appointed by local authorities. A London County Council drama teacher reported working with around 200 regular users of a particular shelter, who were 'completely innocent of all stage art'. Eventually they were performing in a local hall: songs, monologues, and the straightforward one-act play *The Bishop's Candlesticks*, while other shelterers were stage carpenters and electricians.[21] Such activities prompted the Toynbee Hall Settlement in Stepney to organize a drama festival for the amateur groups which had coalesced in the civil defence units, air-raid shelter regulars, and evening classes in the bombed neighbourhoods. The first took place in January 1942 with eighteen companies taking part and the festivals continued throughout the war with thirty participating groups by 1945. Among the initial entries at least 'Shaw was the most popular choice' although comedy, mime and experimental plays were also included.[22] London Unity Theatre formed a group to perform in the tube shelters, with no official sanction but working in liaison with the shelter committees where they had built contacts. Where their shows were able to be effective – not defeated by rival noises from tube trains, noisy crowds or the sound of bombs – it was because they had taken time to establish relationships with the audiences. They provided variety entertainment and community songs, building eventually to satirical turns and a one-act play on German anti-fascist resistance, *Erma Kremer of Ebenstadt*.[23]

The theatre critic Barbara Nixon served with the London civil defence and recalled the social diversity of the wardens: they included post-office sorters, garage hands, lawyers, chorus girls and also men from the clandestine occupations associated with race-track betting. Presumably their amateur drama casts were drawn from similarly diverse groups. As in the pre-war years the adjudicated festival was the ubiquitous means to provide goals and incentives, broaden awareness and raise standards. It also provided an event for a beleaguered population. Nevertheless Nixon also recalls that some air-raid shelters were badly run and chaotic, with no committee structure, and some borough administrations could be suspicious of any organized activity in them. Whereas initiatives like the West Ham Open-Air Theatre received nationwide press coverage on her evidence it is fair to assume that this good practice was not necessarily the standard one.[24] Civil defence theatre was not confined to London. The Port Glasgow CD Drama Group, at least one of whose members had previous experience of amateur theatre, performed programmes of one-act plays for troops and other local audiences. The company was large enough to enter three teams for the Greenock Drama Festival in 1944. Their combination of different pieces included the tragedy *Her Affairs in Order*, which had an all-women cast.[25]

Hostel and factory drama groups

In Northumberland Gordon Lea revisited his pre-war role as a drama adviser to encourage drama groups among the Women's Land Army. This was part of the educational and social events organized by welfare officers for the women living in hostels in rural areas distant from any of the familiar services or amenities. Lea hoped to establish groups at eight hostels by the end of 1944. Once more the drama festival of one-act plays was an incentive, with seven teams taking part before a large audience at the Newcastle People's Theatre in April 1944. At least two of the entries were all-women plays by Muriel and Sydney Box, popular with amateur dramatic groups before the war: *Number Ten*, concerning a mercy killing on a hospital ward, and the family comedy *A Marriage Has Been Disarranged*.[26]

A hostel was the necessary accommodation for a range of munitions and wartime workers besides the Women's Land Army. The factories could often be distant from sources of commercial entertainment and thus, like the smaller civil defence and armed forces bases, a ready if somewhat captive audience. The BDL had approached regional welfare officers and visited factories to facilitate play-reading and acting groups amongst the workforces, particularly where they were accommodated in hostels on site.[27] For example the Viking Players were drawn from a factory in Lancashire and their work echoed that of the industrial theatre groups of the 1920s. Both cast and producer (the latter previously active in amateur theatre) were employees, as was the set designer, and the sets were made in the factory. Having begun in 1941 with play-readings they progressed to shows for their fellow workers and then to performances around the local towns. Unlike the Leeds Industrial Theatre they did not attempt Shakespeare and the classics but contemporary comedies and thrillers by Esther McCracken and Patrick Hamilton. They did act as a catalyst in their area by inviting other groups to perform and organizing a local amateur drama festival each year from 1942 until the end of the war. As with Leeds in the 1920s they enjoyed a sympathetic works management, in this case doubtless part of the efforts to sustain morale in a vital area of production.[28] As was the case with the colliery community drama groups initiated through the Carnegie Trust UK before the war, such factory groups proved sustainable only where an active voluntary producer remained involved.

There were other initiatives besides those for factory hostels. For example, in 1943 Makin, on behalf of Derbyshire RCC, organized and adjudicated a one-act play festival for the Atherton Collieries workforces. He reported that 'the standard was not particularly good' although it had been very popular and 'the spirit for the whole event was excellent'.[29]

Another government scheme for war workers launched in 1942 was for 'holidays at home', supporting local authorities to provide summer recreation where conventional holidays were not practical. Parks became the venues for sport, shows and concerts. CEMA has been credited with 'bringing straight drama to the people' for these programmes, for example the professional Shakespeare performances in London's Richmond Park. In fact local amateur companies were in the forefront. Sunderland Drama Club, for example, performed Shakespeare plays in the open air, between 1942 and 1945, making use of park scenery and a loudspeaker system. Hull's Drasdo Players performed plays for children, and five Shakespeare plays in parks during the war, with one production of *A Midsummer Night's Dream* having an audience of over a thousand schoolchildren. In 1943 the Cardiff scheme included four amateur drama companies with a four-day festival in Roath Park. In Coventry, Nottingham, Rugby and Liverpool too amateur companies performed mixed programmes of comedies, Shaw and Shakespeare to large outdoor park audiences.[30] The war years witnessed a revival of Shakespeare on the professional stage with an increasing number of productions and record audiences.[31] The amateur stage should also be included in the account and possibly it paved the way for the professionals: for example, the visits to Hull by professional Shakespeare companies each September between 1942 and 1945 had been preceded by the park performances during the summer.

Old Vic tours for mining areas

One of the most celebrated initiatives by CEMA was the support for the Old Vic and other professional companies to tour the South Wales and Durham coalfields, and later some munitions factory hostels. By September 1942 nine companies were involved. The first tour – featuring Sybil Thorndike and Lewis Casson in *Macbeth* – visited seventeen different South Wales mining communities during the autumn of 1940. The following year, with a different cast, the company performed *The Merchant of Venice* at sixteen different venues in County Durham, each a miners' welfare hall apart from the Everyman Theatre at the Spennymoor Settlement. These mining communities had been facing dereliction in the 1930s but they were now crucial to the war economy and this probably explained the new attention. The tours were extensively documented and publicized by the

Ministry of Information to explain how state subsidy for theatre helped the war effort. What was not recorded or subsequently acknowledged is the extent to which the success of these tours was built on the pre-war amateur movement.

In South Wales the Old Vic frequently performed in miners' halls and welfare institutes. Only limited properties and scenery could be transported on tour, and so reviews described minimal sets, no use of drop curtains and an imaginative use of small spaces for large-scale scenes. Thus a West End company adapted to the normal circumstances of a social service centre or settlement Little Theatre. Nevertheless the tour was a celebrated success and the responsiveness of the large audiences was striking. Casson told one that 'you gave us the feeling that you were playing the play with us', and Thorndike too was effusive in her descriptions.[32] The groundwork for the shows and the accommodation for the casts were arranged in several cases by educational settlements such as Merthyr and Dowlais. The theatre space at the Maes-yr-haf Settlement, the first of the coalfield educational settlements, was also a performance venue.[33]

In County Durham again the venues determined the style of production, as described by producer Esme Church: 'in most of the places where we act the stage is so small, we have to build an apron, bringing the actors right out into living, intimate contact with the audience – rather like the contact Shakespeare had with the Elizabethans for whom he wrote'. She also emphasised that the cast had been 'particularly thrilled by the way in which the purely mining audiences had responded ... displaying a freshness of appreciation which was a relief and a surprise to the actors'. It was no surprise to at least one press reporter, who was aware that at Spennymoor at least, 'They found an audience trained in appreciation of the best dramatic art'. There is another example of the foundations that had been laid by the Workers' Educational Association (WEA) and the Spennymoor Settlement before the war. Peggy Ashcroft and the Apollo Players toured the Durham coalfield with music, poetry and readings. Later she recalled that, 'The best educated and most responsive audience was a group of miners at their communal theatre at Spennymoor'.[34]

The basis of these successes lay in the pre-war intersections between adult education, drama projects among the unemployed communities and the amateur theatre movements in the coalfields of South Wales and County Durham. This was described in previous chapters. Drama, either through classroom appreciation, participation or watching, had been important feature of adult education in both coalfields. Other relevant elements from the inter-war experience were the Carnegie Trust UK support for taking theatre to coalfield areas, and the adult education imperative to introduce great art to all. As we have seen, *The Merchant of Venice* had been popular in County Durham miners' halls some years previously. It should be acknowledged that CEMA built on the work of the educational settlements, the WEA and the social service centres to build audiences for serious drama before the war.

Another celebrated tour was by Walter Hudd, a well-known stage and screen actor, who formed a company sponsored by CEMA to tour munitions factories and subsequently their outlying towns.[35] After the war the 'startling fact' was recorded that only about 2 per cent of these hostel audiences had ever seen a stage play before; a ready-made audience 'of an entirely unsophisticated kind', it took them time 'to acquire a theatre etiquette'.[36] Despite this, or because of it, Hudd was enthusiastic about these tours. He recounted that companies had performed *Twelfth Night* and *The Shoemaker's Holiday* in the Elizabethan way with no scenery or scene divisions, not even any pauses between the acts, and the audiences, numbering thousands, had found it natural.[37] When touring Shaw and Ibsen in small towns he had found that that the best responses were where 'the pioneering work of building a sound local tradition of dramatic taste' had already been done. The work had already been done by groups like the Viking Players and other, pre-war, amateurs.[38]

However, as historians have shown, the internal reports of CEMA concerts and plays at factories and hostels described an uneven record. Some audiences were responsive and enthusiastic but others much less so. A number of factors could be involved: one that should be remembered is that Walter Hudd and his colleague Wendy Hiller in *Twelfth Night* were famous cinema actors and thus an attraction in their own right. Their effect was noted by Beth Brewer, herself responsible for organizing entertainments at a munitions factory hostel. At first she was enthusiastic about these new audiences for quality drama but later she observed, in the absence of the stars, how audiences reverted back to preferring familiar popular shows. Nevertheless, she also related that there were a small number of people in these audiences who had obviously gained a new appreciation of the theatre and who were likely to remain with it.[39]

Wartime programmes

In many respects amateur groups continued with the staples of the inter-war years, such as Shaw, Shakespeare, Ibsen or Goldsmith, or comedies by A.A. Milne and Esther McCracken. Du Garde Peach's advocacy of material to provide escape from the war without being 'frivolous rubbish' proved apposite. On the amateur stage comedies were popular, such as McCracken's *Quiet Wedding*, as were what contemporary critics called 'intelligent thrillers': those by Emlyn Williams, Patrick Hamilton's *Gaslight*, and Denham and Percy's *Ladies in Retirement*. Many of these plays had been popular films and this probably influenced their attraction for new theatre audiences. This in fact mirrored the West End stage where in 1944 a quarter of the plays performed concerned murder.[40]

Ladies in Retirement, like another common choice *Nine Till Six*, had almost entirely female casts and thus suited the gender balance imposed on theatre groups by military service. Some amateur groups as well as repertory companies performed Shakespeare plays with all-female casts, something accepted as imposed by the war and no barrier to well-received productions. Once more the market responded to a demand for all-female one-act plays and at least one, the tragedy *Her Affairs in Order*, had performances alongside drama and comedies in performances of one-act works. Some groups maintained similar programmes to those before the war as far as personnel allowed. Sunderland Drama Club continued with 'experimental nights' featuring plays by members, and performed *Janet*, another play by their member Nan Richenburg, in which a young working-class woman struggles to combine scholarship ambition with family carer responsibilities. In Wales, Eynon Evans continued to enter comedies for competition and have them performed by Little Theatres.[41]

During the period of communist opposition to the war the surviving groups once associated with the LBCTG performed oppositional material. This highlighted various grievances which had resonance before the Dunkirk crisis. Leeds Unity for example produced a duologue, *Voices Across the Dark*, and a living newspaper, *Let the People Speak*. These productions were largely confined to their own members.[42] In 1941 the Nazi invasion of the Soviet Union propelled the USSR into alliance with the West, and its stubborn resistance to the Nazis caught the public imagination. This was celebrated in official propaganda, pageants and festivals, and it provided new material for the stage which the amateur movement adopted. Left theatre groups now supporting the war effort were operating in the mainstream of political opinion, and thus able to reach wider audiences. Their variety shows, one-act plays and concerts for war workers and civil defence units were now welcome, and included Russian song and dance scenes, or calls for a second front in Europe to assist the Soviets.[43] Once again the regional left groups devised their own material. Leeds schoolteacher Kate Penty produced *Comrade Enemy* for Leeds Unity in 1942, a play she wrote with Leeds Unity activist Alec Barron. The three acts feature soldiers from the British, German and Soviet armies and their families, the German being a left critic of the Nazi regime. The London Unity play clinic had judged that the characterization veered too much between the realistic and the agitprop to be convincing. Nevertheless it attracted large audiences at the Leeds Albert Hall to support the Aid Russia Fund and subsequently toured the area.[44]

One-act plays from the Soviet Union arrived after 1942, generally requiring a single set and a small cast, and therefore suitable for new amateur groups. They were generally stories of the Russian resistance and chimed with the public mood: some were performed by youth club and high school groups around the country.[45] In addition amateur groups unconnected to the left also produced their own material on the drama of the Soviet war effort. The one-act plays presented by the Carfin Hall group in 1942 included *The Day is Coming*, by one of their own members. Concerning the fate of a German soldier outside Smolensk it apparently 'gripped' the audience.[46]

Two contemporary full-length plays by Soviet authors were performed in repertory, and their adoption by the amateur movement ensured a wider reach, often as contributions to local Aid Russia Week fund drives. One of these was *Distant Point*, by Alexei Afinogenev, one of the few Soviet plays to be widely performed in Britain, 'and not just by Russia enthusiasts'. It was originally staged by London Unity Theatre, then in the West End and some other city theatres, and taken up by amateur groups throughout the country.[47] The action of the play takes place over forty-eight hours in a remote station on the Trans-Siberian Railway line. A general's private carriage must stay there for a repair and he, Matvei, his wife, Vera, and his adjutant become acquainted with the diverse characters who live in the village and are all connected to the railway. It emerges that the general is terminally ill. The play is concerned, in essence, with reconciliation to death through the knowledge of a life spent for the common good, and the interests of a community at war taking precedence over personal situations. It was of course taken up by local left theatre groups, who were often the only drama societies to have a modern Russian play available for events such as Aid Russia Weeks. Leeds Unity performed it 'for the first time in the provinces' in 1941, if only for their members. Reigate Unity played it to a large public audience which included the Mayor and drew praise for the quality of the acting despite using only minimal props and no scenery. Bristol too performed it in July 1942 in conjunction with the local WEA Players who had simultaneously decided to stage it. This was hailed as a great success, with packed houses in a 900-seat theatre on three nights. These included bookings of ten from factories, workplaces, schools and large numbers of Co-operative Guilds.[48]

Distant Point was not confined to political groups. It was performed by the Spennymoor Settlement Players in 1942, additional performances being organized later that year at the request of mine workers and arranged to suit their shifts. Producer Bill Farrell saw more in the play than a story of 'our great Soviet ally'. It had 'electrified the company' because it was drama with a social purpose that did not lose its entertainment value. The Shelter Players performed it at the West Ham Open-Air Theatre in 1942, and two years later the Nottingham Playgoers' Club production was sponsored by the local Co-operative Society as part of their centenary celebration. The play was valued as an endorsement of general co-operative values and not simply for its Russian setting.[49]

The other was *Squaring the Circle* by Valentin Kataev, a play that had been performed in 1934 by the Newcastle People's Theatre, and produced there again in 1941. It is a comedy, veering into satire, set in the revolutionary days of the 1920s and a key plot line is the terrible housing shortage in Moscow at the time. The critical response was generally appreciative and revealed 'surprise that the Russians have a sense of humour'.[50] The play was taken up by groups in Sunderland, Ealing, Huddersfield and elsewhere, again often during Aid Russia Weeks. These plays stood on their own merits besides benefiting from the public solidarity with the Russian resistance.

There were attempts to encourage new dramatic writing which engaged with the war and related issues. However, it is not clear how successful they were. Early in 1943 the BDL invited submissions of 'good plays irrespective of theme or tendency, provided only that they conduce to victory and to that cultural progress which should be a result of the War for Freedom'. It was expected that these plays would 'deal constructively with national and international problems arising from the war'. Submitted scripts if approved would be circulated to companies in the amateur movement. Sixty scripts were received in the first month, and by the following year 'a large number of manuscripts dealing particularly with the war and post-war problems were continuing to arrive'. The only further information about the project was that eighty-seven scripts were submitted in 1943, some had been circulated but only two had actually been performed.[51] Unfortunately, and as with the pre-war invitations to prospective dramatists from the left theatres, details were not forthcoming. The titles of the two performed plays are not mentioned, nor how many in total were actually circulated, nor what the general judgement was about the value of the exercise for the amateur movement. Nor, again, whether any new writers received constructive advice on how to continue.

In Glasgow the Citizens Theatre (a new civic theatre supported by CEMA) organized a play-writing competition to seek out fresh material to stage. One hundred and forty-seven entries by both men and women were received, and a 'considerable proportion of the scripts dealt with Scottish life and problems, Highland and Lowland'. However the judges were scathing about the overall quality of the entries, announcing that 'even reasonably competent work shone through like a shaft of light through fog'. This verdict was hardly likely to encourage even the winners (two naval officers) to further efforts. Nevertheless it is clear that many of the entered plays featured 'Scottish life and problems'.[52]

Outside such formal competitions some local societies, certainly in Scotland, performed their own work with a war setting. Besides the Carfin Hall group Tom Minihan of Port Glasgow Civil Defence wrote and produced *Your Son, My Son*, set in a prisoner of war camp. The best-known example is the novelist James Barke's *The Night of the Big Blitz*, for Glasgow Unity Theatre, the successor to the Workers' Theatre Group. Set in the catastrophic Clydebank blitz of 1941 it focussed on the traumatic effects of the bombing on a working-class family with an emotional intensity that caused a key scene to be removed by the censor.[53]

Festivals and politics

Before the war some amateur theatre groups had used what Joe Corrie called 'the freedom of the festival' to perform plays which engaged with the issues of the day. This was also true, to an extent at least, during the different circumstances of the war. *Twentieth Century Lullaby* featured the Anglo-German name of Peter Ulrich Smith and, as we have seen, was anti-war, contrasted dreams for the future with harsh contemporary realities, but ended in hope. It was performed during the war by church groups, youth groups and co-operative societies, being in accord with their values. It provoked different reactions from festival adjudicators. At the Thames Valley Amateur Theatre Festival one stated that 'the play was not a good choice at the moment', whereas at an annual event in Birmingham it was considered 'more than apt to the moment'. It played successfully in a Belfast amateur drama festival too.[54]

In Wales the Pontypridd Drama Week aimed to provide war workers with 'welcome relaxation', but the adjudicator ruled that the four one-act plays performed by Cardiff Unity 'were definitely political propaganda and not entertainment'. These unnamed pieces were performed but 'to practically unanimous approval' not considered for the competition. Glasgow Unity Theatre overcame its pre-war antipathy to the SCDA, or possibly the attitude of the SCDA towards political drama had altered. The group won the prize in the first SCDA wartime festival in 1944 with one act from their own play *Night of the Big Blitz*, on the Clydebank bombing. The following year an excerpt from their production of *The Lower Depths* won them high praise at the festival.[55] Both Bristol and Cardiff Unity had more success with plays that were still political but in a more nuanced form. The Unity entry to the Bristol Drama Festival in 1944 was *Buster*, which will be discussed below. Cardiff earned first prize at the Aberaman Drama Festival in 1945 with J. B. Priestley's *They Came to a City*; again the play will be discussed below but as the press critic remarked it was a 'singularly appropriate' production in the context of 'the current discussion of plans for a better world'.[56]

Although the subjectivity of festival adjudicators has to be taken into account these last two examples illustrate how a new, if inchoate, consensus had emerged during the war. It was based on a rejection of any prospect of a return to the society of the 1930s and a recognition of the need for international efforts to secure lasting world peace. It has been argued that the political education provided through the huge number of Left Book Club (LBC) titles in circulation had a role in building this consensus.[57] The next section examines some further examples of how the amateur movement contributed to this and to engaging audiences in debate about the post-war future.

War aims, reconstruction and where do we go from here?

As in the previous conflict there was public debate over the future shape of society after the war. In contrast, during this war the state appeared to be refusing to engage with the discussion. Playwright J. B. Priestley gave a series of regular radio talks in 1940 and again in 1941 in which he was unequivocal in refusal to return to the social conditions of the 1930s after the war. He was prematurely taken off the air and this was popularly assumed to be at government behest. More telling was the reaction when the Beveridge Report was published in 1942. This plan for a comprehensive system of national insurance and a national health service free at point of use attracted widespread public interest and support. It articulated a rejection of the social neglect of the 1930s at a time when the war had acclimatized British society to state intervention. However, in parliament the Conservatives clearly disagreed, and indeed Prime Minister Churchill discouraged any official discussion of war aims and the post-war future.[58]

Nevertheless a vigorous discussion about the future of Britain after the war took place in civil society. The next section examines four plays, three of which were extensively performed on the amateur stage, and another professional production which was shaped by the pre-war amateur theatre. These both reflected and contributed to the social movement to build a progressive consensus about post-war reconstruction.

Priestley's *They Came to a City*, supported by CEMA on account of its experimental style, ran for eight months in London's West End in 1943 after a provincial tour. Perhaps less well-known is that subsequently 'no play was more widely asked for by amateur societies' when performance rights were released.[59] Thus it was brought to a wider audience outside the capital and the major urban areas with regular theatre provision.

In the play nine characters suddenly find themselves on steps outside a high wall, and this is where all the action takes place. Their conversations reveal that they are archetypes representing different social strata. They comprise a cockney cleaning lady, shop assistant Alice and thoughtful, rebellious merchant sailor Joe. The others are aggressive self-made businessman Cudworth, aristocrats and a middle-class banker with a socially disappointed wife. As dawn breaks they realize that they are looking down on a city (which the audience do not see) and they are able to visit it. The city is a co-operative utopia and it is up to them to join it or return to the lives they came from. The aristocrats (apart from the daughter, seeking her independence) and the banking family abhor the place, finding it impossible to relate to the new social circumstances. Likewise the businessman, who relates what happened when he explained capitalism to a city-dweller:

> **Cudworth**   He said, 'We don't call that work here'. So I said, 'Well, what do you call it, then?' He said, 'We call it *crime*'.[60]

The working-class characters in contrast are overwhelmed by the city. Alice and Joe are now together and as she exclaims to him:

> **Alice**   It's what I'd always hoped for, something I'd always believed was somewhere round the corner, if we could only find it. And there it is. I always hoped that men and women could live like that, if they tried. Life hadn't to be a dog-fight round a dustbin. We'd made it like that, but it needn't be like that.[61]

She is desperate to stay in the city but Joe, who has lost an earlier cynicism about human motive, persuades her that they must leave and return to the world. They have to convince others that this new world is possible if people choose to build it. Priestley thus invites the audience to imagine a better post-war society that is there to be built, and as Maggie B. Gale argues he requires the audience to consider its own role in maintaining the class system and appraise alternative social arrangements as the old order crumbles.[62] The set is fixed with changes done through lighting, but as she observes the play is a challenge in terms of its style and composition, condensed as it is into two acts with the essential action reported or implied, and requiring a high standard of characterization. This 'moving exposition of a new mood that is taking hold of the community' was performed by the Lewis's Stores Sales Managers drama group in Birmingham, by groups in Liverpool and London; the Spennymoor Settlement production 'played to packed houses with people turned away', and was repeated there in June 1945 whilst the general election campaigns were in progress. Amateur productions continued with full houses after the 1945 election and even during the early years of the new Labour government.[63]

A similarly themed but quite different play was *Buster*, performed by London Unity and then at the Arts Theatre in London in 1943, subsequently being taken up by groups around the country. It was written by Ted Willis, a former leader of the Young Communist League, briefly a soldier and by this time a leading spokesman for Unity Theatre. Comprising three acts each scene takes place in a domestic living room and required only minimal set changes, which of course made it straightforward for amateur companies.

The living room is in the home of the King family, and there is an immediate contrast between the unemployed, former Labour councillor Mr King and his son, Buster: he is also unemployed but is street-wise, irreverent and the leader of a gang of young petty thieves. In the opening scene there is a confrontation when a policeman arrives over Buster's thieving.[64] Nevertheless, he later explains to a social worker that he's not work-shy, far from it:

Buster   Don't get me wrong, mister. I've thought of all them things. I ain't no kid and I ain't no mug either. Work don't frighten me. I was helping on a milk round when I was ten, and delivering papers up at five in the morning when I was eleven. When did you start work?[65]

The morning after a night of heavy bombing we learn from others that Buster (having left the shelter early seeking looting opportunities) has behaved heroically in helping to rescue victims. He is later awarded the George Medal ('T'aint gold nor silver. Couldn't get much for it') and the social worker uses this to facilitate his entrance into flying officer training. The rest of the family are now all finally employed due to the war, but Mrs King reacts

Figure 6 Bristol Unity Players performance of *Buster*, 1944. Reproduced with the permission of University of Warwick Modern Records Centre MSS 212/X/2/6.

bitterly to the argument that at least the war has made work for the family and many like them:

> **Mrs King**   ... You can have your war and your work and everything that goes with it. If I was to go out down the main road and break all the shop windows it'd make work. But it wouldn't make sense.[66]

In the event Buster fulfils his wish for pilot training and the play concludes with a positive view of the future. The play has been read as a 'slum-boy redemption narrative'[67] and in a sense it is. This should not distract attention from the consistent message about the human waste caused by the lack of work and other opportunities for working-class people before the war, and the tragedy that it has taken the mass slaughter of the war to bring about change.

Buster was extensively performed in some regions but seemingly only by those groups identifying with the left. Bristol Unity Players, for example, toured army camps, hostels, canteens and community centres with it. The Cambridge Progressive Players reported that they had completed sixty-eight performances of *Buster* in a year, within a sixty-mile radius of Cambridge. Their audiences were mostly British and American forces as well as some in the surrounding villages, again in aid of war charities.[68] Colin Chambers observes that audiences on American bases would presumably have been racially segregated at that time. If this is so it can be added that these theatre groups would have been required to acquiesce with it, and did not comment on segregation in their reports.[69]

Glasgow Unity Theatre staged the three-act play *When the Boys Come Home* in June 1945, shortly before the general election was called. Written again by James Barke it is set in his former workplace of a Clyde shipyard office and demonstrates an ear for dialogue. The first act introduces the characters with workers continually coming in for materials, bantering, complaining about life and their hard-faced manager; a young man soon to join the navy believes that no one in the yard seems to be taking the war seriously. Political discussion is writ large in Act Two, particularly during an imaginative scene featuring a dream sequence: a dense dialogue takes place between Robert Burns, Jean Armour and Karl Marx in which socialist ideals and ideas about Scottish national self-determination are thrown to and fro with humour. The initial scenes in the final act have three or four women shipyard workers in a lunch-break discussion: besides general gossip about rationing and shortages they are complaining about the canteen, and their poor wages in comparison with the women in munitions. The play gives the male workers the explicitly political speeches and reasoning, particularly in the final scene:

> **Peter**   You see what's happening to Scotland now? Now that the war's practically over, the Westminster government shows its hand. Scotland's to become a derelict area again. And I told you that from the beginning.
>
> **Donald**   And do you think the lads of the Fifty-First Division are going to put up with that when they come back home? D'you think they'll put up with a derelict area?[70]

Both the politically minded and those not so minded are united in their different ways, including through the tragedy of a colleague blinded on war service, and also find different ways of articulating the need for common values and a new sense of purpose: 'The soldiers will come home again. But greater battles lie before us.'[71] The play sees the politics of change through a specifically Scottish perspective. This was in line with the public mood given that the Scottish National Party had won its first Westminster seat at a by-election in 1944. Both the wartime Glasgow Unity productions and their post-war success with *The Gorbals Story* demonstrated the vivid dialogue in the local idiom which John Allen had hoped to see in 1938.

In 1940 the Central Council for Army Education had been empowered to establish a programme of both voluntary and compulsory courses for troops, largely discussion-based and led by a regular series of civic studies and current affairs pamphlets. These were produced by a new unit, the Army Bureau of Current Affairs (ABCA). By 1943 some 60 per cent of home-based units were operating the scheme. ABCA staff wished to present their material more effectively and called on Michael MacOwan, a professional theatrical producer who was now an army major. MacOwan had been impressed by the pre-war living newspaper plays of Unity Theatre and established the ABCA Play Unit to use the form for discussion-based learning in the army.[72]

The Play Unit used professional producers and the casts were professional performers. Nevertheless, it was the pre-war amateur theatre that provided the writing personnel – for example, Ted Willis, Miles Tomalin and Jack Lindsay from London Unity Theatre – and it appears that Nora Ratcliff also had an involvement. The Unit used the dramatic techniques that the pre-war amateur theatre had developed. These included, from *Waiting for Lefty*, using every part of the hall, actors entering from any part and seated in the audience; and from the living newspapers combining drama with factual information, and using spotlights to create fast scene changes and flashbacks in the manner of film.

A good example is *Where Do We Go from Here?*, written by Willis and Lindsay, performed to both army and civilian audiences in 1945. The play opens with a group of male and female soldiers learning about the end of the war from the radio, and their conversation turns to what they may be returning to now. One, Steve, recalls in blank verse, what Lindsay called 'heightened prose', his family's sufferings from unemployment before the war. This cuts to a series of short episodes juxtaposing domestic and public scenes, showing industrialists, trade unions and politicians with no control over economic events. Finally, a bemedalled Old Soldier figure appears on stage with a begging bowl, symbolizing the soldiers' fear for the future. Suddenly the spotlight falls on the 'Ladderman', who is perched on a ladder with a commanding view of the stage. He represents Planning, and he comments on a series of fast-moving scenes of life during the war: state intervention and the direction of industry, the end of craft demarcation and the conscription of women as well as men into factories, and the provision of accommodation wherever labour was needed. However, powerful vested interests are seeking to overturn planning after the war and so the Ladderman is seeking the support of the people. In this he makes too many assumptions about how and where ordinary people want to live, and the level of state direction of their lives that they are willing to accept. They revolt, but again in a salutary warning the Old Soldier reappears.

Ladderman   Don't you see – you can't do without me? The kind of job I've been doing in war-time has got to be carried over into the peace . . . It's not going to be any fun you know . . . You've got to get used to the idea of putting up with things for the sake of the peace just as much as you did for the war. Yours is the difficult job, you know. If you can pull yours off – mine's easy.

Steve   All right – we'll take it. But we're not going to have you up there, you know. You've got to stay down to earth and do your planning where we can watch what goes on and have a say in it.[73]

The play promotes a discussion of the need for post-war planning to avoid a return to the deprivations of the 1930s, but with democratic participation and control. The work of Willis is apparent in the naturalistic working-class scenes similar to *Buster*, while Lindsay contributed the verse-like dialogue. After the performances for troops *Where Do We Go From Here?* was performed for factory hostel audiences in Coventry and Northampton. The play was enthusiastically reviewed by the local press, noting that their technique, although originally aimed at the forces, 'had a widespread appeal' that 'was obvious from the acclamation with which it was received'. The promotion of discussion was welcomed, particularly over 'the question uppermost in the minds of all service men and women awaiting demobilisation'. These performances took place shortly before the general election of 1945 was called.[74]

At the end of the war

One metric of amateur theatre activity during the war is the number of groups affiliated to the BDL. In November 1940 this had fallen to 1,749 but by 1945 had reached 4,247. To the BDL this showed 'a remarkable revival in dramatic work and interest throughout the country'.[75] This number was simply the affiliates and so as before the war the total number of active companies would have been far greater. The amateur movement had maintained the existing and grown new audiences. This was because the war had dispersed its large number of experienced members into the forces, civil defence and munitions, where they continued their activities. Several pre-war enablers of amateur drama – Kelly, Lea, Makin, du Garde Peach – pursued their work with new communities and audiences created by the conflict. Such was the scale of the amateur movement it was able to be present in every aspect of wartime life: military service, evacuation, war factory work, resilience to air raids and the home front. The amateur drama in adult education had paved the way for the success of some touring professionals.

By 1945 many progressive commentators believed that CEMA had promoted a democratization of culture, and following this redistribution of cultural resources by the state great art was no longer reserved for an affluent elite. It had taken war to bring Old Vic programmes to working-class communities, and demonstrated their appreciation of them; now there was an aspiration that this should continue in peacetime. As Farrell at Spennymoor observed, 'It has taken a second world war to bust the West End racket, to send the theatre back to the people, back to where it belongs, and I believe the people will not be slow to claim their own again . . .'.[76]

This was the context in which a national theatre conference was convened early in 1948. The final chapter discusses this event before assessing the amateur 'theatre with a purpose' during the inter-war and wartime years.

Conclusion

The Contribution of Theatre with a Purpose

The National Theatre Conference 1948

Once again, the end of a world war which had affected every aspect of British society provided the catalyst for an organized debate over the future of the theatre. As Geoffrey Whitworth, who was involved in both debates, expressed it, 'our situation at the moment as a nation demands that our theatre be properly organised'. Before the National Conference of 1948 future possibilities for the theatre had already been subjects for discussion. In 1943 the British Drama League (BDL) had put forward proposals for state-aided local civic theatres, part of whose role would be to encourage new work by local playwrights, and to tour outlying areas. Local conferences on the future of theatre – sometimes in terms of aspirations for 'people's theatres' – had been taking place to explore the possibilities it was believed were open following the war.[1] As in 1919 this National Conference involved major figures from the theatre, being chaired and largely organized by J. B. Priestley, and attended by 'famous dramatists, actors and actresses' such as Lewis Casson and Sybil Thorndike.[2] One noticeable difference was the absence of representatives from the social and adult education work fields, or at least they do not appear in the reports.

'The first of the conference resolutions to have practical results', it was jocularly claimed, was a clause in the Local Government Act 1948 which gave local authorities the power to finance theatres, galleries, cinemas and orchestras from the rates. Coupled with the continuation of the Council for the Encouragement of Music and the Arts (CEMA) as the Arts Council of Great Britain (ACGB) this established public financial support to maintain drama outside the commercial sector. Other resolutions[3] called for the extension of drama studies in higher education and for the permanent establishment of children's theatres and drama in schools. Amateur theatre was to be supported by a proposal for repertory companies and local education authorities to work with local amateur groups to improve their technical standards. As regards the Arts Council the conference called for 'a very substantial increase' in funding, an extension of the policy of taking theatre to areas without it, and for the Council to pay greater attention to encouraging new dramatists. Early in the war professional producers and theatre managers' associations had lobbied for state support for professional theatre only, arguing that amateur work was 'social, not artistic'.[4] This was as we have seen the policy of CEMA after 1942, and in the post-war years the ACGB concentrated funds on professional and prestigious London venues. Those funds were to have no prospect of 'a very substantial increase': the 1945 government faced major economic problems, to say nothing of an acute housing crisis, and significant funding for theatre in that environment would not be a priority. Nevertheless, many of those who had been enthused by the 'remarkable revival' saw the priorities of the ACGB in terms of missed opportunities.[5]

In any event the decline of British amateur theatre from its inter-war and wartime levels of activity was not the result of neglect by the Arts Council, even if its policies have contributed to neglect by historians. The amateur movement seemed in a healthy position in the immediate post-war years, as indicated perhaps by three initiatives. In 1946 the Guild of Little Theatres was established to further their interests and to exchange experience, and a year later the Guild of Drama Adjudicators was organized by the BDL to accredit festival judges and to promote recognized standards of adjudication. In 1948 the Carnegie Trust UK took financial responsibility for county drama advisor posts even when the matching local authority funding was withdrawn in favour of other, more pressing, priorities.[6] Eventually the amateur drama movement was to reduce and essentially consolidate around the companies with Little Theatres, a process that was not sudden but gradual. Even in 1959 Nora Ratcliff was adjudicating at amateur drama competitions while a Yorkshire journalist recalled that in the 1950s 'almost every commercial company had its drama group' in the county and likewise most of the villages.[7] In time of course leisure patterns were changed through television, and the large workplaces with the critical mass of staff necessary to support drama clubs reduced their workforces through technology, and de-industrialization had its impact on communities.

Once public funding for theatre had been secured and quality drama was no longer at the mercy of commercial pressure the amateurs had less strategic importance. Milling, Holdsworth and Nicholson observe that by this time, with several of its key objectives achieved, the advocacy activities of the BDL were no longer urgent.[8] This would be the appropriate point at which to review what an amateur theatre with a purpose, the examples examined in the previous chapters, had achieved in the years between the two conferences.

Democratic lines

The activists and idealists of the amateur movement, generally meaning those who actually saw it as a movement, had envisaged a 'theatrical revival on democratic lines'. They had been concerned to extend the sense of entitlement to participate in drama, both as audiences and casts, through all sections of British society. For some this participation was analogous to the participation required of active citizenship in democratic societies. Similarly, where opportunities for self-expression and personal development were accompanied by the communal co-operation required by performance, this could be extended to benefit social cohesion in general. Some again saw wide participation as a means to return the theatre to the role in the lives of ordinary people which they believed it had enjoyed in the past. Alongside this they believed that there was an audience for quality drama amongst those generally untouched by theatre provided that it was accessible to them, something the amateur stage could achieve where the commercial theatre could not. In this project amateur theatre was central, it had a purpose and it was valued. It is difficult to assess the efficacy of amateur theatre regarding the more intangible objectives here, but some assessment of their other efforts can be made. One starting point can be to consider some of the negative judgements amateur theatre received during the 1930s and 1940s.

How far, overall, did these different developments widen the 'democratic lines' of the theatre during this period of revival? In the absence of anything resembling a contemporary survey the informed impressions of some of those involved at the time can be reviewed. One such was John Bourne, the experienced producer and festival adjudicator, editor of *The Amateur Theatre and Playwright's Journal* and a commentator on the movement. In his piece where he had welcomed the Left Book Club Theatre Guild he had also described the amateur theatre movement in Britain since 1920 as almost entirely middle-class in composition and outlook. This appears to contradict a newspaper article by him from two years earlier, in which he stressed the social class diversity – 'all sorts and conditions of people' – in amateur theatre. He described the ingenuity deployed, particularly by the unemployed groups, to create performance spaces, and how the social mixing essential to successful performance was a 'great class leveller'.[9] One response to this is to recall the evidence of the earlier chapters, with some of which Bourne was obviously familiar, which queries his later and more polemical statement.

It is clear that participation interlinked with adult education involved a much wider range of occupational groups than the professional ones, or those most likely to be comfortably placed. The Workers' Educational Association (WEA) had always offered a traditional base for culturally aspiring manual workers but the unemployed clubs and coalfield settlements extended this into a new stratum, as was recognized at the time. This route involved some of the most deprived communities in the country in play-making, established local identification with new Little Theatres there, and involved women, themselves not generally part of the culture attached to the local occupational world. It could be argued that these are simply the exceptions that illustrate the rule. Again, it is 'a question of where one stood, geographically, occupationally, socially'. Commentators in both the South Wales and the County Durham press were agreed that the amateur drama movements in their areas had been given additional and welcome momentum by the drama clubs for unemployed people. In more favoured parts of the country this would not have been the case. Although many of these projects came from an outside catalyst they were taken up with enthusiasm.

However, the adult education tradition did not generally feature creative writing, and the left theatre seems to have privileged only those works which met its approval. Neither was likely to offset the structural inequalities which resulted in the under-representation of working-class people in cultural production relative to their numbers. This book has provided some examples of working-class playwrights who are little-known, or completely unknown, but in terms of recorded work too few to constitute a genre.

'Social, not artistic'?

As was noted initially, in 1947 Norman Marshall had been dismissive of the amateur movement between the wars. His critique quotes another opinion from Bourne voiced at the end of the 1930s. Writing of amateur performers Bourne felt that they were not serious about their activity and their motive was 'the spontaneous and unconsidered desire to don the motley and have fun and games in doing so'. They did not attend or study the theatre, and unless amateur actors 'were actually concerned with a production' their interest would flag. Allardyce Nicoll too had lamented the amateur movement's 'lack of a sense of purpose' as companies appeared to 'drift from performance to performance with no other object in mind'.[10] Bourne had obviously concluded that many amateur companies did not share the sense of mission which had animated the activists of the BDL and others, or the conception of a theatre with a purpose held by movements such as the Left Book Club Theatre Guild (LBCTG). Recreation was still a dominant motivator for the amateur, and as Cochrane points out this recreational strength was of course one key to sustainability. Purpose does not relegate enjoyment. Here some useful evidence is the report of a questionnaire survey issued to 11,000 readers by the journal *Theatrecraft* in 1939. This was concerned with the attitudes of members of amateur clubs to their activity. There is little information in the report by which to judge the robustness of the survey, despite the claim that it reflected 'the opinions of a solid cross-section of actors and producers'. Nevertheless, it appears to be the only survey of its kind (other than that by the LBCTG of its affiliates) during the period. Of those respondents identifying as actors and actresses most, by a wide margin, reported that they took part because they personally enjoyed it rather than because they sought to interest the public in stage work and plays. This would tend to confirm Bourne's judgement. In contrast, respondents identifying as producers reported, again by a wide margin, that their motive was primarily to interest the public in drama. The practice of the theatre with a purpose clearly depended on the producer first and foremost and this is not surprising.[11]

The evidence from the earlier chapters supports the centrality of the producer: for example Edwards, Ratcliff, Tuckett, Stewart, Learner; the Farrells, Newton, Makin, Barber and Lea. Each of them was to some extent in a professional capacity or had previous theatre training, and this illustrates more commonality than division between amateur and professional in these cases. Alongside the conventional role of the producer they networked for assistance and resources, negotiated with funding bodies, liaised with trade unions and campaign groups, and in Edwards's case also advocated with labour exchanges. The choice of play was obviously in their hands and they were prepared to use the more challenging material to develop their actors and technicians. These producers certainly were animated by a vision for regenerating the theatre.

Marshall's dismissal had concluded that 'the growth of the amateur movement in the years before the war was awe-inspiring', the support from the BDL had been considerable, and it had undoubted value for many participants, but nevertheless 'it had contributed little of importance to the theatre as a whole'.[12] In this respect he echoes the claim of the wartime commercial managers that amateur drama was 'social, not artistic'. A 'contribution to the theatre as a whole' of course can take different forms. Nicholson, Holdsworth and Milling understand theatre to be an eco-system of inter-dependent elements. In this perspective the examples discussed here certainly contributed. Playwrights were financially supported by the amateur one-act play market, and from royalties. Opportunities were created for professionals, or the professionally trained, to work with amateurs. New performance spaces were created – in some cases permanently – outside cities and major towns, and audiences for live theatre were both sustained and introduced to some important works of drama as well as popular material.

Another contribution to the theatre can be seen as the writing, performance and production of plays, and this may be what Marshall had chiefly in mind. Again, this conforms to the convention by which the innovative and the exceptional is to be valued at the expense of the bedrock or the standard. Nevertheless by this criterion several of the initiatives associated with the amateur theatre with a purpose challenge his dismissal. Some producers with casts of unemployed people drew on improvisation as the core of making a play. In these examples it was the very circumstance of amateur production which made this necessary and through it improvisation was absorbed into mainstream actor training in Britain. Another frequent circumstance of amateur production was the performance style imposed by the non-theatrical venues in which it took place. This can be seen as a forerunner of the touring professional community theatre of later years. As we have seen, the one-act form was developed by some playwrights who avoided naturalism in favour of verse or fantasy forms. This was to express warnings about the threat and consequences of war without compromising the dramatic effect of the play. The amateur movements in Scotland and Wales nurtured playwrights who portrayed the life of their nations, something sought after by critics at the time, albeit in these examples it was articulated through working-class experience. An example of the techniques pioneered by the amateurs contributing to professional play-making is *Cockpit*, written by Bridget Boland and produced by Malcolm MacOwan in the West End in 1948. The play was concerned with the huge number of refugees and displaced persons then in Europe. The action took place all around the auditorium and involved the audience by treating them as displaced persons, shouted at by guards arriving from outside the hall. These techniques are clearly taken from MacOwan's earlier productions with the ABCA Play Unit, where Boland had also been a writer; in turn they derived from the amateur performances of *Waiting for Lefty* which MacOwan had witnessed before the war.[13]

Achievements

The different models of educational settlements examined here had drama at the centre of their adult education practice, one that had been officially sanctioned since at least 1919. They were capable of high standards of performance with ambitious choices of material; they offered opportunities for play-making to people with little formal education, and to a wide range of manual workers, and those opportunities were taken up. This provided the basis for local amateur drama societies in mining villages and attracted local audiences. They made full use of the by-products of participation to promote the values of co-operation, and of theatre studies as a route to education in other fields. There are examples of adult education classes studying plays as performance and not simply as a literary text, an approach adopted in higher education in later years. Raymond Williams's *Drama in Performance*, first published in 1954 and considered a pioneering example of this, was derived from his experience as a WEA tutor.

The clubs for unemployed people, which included those attached to settlements, were contentious at the time and regarded by some as a palliative distraction from the causes of worklessness. Nevertheless some space was created for political discussion through the medium of adult education, and play-making was organized successfully. The plays performed were not necessarily trivial or politically safe, and some unemployed people became playwrights who drew on their own experience. In some cases innovative techniques of improvisation were developed. At least some of the drama producers and enablers were alert to the sensitivities which could potentially arise from their positions. Some too advocated the integration of unemployed drama groups into the mainstream movement, with what success is difficult to gauge. Both the settlements and the unemployed clubs extended the range of the Little Theatre movement to new communities and audiences.

The competitions and festivals which featured in almost every sphere of amateur drama, and generated a cottage industry of one-act playwrighting, produced mixed reflections from some of those at the centre of them. There was enough anecdotal evidence to sustain the view that festivals were raising standards of acting and production, and by extension furthering the education of audiences in what to look for in plays. On the other hand the structure of the competitions, and an assessment bias towards technical skills at the expense of choice of play obstructed, it was argued, the development of playwrighting beyond the one-act form, and the furtherance of new dramatic exploration. Nevertheless, some writers pushed the one-act play in new directions largely in response to the social movement coalescing around the threat of war. The festival competitions (together with the local Peace Festivals) were an opportunity for theatre groups unconnected with the political left to stage work that was engaged with the social issues of the time. This queries any assumed binary opposition between political theatre and the amateur movement.

In just three years the LBCTG built a not insignificant, if uneven, presence across the country. As a part of the major social and political movements of the day it linked with some activists of the amateur stage, and promoted training and education to develop technical standards. At least some local Guilds built constructive relationships with their local amateur societies and the BDL. In addition their entries to festivals gave support to those using them to provide socially engaged plays to mainstream audiences. The mass declamations, living newspapers and the techniques of the American left theatre used by Guild groups were breaking new ground. Whereas innovative drama might have been confined to London and specialist arts theatres, the local Guild affiliates gave them audiences around the country. They helped to reach non-theatrical audiences through trade unions and campaigning organizations. In so doing they provided a confirmatory function for activists and potentially drew nominal supporters into activity.

The range and strong roots of British amateur drama were evident during the Second World War when its presence supported every aspect of wartime life: military service, war industry work and holidays, evacuated children and families, and resilience during and after bombing raids. The numbers of people experienced in theatre who made this possible were the products of the pre-war movement. The value of its work allied to adult education in the coalfield communities of South Wales and County Durham was evident in the responses to the Old Vic tours. As with the CEMA tours the amateurs too played a part in reaching new audiences for classic drama Amateur drama successfully pursued different purposes: distraction, support, community integration and building new audiences for live theatre performance. It also contributed to the progressive consensus for the post-war world which delivered a Labour government in 1945. British amateur drama in its heyday drew on those for whom theatre had a purpose.

Notes

Introduction: Amateur Theatre and History

1 PGL: SPE 1/C/5/12/3-5 Bill Farrell, *Art for Everyone*, BBC Pacific Service, 9 April 1945.
2 Numbers in John Bourne, 'The One-Act Play in England', in William Kozlenko (ed.), *The One-Act Play Today: A Discussion of the Technique, Scope and History of the Contemporary Short Drama* (London: George Harrap, 1939), 221; Michael Dobson, *Shakespeare and Amateur Performance: A Cultural History* (Cambridge: Cambridge University Press, 2013), 107.
3 Helen Nicholson, Nadine Holdsworth and Jane Milling, *The Ecologies of Amateur Theatre* (London: Palgrave Macmillan, 2018), 46–7; on belittling see Taryn Storey, 'Village Hall Work Can Never Be "Theatre": Amateur Theatre and the Arts Council of Great Britain, 1945–56', *Contemporary Theatre Review*, vol. 27, no. 1 (2017): 76–91; Norman Marshall, *The Other Theatre* (London: John Lehman, 1947), 86–7.
4 Claire M. Tylee, Agnes Cardinal and Elaine Turner, *War Plays by Women: An International Anthology* (London: Routledge, 2000), 111.
5 R. C. Sherriff, *No Leading Lady: An Autobiography* (London: Victor Gollancz, 1969), 195.
6 Rebecca D'Monte, *British Theatre and Performance 1900–1950* (London: Bloomsbury 2015); Linda Mackenney, *The Activities of Popular Dramatists and Drama Groups in Scotland, 1900–1952* (Lampeter: Edwin Mellen Press, 2000); Alyce Von Rothkirch, *J.O. Francis, Realist Drama and Ethics: Culture, Place and Nation* (Cardiff: University of Wales Press, 2014); Mick Wallis, 'Amateur Village Drama and Community in England 1900–50', *New Theatre Quarterly*, vol. 38, no. 3 (2022): 270–82; Nicholson et al, *The Ecologies*.
7 Claire Cochrane, *Twentieth Century British Theatre: Industry, Art and Empire* (Cambridge: Cambridge University Press, 2011).
8 On left theatre see Raphael Samuel, Ewan MacColl and Stuart Cosgrove, *Theatres of the Left 1880–1935: Workers' Theatre Movements in Britain and America* (London: Routledge & Kegan Paul, 1985); Richard Stourac and Kathleen McCreery, *Theatre as a Weapon: Workers' Theatre in the Soviet Union, Germany and Britain 1917–1934* (London: Routledge & Kegan Paul, 1986); Colin Chambers, *The Story of Unity Theatre* (London: Lawrence & Wishart, 1989).
9 John Burnett, *Idle Hands: The Experience of Unemployment, 1790–1990* (London: Routledge, 1994), 202.

10 David Coates, 'Mapping London's Amateur Theatre Histories', in Claire Cochrane and Jo Robinson (eds), *The Methuen Drama Handbook of Theatre History and Historiography* (London: Methuen Drama, 2020), 126–39.

11 On Sheffield see SUSC: Winifred Albaya, *Through the Green Door: An Account of the Sheffield Educational Settlement 1918–55 Part One* (Sheffield: Sheffield District Education Committee, 1977), 4; on Rock House see *Sunderland Echo*, 29 July 1965: 10.

12 Ross McKibbin, *Classes and Cultures: England 1918–1951* (Oxford: Oxford University Press, 1998), 504–5; du Garde Peach in *Theatrecraft*, vol. 1, no.1 (December 1938): 19.

13 Helen Freshwater, *Theatre & Audience* (London: Palgrave Macmillan, 2009), 35–7.

1 'A theatrical revival on democratic lines': Drama and the People after the Great War

1 For a contextualized discussion of the Report see Jude Murphy and Nigel Todd, 'Educating the Peace: Adult Education Responses to 1919', in Matt Perry (ed.), *The Global Challenge of Peace: 1919 as a Contested Threshold to a New World Order* (Liverpool: Liverpool University Press, 2021), 217–33.

2 Ministry of Reconstruction, *Final Report of the Adult Education Committee of the Ministry of Reconstruction* (London: HMSO, 1919), 7.

3 Eric Hobsbawm, *The Age of Extremes, 1914–1991* (London: Abacus, 1995), 67.

4 *Final Report of the Adult Education Committee*, 7, 5, 90–1.

5 *Daily Herald*, 23 May 1919: 8.

6 *The Stage*, 5 June 1919: 15.

7 *The Stage* 5 June 1919: 15. See also Geoffrey Whitworth, *The Making of a National Theatre* (London: Faber and Faber, 1951), 148–9.

8 Margaret Leask, *Lena Ashwell: Actress, Patriot, Pioneer* (Hatfield: University of Hertfordshire Press/Society for Theatre Research, 2012).

9 Quoted in the *Daily Herald*, 4 June 1919: 5.

10 Quoted in Whitworth, *The Making of a National Theatre*, 152.

11 Maggie B. Gale, 'The London Stage, 1918–1945', in Baz Kershaw (ed.), *The Cambridge History of British Theatre Vol. 3: Since 1895* (Cambridge: Cambridge University Press, 2004), 143–66.

12 *The Stage*, 5 June 1919: 15. Christopher Hilliard, *To Exercise Our Talents: The Democratization of Writing in Britain* (Cambridge, MA: Harvard University Press, 2006), 6.

13 See Simon Shepherd (ed.), *The Unknown Granville Barker: Letters to Helen and Other Texts 1915–18* (London: Society for Theatre Research, 2021), 19.

14 Ross McKibbin, *Classes and Cultures: England 1918–1951* (Oxford: Oxford University Press, 1998), 419–22.

15 Patrick Carleton, 'The Revolt from Hollywood', in Patrick Carleton (ed.), *The Amateur Stage: A Symposium*, (London: George Bles, 1939), 17 and 19; Ashwell in the *Daily Herald*, 27 June 1927: 6.

16 See Maureen Callcott (ed.), *A Pilgrimage of Grace: The Diaries of Ruth Dodds 1905–1974* (Whitley Bay: Bewick Press, 1995), 85; Chris Waters, *British Socialists and the Politics of Popular Culture, 1884–1914* (Manchester: Manchester University Press, 1990).

17 Whitworth, *The Making of a National Theatre*, 154.

18 Ibid., 156.

19 *Drama*, vol 6, no. 4 (1928): 61–2; on Northern Ireland see *Northern Whig*, 24 July 1923: 7. On Kelly's work see Mick Wallis, 'Unlocking the Secret Soul: Mary Kelly, Pioneer of Village Theatre', *New Theatre Quarterly*, vol. 16, no. 4 (2000): 347–58; Helen Nicholson, Nadine Holdsworth and Jane Milling, 'Valuing Amateur Theatre' in *The Ecologies of Amateur Theatre* (London: Palgrave Macmillan, 2018), 25.

20 *Yorkshire Post*, 27 October 1934: 9.

21 *Daily Herald*, 16 January 1934: 3; *Daily Gleaner*, 16 December 1936: 7; Delia Jarrett-Macauley, *The Life of Una Marson 1905–65* (Manchester: Manchester University Press, 1998), 93–4.

22 *Newcastle Journal*, 22 August 1928: 10.

23 *Sunday Mirror*, 3 October 1920: 4; *Daily Herald*, 4 October 1920: 5.

24 Adult Education Committee of the Board of Education, *The Drama in Adult Education* (London: HMSO, 1926), 23. See also *The Stage*, 29 April 1926: 16. *Drama*, vol. 4 no. 11 (1926): 141.

25 Claire Cochrane, *Twentieth Century British Theatre: Industry, Art and Empire* (Cambridge: Cambridge University Press, 2011), 131–5; Peter D. Lathan, *Fifty Years On: Sunderland Drama Club 1925–75* (Newcastle upon Tyne: Campbell Graphics, 1975), 4–5; Norman Veitch, *The People's: Being a History of The People's Theatre Newcastle upon Tyne 1911–1939* (Gateshead: Northumberland Press, 1950), 100–2.

26 Rebecca D'Monte, *British Theatre and Performance 1900–1950* (London: Bloomsbury 2015), 99–100; on Southport see *Liverpool Weekly Post*, 2 October 1937: 8; Lathan, *Fifty Years On*, 3–6; Veitch, *The People's*, 198–200.

27 Lathan, *Fifty Years On*, 9.

28 *Merthyr Express*, 31 July 1937: 24, 5 November 1932: 15; *Western Mail*, 25 July 1936: 13 and 28 December 1936: 13.

29 Lathan, *Fifty Years On*, 5, 12.

30 The views of a well-known critic and observer of the amateur theatre in north-west England at the time, Oscar L. Turner; see *Liverpool Weekly Post*, 2 October 1937: 8 and 9 October 1937: 8.

31 Nicholson et al., *The Ecologies*, 8–78.

32 Maggie Andrews, *The Acceptable Face of Feminism: The Women's Institute as a Social Movement* (London: Lawrence & Wishart, 1997).

33 Nora Ratcliff, *Rude Mechanicals: A Short Review of Village Drama* (London: Thomas Nelson, 1938), 26–7.

34 Mick Wallis, 'Amateur Village Drama and Community in England 1900–50', *New Theatre Quarterly*, vol. 38, no. 3 (2022): 274.

35 *Kilmarnock Herald*, 4 May 1933: 1.

36 *Sussex Express*, 17 June 1927: 5; *Newcastle Journal*, 14 September 1928: 10.

37 *Sussex Express*, 23 March 1928: 5.

38 *Surrey Mirror*, 11 May 1928: 12.

39 Ros Merkin, 'The Religion of Socialism or a Pleasant Sunday Afternoon? The ILP Arts Guild', in Clive Barker and Maggie B Gale (eds), *British Theatre between the Wars, 1918–1939* (Cambridge: Cambridge University Press, 2000), 162–90.

40 Samuel, 'Theatre and Socialism in Britain (1880–1935)', in Samuel et al., *Theatres of the Left*, 29.

41 GA: *Progressive Players Diamond Jubilee 1920–1980* (Gateshead: Gateshead Little Theatre, 1980).

42 On the Gateshead Progressive Players see Maureen Callcott and Margaret 'Espinasse, 'Ruth Dodds (1890–1976): Socialist and Labour Councillor', in Joyce M. Bellamy and John Saville (eds), *Dictionary of Labour Biography Vol. VII* (London: Macmillan Press, 1984), 63–7; Samuel, 'Theatre and Socialism in Britain', 27.

43 M. H. Dodds, 'Our Aristocratic Drama', *Drama*, no. 26 (1923): 113–15.

44 Andrew Davies, *Other Theatres: The Development of Alternative and Experimental Theatre in Britain* (London: Macmillan, 1987), 100.

45 GA: *Gateshead Labour Herald*, no. 110 (May 1938): 4.

46 Nicholson et al. *The Ecologies*, 166. Robert Snape, *Leisure, Voluntary Action and Social Change in Britain, 1880–1939* (London: Bloomsbury Academic, 2018), 133; on BDL support for Welfare Departments see *Drama*, no. 7 (1921): 51.

47 See, for example, *Birmingham Daily Gazette*, 29 May 1937: 7.

48 *Liverpool Weekly Post*, 6 November 1937: 8 and 3 December 1938: 8.

49 Angela Tuckett, *The People's Theatre in Bristol 1930–45* (London: Our History Pamphlet, no. 45, 1980), 6; *Drama*, no. 27 (1923): 122; Jonathon Rose, *The Intellectual Life of the British Working Classes* (New Haven, CT: Yale University Press, 2021), 81.

50 See *West London Observer*, 9 February 1923: 2; *The Drama in Adult Education*, 57.

51 *Drama*, no. 7 (1921): 51; *The Drama in Adult Education*, 57.

52 James Gregson, *The Autobiography of James Gregson* (Brighouse: ER Smith Publications, 2011), 67–70.

53 Ibid., 105.

54 Ibid., 104; *Daily Herald*, 30 April 1923: 2.

55 Gregson, *The Autobiography*, 106; *Daily Herald*, 30 April 1923: 2; *Shields News*, 7 September 1922: 8; *Yorkshire Evening Post*, 21 February 1922: 4.

56 *Yorkshire Evening Post*, 2 December 1921: 5.

57 *Daily Herald*, 30 April 1923: 2; Rose, *The Intellectual Life of the British Working Classes*, 83.

58 Steve Nicholson, 'A Critical Year in Perspective: 1926', in Baz Kershaw (ed.), *The Cambridge History of British Theatre Vol. 3: Since 1895* (Cambridge: Cambridge University Press, 2004), 127–43.

59 *The Drama in Adult Education*, 170; *John Bull*, 16 January 1926: 11.

60 Jeremy Burchardt, 'State and Society in the English Countryside: The Rural Community Movement 1918–39', *Rural History*, vol. 23, no. 1 (2012): 81–106.

61 NA: DD/RC/3/1 Minutes of the Nottinghamshire Rural Community Council Adult Education Committee, 12 December 1929 and 17 November 1931.

62 NA: DD/RC/3/1 Minutes of the Nottinghamshire Rural Community Council Adult Education Committee, 20 March 1931; Secretary's Report on Adult Education Work in the Villages 1933/34; Inspection report by Director of Education 1935/36.

63 *Nottingham Journal*, 13 February 1933: 5; 12 March 1936: 5; 24 September 1937: 5 and 29 September 1937: 4.

64 DA: D8 72/1/1-3 Minutes of Derbyshire Rural Community Council Music and Drama Sub-Committee, and Executive Committee, 1 November 1926 to 16 March 1931.

65 DA: D8 72/1/3 Minutes of Derbyshire Rural Community Council Music and Drama Sub-Committee, and Executive Committee, 8 March 1937 to 13 June 1938; *Derbyshire Evening Telegraph*, 30 June 1938: 6.

66 *Belper News*, 22 October 1937: 12.

67 On the German visit see *Derby Daily Telegraph*, 7 October 1937: 4; on his work with the Czech refugees see *Derby Daily Telegraph*, 27 October 1939: 3.

68 For example Allardyce Nicoll, *The English Theatre: A Short History* (London: Thomas Nelson, 1936), 208–9.

69 *Yorkshire Post*, 27 October 1934: 8.

70 For an economic history of the recessions see, for example, John Burnett, *Idle Hands: The Experience of Unemployment, 1790–1990* (London: Routledge, 1994), 199–204.

71 Ruth Dodds, *The Pitman's Pay: A Historical Play in Four Acts* (London: The Labour Publishing Company, 1923).

72 GA: *Gateshead Labour Party and Trades Council Monthly Circular*, no. 75 (December 1922): 4; Callcott (ed.), *A Pilgrimage of Grace*, 90. On Ruth Dodds as playwright see Ros Merkin, 'No Space of Our Own? Margaret Macnamara, Alma Brosnan, Ruth Dodds and the ILP Arts Guild', in Maggie B. Gale and Viv Gardner (eds), *Women, Theatre and Performance: New Histories, New Historiographies* (Manchester: Manchester University Press, 2000), 180–98.

73 Joe Corrie, *In Time O' Strife* (London: Bloomsbury, 2013). First published in 1926.

74 Ibid.

75 Linda Mackenney, *The Activities of Popular Dramatists and Drama Groups in Scotland, 1900–1952* (Lampeter: Edwin Mellen Press, 2000), 45–6; on the Bowhill Players, their tours and Corrie's involvement see 37–62.

76 Leask, *Lena Ashwell*, 174. On unemployment relief controversies see Noreen Branson, *Poplarism 1919–1925: George Lansbury and the Councillors' Revolt* (London: Lawrence & Wishart, 1979).

77 GA: *Progressive Players Diamond Jubilee 1920–1980*, 2.

78 Gregson, *The Autobiography of James Gregson*, 135.

2 'A co-operative community effort': Educational Settlement Theatre

1 Robert Snape, *Leisure, Voluntary Action and Social Change in Britain, 1880–1939* (London: Bloomsbury Academic, 2018), 35–49.

2 A comprehensive account of the educational settlement movement has been provided by Mark Freeman, '"No Finer School than a Settlement": The Development of the Educational Settlement Movement', *History of Education*, vol. 31, no. 3 (2002): 245–62.

3 *The Drama in Adult Education*, 2, 78. Drama groups are referred to in some local accounts, of which the most comprehensive is Robert McManners and Gillian Wales, *Way to the Better: The Spennymoor Settlement* (Durham: Gemini Publications, 2008).

4 Final Report of the Adult Education Committee, 91.

5 F. W. D. Manders, *A History of Gateshead* (Gateshead: Gateshead Corporation, 1973), 236, 173, 48.

6 TWAS: SX51/1 Bensham Grove Settlement: *Second Annual Report 1921–23*, 2.

7 Horace Fleming, *Beechcroft: The Story of the Birkenhead Settlement 1914–1924* (London: Educational Settlements Association, 1938), 11; quoted in Winifred Albaya, *Through the Green Door: An Account of the Sheffield Educational Settlement 1918–55 Part One* (Sheffield: Sheffield District Education Committee, 1977), 25. *Sheffield Independent*, 23 November 1935: 6.

8 Mary Stocks, *Fifty Years in Every Street: The Story of the Manchester University Settlement* (Manchester: Manchester University Press, 1945), 18, 51; Joan Littlewood, *Joan's Book: Joan Littlewood's Peculiar History, As She Tells It* (London: Methuen, 1994), 101.

9 Albaya, *Through the Green Door: Part One,* 19, 22; on York, *Leeds Mercury*, 14 February 1925: 10.

10 *Sunderland Echo*, 19 January 1932: 3, 5 May 1932: 7, and 7 July 1936: 2.

11 Quoted in Keith Armstrong (ed.), *Homespun: The Story of Spennymoor and its Famous Settlement, told by Local People* (North Shields: Northern Voices, 1992), 40–1. PGL/SPE 1/A/24/1 Spennymoor Settlement *Eighth Annual Report 1938/39*, 1; *North Eastern Gazette*, 31 March 1939: 1. The Pilgrim Trust sponsored one of the classic studies of unemployment in Britain in the 1930s, *Men Without Work* (Cambridge: Cambridge University Press, 1938).

12 Jonathon Rose, *The Intellectual Life of the British Working Classes* (New Haven, CT: Yale University Press, 2021), 79–80. On the Mansfield House Settlement in London see the *Daily Herald*, 1 March 1930: 5.

13 Armstrong (ed.), *Homespun*, 29; McManners and Wales, *Way to the Better*, 122.

14 *Motherwell Times*, 21 December 1934: 6.

15 Katharine Dewar, 'Report of Harkness House', *Social Service Review*, vol. 13, no. 8 (1932): 150–1.

16 *Edinburgh Evening News*, 14 October 1933: 6; *The Scotsman*, 9 February 1935: 14.

17 Barrie Naylor, *Quakers in the Rhondda 1926–1986* (Malthouse: Maes-yr-haf Educational Trust, 1986). Bernard Harris, 'Responding to Adversity: Government–Charity Relations and the Relief of Unemployment in Inter-War Britain', *Contemporary British History*, vol. 9, no. 3 (1995): 529–61.

18 Naylor, *Quakers in the Rhondda*, 91.

19 John McIlroy, 'Independent Working-Class Education and Trade Union Education and Training', in Roger Fieldhouse (ed.), *A History of Modern British Adult Education* (Leicester: National Institute of Adult and Continuing Education, 1998), 264–90.

20 Naylor, *Quakers in the Rhondda*, 28.

21 Fleming, *Beechcroft*, 59; Richard Lewis, 'The WEA and Workers' Education in Early Twentieth Century Wales', in Stephen K. Roberts (ed.), *A Ministry of Enthusiasm: Centenary Essays on the Workers' Educational Association* (London: Pluto Press, 2003), 198–215; Daryl Leeworthy, *Labour Country: Political Radicalism and Social Democracy in South Wales 1831–1985* (Cardigan: Parthian Press, 2018), 389.

22 Naylor, *Quakers in the Rhondda*, 36; *Sunderland Echo*, 19 January 1932: 3.

23 *Harkness House Hotch-Potch*, no. 1 (1934): 6–7. There were other issues of this annual publication but 1934 appears to be the sole survivor. On the Welsh settlements and international affairs courses see Leeworthy, *Labour Country*, 389.

24 TWAS: SX51/18/10 Bensham Grove Settlement *Annual Report 1936/37*, 6; PGL/SPE/1/A/16/1 Spennymoor Settlement Report, 11 November 1932, 3; CUSC: Merthyr Tydfil Settlement *Sixth Annual Report 1936/1937*, 8.

25 PGL/SPE: 1/A/24/1 Spennymoor Settlement *Eighth Annual Report 1938/1939*, 3.

26 Freeman, '"No Finer School"': 258.

27 Beechcroft Settlement, *Sixth Annual Report 1919–20*, 5; quoted in Keith Armstrong, *Common Words and the Wandering Star: A Biographical Study of Culture and Social Change in the Life and Work of Writer Jack Common, 1903–1968* (Sunderland:

University of Sunderland Press, 2009), 79; *Sunderland Echo*, 25 March 1935: 7; quoted in Armstrong (ed.), *Homespun*,19; PGL/SPE: 1/A/24/1 Spennymoor Settlement *Eighth Annual Report 1938/1939*, 4–5; *Harkness House Hotch-Potch*, no.1 (1934): 4.

28 PGL/SPE: 1/A/24/1 Spennymoor Settlement *Eighth Annual Report 1938/1939*, 3; Leeworthy, *Labour Country*, 389; CUSC: Merthyr Tydfil Settlement *Sixth Annual Report 1936/1937*, 7–8.

29 Katherine Dewar, 'Report of Harkness House': 150; PGL/SPE: 1/A/19 Spennymoor Settlement *Third Annual Report 1933/34*, 3; Naylor, *Quakers in the Rhondda*, 44.

30 *The Woman's Leader*, 15 November 1929: 318.

31 Frida Stewart, *Firing a Shot for Freedom: The Memoirs of Frida Stewart* (London: The Clapton Press, 2020), 68; Mary Stocks, *Fifty Years in Every Street*, 96. The Stewart memoir was first published in 1940.

32 William Robertson, *Welfare in Trust: A History of the Carnegie United Kingdom Trust 1913–1963* (Dunfermline: The Carnegie United Kingdom Trust, 1964), 100–1.

33 TWAS: SX51/18/2 Bensham Grove Settlement *Annual Report 1928/29*, 5, 10; Eric Barber, 'Durham and Northumberland', *Drama*, vol. 11, no. 10 (1933): 173–4.

34 *Sunderland Echo*, 18 April 1938: 4, and 20 September 1937: 7.

35 *Sunderland Echo*, 11 February 1934: 7; 6 June 1935: 9; 27 March 1935: 4.

36 *Western Mail*, 16 May 1936: 7; Naylor, *Quakers in the Rhondda*, 91; *Motherwell Times*, 1 April 1938: 2; Mackenney, *The Activities of Popular Dramatists in Scotland*, 75.

37 On Barber see *Sunderland Echo*, 21 September 1935: 2; Stewart, *Firing a Shot for Freedom*, 110–11; on Morgan see *Hull Daily Mail*, 22 June 1926: 8.

38 *The Drama in Adult Education*, 77; *Leeds Mercury*, 16 September 1937: 3; *Sunderland Echo*, 23 February 1932: 3.

39 *Drama*, vol. 10, no. 2 (1931): 27.

40 On Beechcroft see *The Stage*, 23 December 1926: 22 and 24 March 1927: 22; Naylor, *Quakers in the Rhondda*, 90; Farrell, 'Drama in Occupation Centres', *National Council of Social Service News Sheet* September 1933: 1; PGL/SPE: 1/C/5/12 Farrell, *Art for Everyone*, 4.

41 Quoted in Armstrong (ed.), *Homespun*, 38.

42 *South Yorkshire Times*, 24 June 1927: 9; 21 December 1928: 8; *Sheffield Independent*, 23 November 1935: 6. A complete list of performances is provided in SUSC: Winifred Albaya, *Through the Green Door: An Account of the Sheffield Educational Settlement 1918–55 Part Two* (Sheffield: Sheffield District Education Committee, 1980), 169–73.

43 Stewart, *Firing a Shot for Freedom*, 68–72; Stocks, *Fifty Years in Every Street*, 96–7.

44 Eric Barber, 'Durham and Northumberland': 174; *Sunderland Echo*, 26 May 1936: 2 and 14 February 1936: 8.

45 *Leeds Mercury*, 14 February 1925: 10; and 25 March 1926: 3; Veitch, *The People's*, 87; Colin Chambers, *The Story of Unity Theatre* (London: Lawrence & Wishart, 1989), 25.

46 *Yorkshire Evening Post*, 7 March 1927: 3 and 14 January 1932: 7; *Leeds Mercury*, 17 February 1939: 3.

47 *Bellshill Speaker*, 5 February 1937: 5.

48 Adult Education Committee *Final Report*, 90; statement on a Settlement theatre programme 1928, included in John Roberts, *The Sheffield Educational Settlement 1918–1955* (MA diss., Faculty of Education, Sheffield University, 1961), 204; on the WEA and creative writing see Hilliard, *To Exercise Our Talents*, 114, and Derek Tatton, 'Literature, Cultural Studies and the WEA', in Roberts (ed.), *A Ministry of Enthusiasm*, 238–59.

49 *Motherwell Times*, 1 April 1938: 2.

50 Ibid.

51 *Merthyr Express*, 31 March 1934: 19.

52 On Jones's life and work see Keri Edwards, *Writers of Wales: Jack Jones* (Cardiff: University of Wales Press, 1974) and Jones's autobiography, *Unfinished Journey* (New York: Oxford University Press, 1937). This describes his maverick political career.

53 Jack Jones, *Land of My Fathers* (London: Samuel French, 1937), 10.

54 *Merthyr Express*, 16 April 1938: 20; on the local politics see Leeworthy, *Labour Country*, 343–7.

55 *The Drama in Adult Education*, 204.

56 Fleming, *Beechcroft*, 50–2; Beechcroft Settlement, *Thirteenth Annual Report 1926/27*, 12, and *Fourteenth Annual Report 1927/28*, 7.

57 Barber, 'Durham and Northumberland': 173.

58 PGL/SPE: 1/C/5/12 Farrell, *Art for Everyone*, 4.

59 Albaya, *Through the Green Door: Part One*, 65.

60 *Sunderland Echo*, 23 February 1932: 3; TWAS: SX51/18/1 Bensham Grove Settlement *Annual Report 1926/27*, 7–8; TWAS: SX51/6/1 Bensham Grove Scrapbooks 1919–1936; *Annual Report 1921/23*, 9 and *Annual Report 1925/26*, 5.

61 *The Drama in Adult Education*, 182.

62 *Sheffield Independent*, 11 December 1935: 7.

63 PGL/SPE: 1/C/3/1 Programme Booklet for *Cradle Song*, 1934, 5; PGL/SPE: 1/C/5/12 Farrell, *Art for Everyone*, 3. An analysis of *Everyman* is in Raymond Williams, *Drama in Performance* (London: Pelican Books, 1972), 52–9. He regards it as an early masterpiece of dramatic literature.

64 Nicholson et al., *The Ecologies*, 8; quoted in Armstrong (ed.), *Homespun*, 38–9.

65 PGL/SPE: 1/A/17 *Spennymoor Settlement First Annual Report 1932/3*, 3.

66 Stocks, *Fifty Years in Every Street*, 96; review quoted in Michael E. Rose and Anne Woods, *Everything Went On at the Round House: A Hundred Years of the Manchester*

University Settlement (Manchester: Manchester University, 1995), 53. *Sheffield Independent*, 23 November 1935: 6.

67 For examples of reviewing individual actors see the *Merthyr Express*, 31 March 1934: 19; critical appreciations of Beechcroft in *Liverpool Echo*, 19 October: 2 and 14 December 1929: 10; on York the *Daily Herald*, 7 December 1925: 1.

68 *Bellshill Speaker*, 5 February 1937: 5; 19 November 1937: 2 and 28 January 1938: 2.

69 TWAS: SX51/18/1 Bensham Grove Settlement *Annual Report 1926/27*, 12, *Annual Report 1925/26*, 12, and *Annual Report 1934/35*, 11.

70 Quoted in Rose and Woods, *Everything Went On at the Round House*, 58. See also K. Swinstead-Smith, 'Players at Ancoates', *Social Services Review*, vol. 15, no. 10 (1934): 172–3. As Freeman ('"No Finer School"': 262) notes, the voices of those for whom activities were organized are generally missing from the narratives about them. Some exceptions are Winifred Albaya, who was a student at the Sheffield Settlement in the 1930s, and the County Durham students quoted by Keith Armstrong.

71 Stewart, *Firing a Shot for Freedom*, 68–9; *Liverpool Echo*, 6 November 1936: 8.

72 Roberts, *The Sheffield Educational Settlement*, 204, 165.

73 *Sheffield Independent*, 23 November 1935: 6, and 5 January 1937: 7. *Daily Herald*, 7 April 1924: 5.

74 *North Eastern Gazette*, 31 March 1939: 3; *Bellshill Speaker*, 30 March 1934: 1; Orr quoted in Linda Mackenney, *The Activities of Popular Dramatists and Drama Groups in Scotland, 1900–1952* (Lampeter: Edwin Mellen Press, 2000), 75.

75 *Yorkshire Evening Post*, 23 May 1929: 10.

3 Social Control or Self-Expression? Amateur Theatre and the Unemployment Crisis

1 John Burnett, *Idle Hands: The Experience of Unemployment, 1790–1990* (London: Routledge, 1994), 199–202. See also Keith Laybourn, *Britain on the Breadline: A Social and Political History of Britain 1918–1939* (Stroud: Sutton Publishing, 1998), 7–69.

2 On the NUWM see Richard Croucher, *We Refuse to Starve in Silence: A History of the National Unemployed Workers' Movement, 1920–1946* (London: Lawrence & Wishart, 1987).

3 Noreen Branson and Margot Heinemann, *Britain in the Nineteen Thirties* (London: Weidenfield & Nicolson, 1971), 57–60; John Stevenson and Chris Cook, *The Slump: Society and Politics during the Depression* (London: Quartet Books, 1979), 64–5.

4 Statistics quoted in Robert Snape, *Leisure, Voluntary Action and Social Change in Britain, 1880–1939* (London: Bloomsbury Academic, 2018), 125. These centres

should not be confused with the compulsory 'transfer instructional centres' established in 1934.

5 Wal Hannington, *The Problem of the Distressed Areas* (London: Victor Gollancz Left Book Club edition, 1937), 194–216; on donors to clubs see Richard Flanagan, *'Parish-Fed Bastards': A History of the Politics of the Unemployed in Britain, 1884–1939* (New York: Greenwood Press, 1991), 213; Margaret Brasnett discusses trade union hostility in *Voluntary Social Action: A History of the National Council of Social Service 1919–1969* (London: National Council of Social Service, 1969), 74–5.

6 Editorial, 'Drama and Unemployment', *Drama*, vol. 11, no. 6 (1933): 103; George Makin, 'Drama among the Unemployed' in Carleton (ed.), *The Amateur Stage: A Symposium*, 163; Gregson in *Yorkshire Post*, 22 February 1934: 7. On assumptions about unemployment see Andrej Olechnowicz, 'Unemployed Workers, "Enforced Leisure" and Education for the "Right Use of Leisure" in Britain in the 1930s', *Labour History Review*, vol. 70, no. 1 (2005): 27–52.

7 *Nottingham Journal*, 13 February 1933: 8 and 29 September 1937: 8.

8 NA: DD/RC/3/1 'Work with Social Service Drama Groups', Report to Nottinghamshire Rural Community Council Adult Education Committee for Year End 31 March 1938; *Nottingham Journal* 13 February 1933: 8; on Belfast, *Northern Whig*, 28 March 1933: 3.

9 TWAS: SX51/18/5 Bensham Grove Settlement *Annual Report 1931*, 4.

10 Farrell quoted in Robert McManners and Gillian Wales, *Way to the Better: The Spennymoor Settlement* (Durham: Gemini Publications, 2008), 17.

11 Tyneside Council of Social Service, *Eighth Annual Report 1936/37*, 28–9.

12 Pilgrim Trust, *Men Without Work*, 352.

13 *Western Mail*, 22 December 1933: 9; *Aberdeen Press and Journal*, 28 October 1938: 8.

14 *The Clydebank Press*, 18 May 1934: 1; *Derbyshire Evening Telegraph*, 15 October 1937: 1; *Nottingham Journal*, 13 February 1933: 4; *Lancashire Evening Post*, 22 January 1935: 4.

15 *Shields Daily News*, 14 April 1934: 4; *Northern Daily Mail*, 7 May 1938: 2; Makin, 'Drama among the Unemployed', 180.

16 *Shields Daily News*, 14 April 1934: 4 and 13 May 1933: 4; *Northern Whig*, 28 March 1933: 3.

17 *Newcastle Evening Chronicle*, 3 March 1939: 5; NA: DD/RC/3/1 'Work with Social Service Drama Groups'; PGL: SPE1/A/18 Spennymoor Settlement, *First Annual Report 1932/33*, 9.

18 Gordon Lea, 'Music and Drama amongst the Unemployed, an Experiment', *Social Services Review*, vol. 16, no. 1 (1935): 9. *Merthyr Express*, 29 December 1934: 7.

19 Frida Stewart, *Firing a Shot for Freedom: The Memoirs of Frida Stewart* (London: The Clapton Press, 2020), 70; Lea, 'Music and Drama amongst the Unemployed', 9.

20 *Daily Herald*, 18 April 1934: 15. This Kathleen Edwards should not be confused with a stage and screen actress of the 1930s named Kathleen Edwardes.

21 *The Unemployed Drama News*, introductory issue 1936: 5–7. The 'introductory issue' appears to have been the only issue of this publication, which was intended to raise funds.

22 Farrell, 'Drama in the Occupation Centres': 1; Nora Ratcliff, *Rude Mechanicals: A Short Review of Village Drama* (London: Thomas Nelson, 1939), 81; on Copeau see Anthony Frost and Ralph Yarrow, *Improvisation in Drama, Theatre and Performance: History, Practice, Theory* (London: Macmillan, 1990), 20.

23 *Berks and Oxon Advertiser*, 2 August 1935: 8.

24 *The Unemployed Drama News*: 10–13; *Drama*, vol. 14, no. 5 (1936): 13; *Western Mail*, 28 August 1934: 7

25 *Western Mail*, 16 August 1934: 13, 25 August 1934: 11 and 31 August 1934: 13; *Merthyr Express*, 25 August 1934: 9.

26 Gavin Bolton, *Acting in Classroom Drama: A Critical Analysis* (Portland: Calendar Island Publishers, 1999), 82–3. On actor training see Frost and Yarrow, *Improvisation in Drama, Theatre and Performance*, 24.

27 Robert G. Newton, *Acting Improvised* (London: Thomas Nelson, 1937), ix, 5, 42.

28 Makin, 'Drama among the Unemployed', 176–7.

29 Newton, *Acting Improvised*, 4; Makin, 'Drama among the Unemployed', 183–3.

30 Ratcliff, *Rude Mechanicals*, 80–1; *Yorkshire Post*, 17 February 1934, 7; Stewart, *Firing a Shot for Freedom*, 69; Farrell, 'Drama in the Occupation Centres': 1; NA: DD/RC/3/1 'Work with Social Service Drama Groups'; *Shields Daily News*, 18 April 1934: 8.

31 Henry A. Mess, 'Social Service with the Unemployed', in Henry A. Mess (ed.), *Voluntary Social Services since 1918* (London: Kegan Paul, 1947), 46; John Allen, 'The Socialist Theatre', *Left Review*, vol. 3, no. 7 (1937): 417.

32 J. B. Priestley, *English Journey* (Ilkley: Great Northern Books, 2009), 258–60; TWAS: SX51/18/9 Bensham Grove Settlement *Annual Report 1935/36*, 4–6. 8; CUSC: Aberdare Valley Educational Settlement *Monthly Bulletin*, October 1938, 2; *Western Mail*, 25 October 1939: 8. Cochrane, *Twentieth Century British Theatre*, 123.

33 Lea, 'Music and Drama Amongst the Unemployed': 10; CUSC: Merthyr Tydfil Settlement *Sixth Annual Report 1936/37*, 7.

34 Tyneside Council of Social Service *Seventh Annual Report 1935/36*, 21 and *Eighth Annual Report 1936/37*, 28–9; *Nottingham Evening Post*, 19 February 1936: 7; NA: DD/RC/3/1 'Work with Social Service Centre Drama Groups'; *Ripley and Reanor News*, 19 April 1938: 2.

35 Elsie Entwistle, *Life's Day* (London: W. Deane, 1935); *Derbyshire Times*, 3 March 1939: 23.

36 *The Clydebank Press*, 4 January 1935: 8.

37 *Nottingham Journal*, 8 July 1936: 7 and 29 September 1937: 9; *Newcastle Journal*, 17 November 1937: 10, *Sunderland Echo*, 10 May 1938: 7.

38 John Bewaldeth, *The Yard* (unpublished script, BL/LCP 1934/43).

39 Ibid.; reviews in *Lancashire Evening Post*, 30 January 1934: 4 and 24 September 1935: 4.

40 On Bangor see *Belfast Telegraph*, 12 February 1936: 9; on Barnsley *Leeds Mercury*, 31 March 1939: 3, *Liverpool Echo*, 22 April 1939: 2, *South Yorkshire Times*, 9 July 1939: 16; Steve Nicholson, *British Theatre and the Red Peril: The Portrayal of Communism 1917–1945* (Exeter: University of Exeter Press, 1990), 43–5. On *Firedamp* see *Liverpool Weekly Post*, 15 April 1939: 8.

41 *Shields Daily News*, 5 December 1933: 3; Tyneside Council of Social Service *Seventh Annual Report 1935/36*, 28; *Newcastle Evening Chronicle*, 29 March 1939: 10.

42 *Sunderland Echo*, 1 May 1936: 2.

43 Programme included in Roberts, *The Sheffield Educational Settlement*, 204.

44 Flanagan, *'Parish-Fed Bastards'*, 219. For an account of these novelists see Andy Croft, *Red Letter Days: British Fiction in the 1930s* (London: Lawrence & Wishart, 1990).

45 Makin, 'Drama among the Unemployed', 176–7; *Derbyshire Times*, 7 July 1939: 18 and 15 December 1939: 11; *Nottingham Journal*, 8 July 1936: 7.

46 Frank Farnin, *The War Memorial* (unpublished script, BL/LCP 1938/5); *Bellshill Speaker*, 28 January 1938: 2. On ghosts and war in drama see Clive Barker, 'The Ghosts of War: Stage Ghosts and Time Slips as a Response to War', in Clive Barker and Maggie B. Gale (eds), *British Theatre between the Wars, 1918–1939* (Cambridge: Cambridge University Press, 2000), 215–43.

47 *The Scotsman*, 22 May 1933: 11; Stewart, *Firing a Shot for Freedom*, 69; *Manchester Evening News*, 27 January 1939: 8.

48 Allen, 'The Socialist Theatre': 417.

49 *Sunderland Echo*, 4 April 1938: 2; Pilgrim Trust, *Men Without Work* (Cambridge: Cambridge University Press, 1938), 352; *Merthyr Express*, 31 December 1938: 16 and 4 June 1938: 9; Naylor, *Quakers in the Rhondda*, 44–5; CUSC: Aberdare Valley Educational Settlement *Monthly Bulletin*, November 1938, 1.

50 *Sunderland Echo*, 14 March 1936: 3; Makin, 'Drama among the Unemployed', 186.

51 Ellen Wilkinson, *The Town That Was Murdered: The Life Story of Jarrow* (London: Merlin Press, 2019), 174–80. First published in 1939.

52 Makin, 'Drama among the Unemployed', 164, 182.

53 NA: DD/RC/3/1 'Work with Social Service Drama Groups'; *Nottingham Journal*, 8 July 1936: 7; Makin, 'Drama among the Unemployed', 173.

54 *Shields Daily News*, 15 February 1935: 2; *Newcastle Journal*, 17 November 1937: 7.

55 *Sunderland Echo*, 4 February 1932: 1; quoted in John Davies, 'John Davies and the Workers' Educational Association in South Wales', *Llafur*, vol. 8, no. 1 (2000): 55; Makin, 'Drama among the Unemployed', 182; Euan McArthur, *Scotland, CEMA and the Arts Council, 1919–1967: Background, Politics and Visual Art Policy* (Abingdon:

Routledge, 2016), 30–1; *Motherwell Times*, 24 September 1937: 7; The Pilgrim Trust *Third Annual Report 1933*, 7.

56 Tyneside Council for Social Service *Eighth Annual Report 1936/37*, 29; The Pilgrim Trust *Fifth Annual Report 1935*, 6; McArthur, *Scotland, CEMA and the Arts Council*, 31.

57 Leeworthy, *Labour Country*, 389; CUSC: Merthyr Tydfil Settlement *Sixth Annual Report 1937*, 6; Bernard Harris, 'Responding to Adversity: Government–Charity Relations and the Relief of Unemployment in Inter-War Britain', *Contemporary British History*, vol. 9, no. 3 (1995): 552.

58 Alyce Von Rothkirch, *J.O. Francis, Realist Drama and Ethics: Culture, Place and Nation* (Cardiff: University of Wales Press, 2014), 42.

59 CUSC: Merthyr Tydfil Settlement *Sixth Annual Report 1937*, 9; PGL: SPE1/C/5 Farrell: *Art for Everyone*, 4; NA: DD/RC/3/1 'Work with Social Service Drama Groups'.

60 Stewart, *Firing a Shot for Freedom*, 70–1.

61 PGL: SPE1/A/24 Spennymoor Settlement *Eighth Annual Report 1938/39*, 4–5.

4 Competitions, Festivals, Politics

1 Claire Cochrane, *Twentieth Century British Theatre: Industry, Art and Empire* (Cambridge: Cambridge University Press, 2011), 112.

2 Sydney Box, 'The Drama Festival', in Carleton (ed.), *The Amateur Stage: A Symposium* (London: George Bles, 1939), 72–3.

3 *Liverpool Weekly Post*, 29 January 1938: 8; on the Welsh company see Alyce Von Rothkirch, *J.O. Francis, Realist Drama and Ethics: Culture, Place and Nation* (Cardiff: University of Wales Press, 2014), 55.

4 This comment on drama festivals is from *The Amateur Stage*, vol. 1, no. 1 (1946): 10; Patrick Carleton, 'The Revolt from Hollywood', in Patrick Carleton (ed.), *The Amateur Stage: A Symposium*, (London: George Bles, 1939), 40–2. For drama groups' improved performances following an adjudicator's assessment see John Bourne, *Drama Festivals and Competitions* (London: Pitman & Sons, 1939), 3 and Box, 'The Drama Festival', 108.

5 Bourne quoted in *Liverpool Weekly Post*, 26 November 1938: 8.

6 Box, 'The Drama Festival', 63–109; John Bourne, *Drama Festivals and Competitions*, 12–18.

7 *The Scotsman*, 8 February 1937: 14; *Liverpool Weekly Post*, 16 October 1937: 8; Thorndike interviewed in *Theatre Newsletter*, no. 17 (1947): 7.

8 Linda Mackenney, *The Activities of Popular Dramatists and Drama Groups in Scotland, 1900–1952* (Lampeter: Edwin Mellen Press, 2000), 72.

9 John Bourne, 'The One-Act Play in England', in William Kozlenko (ed.), *The One-Act Play Today: A Discussion of the Technique, Scope and History of the Contemporary Short Drama* (London: Harrap, 1939), 222.

10 DA: D8 72/1/1 Derbyshire Rural Community Council Music and Drama Sub-Committee Minutes, 24 August 1928; *Liverpool Weekly Post*, 9 October 1937: 8.

11 Muriel and Sydney Box, *Ladies Only* (London: George Harrap, 1934), 11. Flora Robson's comment is in her introduction to this collection, 8.

12 Amateur *Theatre and Playwrights' Journal*, vol. 3, no. 55 (1936): 13; Mackenney, *The Activities of Popular Dramatists in Scotland*, 79; Bourne, 'The One-Act Play in England', 219–43.

13 Bourne, 'The One-Act Play in England', 234–5. Details of festival adjudication are in Bourne, *Drama Festivals and Competitions*, 60–73, 102–8.

14 Unattributed press cutting circa 1928 in Gregson, *The Autobiography*, 241.

15 Helen Nicholson, Nadine Holdsworth and Jane Milling, *The Ecologies of Amateur Theatre* (London: Palgrave Macmillan, 2018), 88.

16 Muriel Box, *Odd Woman Out* (London: Leslie Frewin, 1974), 140.

17 Box, 'The Drama Festival', 104.

18 Review in *Hull Daily Mail*, 4 March 1935: 7.

19 Andrew Spicer: *British Film Makers: Sydney Box* (Manchester: Manchester University Press, 2006), 12.

20 Published in Hugh S. Quekett (ed.), *Eight Prize-Winning One-Act Plays* (London: George Harrap, 1936), 199–221.

21 Box, 'The Technique of the Experimental One-Act Play', in Kozlenko (ed.), *The One-Act Play Today*, 63–9.

22 On the number of performances see Quekett (ed.), *Eight Prize-Winning One-Act Plays*, 6. On the 1936 Welsh final see *Western Mail*, 26 May 1936: 7.

23 *Leeds Mercury*, 10 December 1937: 3; *Hull Daily Mail*, 5 October 1937: 3; *Birmingham Daily Gazette*, 16 November 1937: 7, 27 April 1937: 8 and 19 January 1938: 3; *Left News*, no. 29 (1938): 981; *Western Mail*, 5 August 1936: 6 and 7 December 1938: 12; *Belfast Telegraph*, 1 May 1939: 5.

24 *Mid Sussex Times*, 13 October 1936: 7; *Belfast Newsletter*, 4 January 1939: 3.

25 Text in John Bourne (ed.), *Twenty-Five Modern One-Act Plays* (London: Victor Gollancz, 1938), 473–91.

26 *Berwickshire News*, 18 April 1939: 5.

27 Text in Bourne (ed.), *Twenty-Five Modern One-Act Plays*.

28 *Birmingham Daily Gazette*, 29 May 1937: 7; *Liverpool Echo*, 12 March 1938: 2; *Hull Daily Mail*, 17 February 1939: 11.

29 *Lancashire Evening Post*, 28 June 1937: 3; *Yorkshire Evening Post*, 8 March 1938: 6; *Liverpool Daily Post*, 28 January 1939: 10; *Coventry Herald*, 11 March 1939: 4; *Bedfordshire Times*, 10 March 1939: 10.

30 Bourne, *Drama Festivals*, 99; *Daily Record*, 9 February 1939: 7 and *Warwick Advertiser*, 8 April 1939: 8.

31 Mackenney, *The Activities of Popular Dramatists in Scotland*, 103–8; see also Jan McDonald, 'Towards National Identities: Theatre in Scotland', in Baz Kershaw (ed.), *The Cambridge History of British Theatre Vol. 3: Since 1895* (Cambridge: Cambridge University Press, 2004), 200–1. Karen Anne Marshalsey, 'The Quest for a Truly Representative Scottish National Drama: The Scottish National Players', *Theatre Research International*, vol. 17, no. 2 (1992): 109–16.

32 Mackenney, *The Activities of Popular Dramatists in Scotland*, 148–9, 76–7, 103–10, 88–90; comment on anti-Corrie bias in *The Amateur Theatre and Playwrights' Journal*, vol. 5, no. 91 (1938): 23.

33 *Leeds Mercury*, 14 February 1938: 5; *Western Morning News*, 26 March 1938: 10; *Liverpool Daily Post*, 27 January 1939: 6.

34 Bourne quoted in *Merthyr Express*, 6 April 1935: 24; Von Rothkirch, *J.O. Francis*, 49–51. See also Ioan Williams, 'Towards National Identities: Welsh Theatres', in Baz Kershaw (ed.), *The Cambridge History of British Theatre Vol. 3*, 250–1.

35 *Coventry Evening Telegraph*, 1 April 1938: 22.

36 *Glamorgan Advertiser*, 17 February 1939: 4 and *Western Mail*, 24 June 1939: 7.

37 Rebecca D'Monte, *British Theatre and Performance 1900–1950* (London: Bloomsbury 2015), 102.

38 E. Eynon Evans, *Cold Coal* (London: Samuel French, 1939). Reviews in *Western Mail*, 24 February 1939: 13 and *Merthyr Express*, 26 February 1938: 7. The play was certainly well-discussed locally: see *Merthyr Express*, 5 February 1938: 6, 12 February 1938: 3 and 19 February 1938: 3.

39 *Western Mail*, 22 November 1934: 10.

40 *Merthyr Express*, 26 February 1938: 7; *Caerphilly Journal*, 29 January 1938: 5.

41 *Glamorgan Gazette*, 19 May 1939: 3.

42 Joe Corrie, 'Use the Freedom of the Festival', *The Amateur Theatre and Playwrights' Journal*, vol. 3, no. 66 (1937): 7–8. On Corrie generally see Mackenney: *The Activities of Popular Dramatists in Scotland*, 77–104.

43 R. Vernon Beste, 'Community Theatre Festival', *New Theatre*, no. 1, 1939): 12; on the final see *The Stage*, 25 May 1939: 9.

44 Barbara Nixon, 'Theatre Now', *Left Review*, vol. 2, no. 3 (1935): 105; John Allen, 'The Socialist Theatre', *Left Review*, vol. 3, no. 7 (1937), 417.

45 *The Scotsman*, 1 June 1936: 14; *Daily News*, 26 May 1936: 7. Neil Grant, *The Last War*, in J. Marriott (ed.), *The Best One-Act Plays of 1933* (London: George Harrap, 1934), 243–65. Joe Corrie, *And So to War* (Glasgow: Bone & Hulley, 1936).

46 *Daily Herald*, 1 June 1937: 9. *Hewers of Coal* appears in Joe Corrie, *Plays, Poems and Theatre Writings* (Edinburgh: 7:84 Publications, 1985), 99–119.

47 *Leicester Mercury*, 20 January 1939: 3. On *The Trial of a Judge* and the Group Theatre see Michael J. Sidnell, *Dances of Death: The Group Theatre in the Thirties*

(London: Faber, 1984), 227–38; *Western Daily Press*, 12 April 1938: 7 and 2 May 1938: 7.

48 On Corrie see *Amateur Theatre and Playwright's Journal*, vol. 3, no. 55 (1936): 19; comment on social drama in *Liverpool Weekly Post*, 20 May 1939: 9.

49 Hal D. Draper in *Amateur Theatre and Playwrights' Journal*, vol. 3, no. 60 (1936): 13.

50 *Glamorgan Advertiser*, 12 July 1939: 13 and 14 July 1939: 1. On the Trecynon Players see *Merthyr Express*, 20 February 1937: 15.

51 *The Scotsman*, 13 September 1937: 11; *Coatbridge Leader*, 4 September 1937: 3; *The Scotsman*, 1 April 1939: 17.

52 *Airdrie and Coatbridge Advertiser*, 1 October 1938: 4; On *The Path to Glory* see *Leeds Mercury*, 17 November 1933: 9.

53 On the Bootle controversy see Jerry Dawson, *Left Theatre: Merseyside Unity Theatre – a Documentary Record* (Liverpool: Merseyside Writers, 1985), 14–15.

54 *Liverpool Evening Express*, 13 April 1939: 3; *Walsall Observer*, 18 February 1939: 13. See Steve Nicholson, *The Censorship of British Drama 1900–1968: Volume Two: 1933–1952* (Exeter: Exeter University Press/Society for Theatre Research, 2020), 127–8.

55 In Muriel and Sydney Box, *Ladies Only*, 16–30.

56 Muriel Box, 'Angels of War' in Claire M. Tylee (ed.), Agnes Cardinal and Elaine Turner, *War Plays by Women: An International Anthology* (London: Routledge, 2000), 115–39. *Angels* was first published in 1935. For a feminist criticism see D'Monte, *British Theatre and Performance*, 131–2.

57 Reviews of *Angels* in *Rugby Advertiser*, 28 February 1936: 16; *Birmingham Gazette*, 14 December 1936: 7. Quoted in Nicholson, *The Censorship of British Drama 1900–1968*, 128. On the WI and anti-war sentiment see Maggie Andrews, *The Acceptable Face of Feminism: The Women's Institute as a Social Movement* (London: Lawrence & Wishart, 1997), 60.

58 *Dundee Courier*, 13 April 1939: 3; *The Scotsman*, 20 February 1939: 11 and 13 April 1939: 11.

59 On *Tin Soldiers* see the *Thanet Advertiser*, 3 September 1937: 3. *The Pen Is Mightier* in *The Amateur Theatre and Playwright's Journal*, vol. 4, no. 79 (1937): 323–7.

60 *Liverpool Echo*, 7 May 1938: 10; *Birmingham Daily Post*, 6 February 1939: 11; *Tamworth Herald* 9 April 1938: 3 and *Gloucestershire Echo*, 3 December 1937: 3.

61 *Shells*, in Bourne (ed.), *Twenty-Five Modern One-Act Plays*, 176–97. A review is in the *Daily Record*, 31 March 1939: 1 and 3.

62 *Sheffield Independent*, 13 November 1937: 5 and 16 November 1937: 5.

63 Mackenney, *The Activities of Popular Dramatists in Scotland*, 71; *The Scotsman*, 11 February 1939: 14 and 16 March 1939: 12. On the Jewish Institute Players see Paul Maloney and Adrienne Scullion, 'From the Gorbals to the Lower East Side: The Theatrical and Social Cosmopolitanism of the Glasgow Jewish Institute Players', *New Theatre Quarterly*, no. 34, vol. 1 (2018): 58–73.

64 Mackenney, *The Activities of Popular Dramatists in Scotland*, 108–9.

65 *New Theatre*, no. 1 (August 1939): 5; For Ratcliff plays see *Daily Herald*, 11 November 1938: 15 and *Sheffield Independent*, 17 August 1938: 7.

66 William Kozlenko, 'The Federal Theatre', *The Amateur Theatre and Playwrights' Journal*, vol. 4, no. 78 (1937): 474; Raymond Birt, 'Left Turn Among the Amateurs', *The Amateur Theatre and Playwrights' Journal*, vol. 4, no. 79 (1937): 511.

67 Birt, ibid.; John Bourne, 'The One-Act Play in England', 239–41.

5 'The terribly urgent struggle': the Left Book Club Theatre Guild, 1936–9

1 Branson and Heinemann, *Britain in the Nineteen Thirties* (London: Weidenfeld & Nicolson, 1971), 297–323.

2 Gollancz quoted in LHASC: CP/ORG/MISC/03/08) *The Tasks of the Left Book Club Theatre Guild, Discussion Paper* (1938): 1. The official history of the Club is John Lewis, *The Left Book Club: An Historical Record* (London: Victor Gollancz, 1970); for a selection from the Left Book Club choices see Paul Laity (ed.), *Left Book Club Anthology* (London: Victor Gollancz, 2001). There is a concise account of the Left Book Club Theatre Guild in Colin Chambers, *The Story of Unity Theatre* (London: Lawrence & Wishart, 1989), 93–104 and a brief one in Andrew Davies, *Other Theatres: The Development of Alternative and Experimental Theatre in Britain* (London: Macmillan, 1987), 119–21.

3 For an analysis of the Club in terms of popular front politics see Kevin Morgan, *Against Fascism and War: Ruptures and Continuities in British Communist Politics 1935–41* (Manchester: Manchester University Press, 1989), 254–76.

4 The number of affiliated theatre groups stated in Lewis, *The Left Book Club*, 46. Survey reported in LHASC: CP/ORG/MISC/03/08 *Theatre for the People*, no. 2 (April 1939): 1.

5 1938 pamphlet quoted in Linda Mackenney, *The Activities of Popular Dramatists and Drama Groups in Scotland, 1900–1952* (Lampeter: Edwin Mellen Press, 2000), 133; Angela Tuckett, *The People's Theatre in Bristol 1930–45* (London: Our History Pamphlet, no. 45, 1980), 8; Jerry Dawson, *Left Theatre: Merseyside Unity Theatre – a Documentary Record* (Liverpool: Merseyside Writers, 1985), 1; interview in Don Watson, 'To the Head through the Heart: the Newcastle Left Book Club Theatre Guild', *North East Labour History*, no. 23 (1989): 8.

6 Chambers, *The Story of Unity Theatre*, 97; GUSC: STA GEN 6 Glasgow Workers' Theatre Group Minute Book, LBCTG National Committee Meeting Birmingham, 23 October 1938, 2–3; MRC: BUP212/A/1/7, Bristol Unity Players, Secretary's Report to the AGM, 30 June 1943.

7 Examples are Tom Jeffrey: *Mass Observation: A Short History* (Mass Observation Archive Occasional Paper no. 10, Brighton: University of Sussex Library, 1999), 13–14; Gary McCulloch, 'Teachers and Missionaries: The Left Book Club as an Educational Agency', *History of Education*, vol. 14, no. 2 (1985): 137–53. On working-class involvement see Laity (ed.), *Left Book Club Anthology*, xxv–xxvi.

8 Interview in Watson: 'To the Head through the Heart': 8; *Liverpool Daily Post*, 12 January 1939: 8. On the Chester incident see Jerry Dawson, *Left Theatre*, 12–14.

9 Tuckett, *People's Theatre in Bristol*, 7; Mackenney, *The Activities of Popular Dramatists in Scotland*, 132–3; Maurice Ridley, 'Making a Contribution', in Keith Armstrong (ed.), *But the World Goes on the Same: Changing Times in a Durham Pit Village* (Whitley Bay: Strong Words, 1979), 66.

10 Tuckett, *People's Theatre in Bristol*, 10; V&A: THM/9/6/1/6 Letters from Norman Draper on the History of Cardiff Unity Theatre; Mackenney, *The Activities of Popular Drama Groups in Scotland*, 132.

11 Barbara Nixon, 'Theatre Now', *Left Review*, vol. 2, no. 3 (1935): 105; John Allen, 'The Socialist Theatre', *Left Review*, vol. 3, no. 7 (1937): 105.

12 *Left News*, no. 16 (August 1937): 440; no. 17 (September 1937): 454; Chambers, *The Story of Unity Theatre*, 137. The ILP Arts Guild had also held such courses in the 1920s; see Ros Merkin, 'The Religion of Socialism or a Pleasant Sunday Afternoon? The ILP Arts Guild', in Clive Barker and Maggie B Gale (eds), *British Theatre between the Wars, 1918–1939* (Cambridge: Cambridge University Press, 2000), 168.

13 *Left News*, no. 38 (June 1939): 1314; no. 31 (November 1938): 1068; SUSC: Winifred Albaya, *Through the Green Door: An Account of the Sheffield Educational Settlement 1918–55 Part One* (Sheffield: Sheffield District Education Committee, 1977), 88–9.

14 LHASC: CP/ORG/MISC/03/08) *Theatre for the People*, no.1 (February 1939): 3–7.

15 Interview in Watson, 'To the Head Through the Heart': 9.

16 Mackenney, *The Activities of Popular Dramatists in Scotland*, 139; MRC: BUP212/A/1/11, Joan Tuckett, Producer's Report November 1938; Ewan MacColl, 'Introduction', in Howard Goorney and Ewan MacColl, *Agit-Prop to Theatre Workshop: Political Playscripts 1930–50* (Manchester: Manchester University Press, 1986), xxxviii; *Left News*, no. 24 (April 1938): 784.

17 Allen, 'The Socialist Theatre', 418; *Left News*, no. 28 (August 1938): 948; *Left News*, no. 37 (May 1939): 1281–2; LHASC: CP/ORG/MISC/03/08 *Theatre for the People*, no. 2 (April 1939): 4.

18 Nora Ratcliffe, 'The Soviet Theatre Revisited', *The Amateur Theatre and Playwrights' Journal*, vol. 4, no. 74 (1937): 304–6; *Sheffield Independent*, 22 October 1937: 4 and 14 November 1936: 8. For her own plays see *Daily Herald*, 11 November 1938: 15 and *Sheffield Independent*, 17 August 1938: 7.

19 Angela Jackson, *British Women and the Spanish Civil War* (London: The Clapton Press, 2020), 60–1.

20 LHASC: CP/ORG/MISC/03/08 *Theatre for the People*, no. 2 (April 1939): 4.

21 *On Guard for Spain* was first published in 1937. It is included in Jack Lindsay, *Who Are the English? Selected Poems 1935–1981* (Middlesbrough: Smokestack Books, 2014), 42–54. Written texts cannot do justice to performances of *On Guard for Spain* although some idea can be gained from acting scripts, for example that used by Bristol Unity Players, MRC: BUPMSS 212/L/1/8/1.

22 R. Vernon Beste, 'Mass Declamations', *Our Time*, vol. 2, no. 11 (1943): 5–6.

23 Interview in Watson, 'To the Head through the Heart': 15–16.

24 Ibid.

25 LHASC: CP/ORG/MISC/03/08) Margaret Leona in *Theatre for the People*, no. 2 (April 1939): 12–13; *Western Morning News*, 26 April 1939: 5, and 6 May 1939: 7.

26 Enid Windsor, *Crossing the Frontier* (unpublished script, BL/LCP 1939/11).

27 *Croydon Advertiser*, 7 April 1939: 7.

28 *Belfast Telegraph*, 24 February 1939: 14, *Edinburgh Evening News*, 29 April 1939: 17, *Merthyr Express*, 19 June 1937: 18, and *Western Mail*, 17 June 1937: 11. Play text in *Famous Plays of 1936*, (London: Victor Gollancz, 1937), 503–68.

29 *Left News*, no. 21 (January 1938): 671.

30 Goorney and MacColl, *Agitprop to Theatre Workshop*, xxxviii–xix; Tuckett, *People's Theatre in Bristol*, 10; Dawson, *Left Theatre*, 14–15.

31 Nixon, review of *Ten Peace Plays*, *Daily Worker*, 20 April 1938: 7.

32 'Bury the Dead', *Best One-Act Plays of 1936* (London: Victor Gollancz, 1937), 327–89. See discussion in Steve Nicholson, 'Irritating Tricks: Aesthetic Experimentalism and Political Theatre', in Keith Williams and Steven Mathews (eds), *Re-Writing the Thirties: Modernism and After* (London: Longman, 1997), 157–9. Press cutting in MRC: BUP212/X/2/2; *Liverpool Weekly Post*, 11 March 1939: 8; SUSC: Betty Hunt Papers Box 1: letter from Fred Hughes to Betty Hunt, 1973.

33 Chambers, *The Story of Unity Theatre*, 149–50; Lynn Mally, 'The Americanization of the Soviet Living Newspaper', *The Carl Beck Papers in Russian and East European Studies*, no. 1903 (2008): 1–44.

34 SUSC: Betty Hunt Papers Box 3: Press cutting 3 December 1938.

35 Tuckett, *The People's Theatre in Bristol*, 14–15; *Western Daily Press*, 3 July 1939: 11.

36 GA: *Gateshead Labour Herald*, no. 97 (April 1937): 4; unpublished script, extract in SUSC: Betty Hunt Papers Box 1; *Sheffield Independent*, 24 August 1938: 7.

37 The script is in Laity (ed.), *Left Book Club Anthology*, 101–14. It was a supplementary Left Book Club choice in 1937. For the London Unity production see Chambers, *The Story of Unity Theatre*, 61–3; Nicholson, Steve Nicholson, *The Censorship of British Drama 1900–1968: Volume Two: 1933–1952* (Exeter: Exeter University Press/Society for Theatre Research, 2020), 124.

38 Goronwy Rees, 'Politics on the London Stage', in John Lehman (ed.), *New Writing*, vol. 7, no.1 (1939): 112.

39 George Fullard, *Clogs* (unpublished script, BL/LCP 1938/59).

40 *Sheffield Telegraph*, 19 December 1938: 4.

41 MRC: BUPMSS 212/L/1/57 *Union Button* (unpublished script). Circa 1938. No author credited.

42 SUSC: Betty Hunt Papers Box 1: letter from Norman Brown to Betty Hunt, 1973; *Sheffield Daily Telegraph*, 11 March 1939: 7; *Birmingham Daily Gazette*, 19 January 1938: 3; *Left News*, no. 20 (December 1937): 632.

43 Baz Kershaw, *The Politics of Performance: Radical Theatre as Cultural Intervention* (London: Routledge, 2005), 29–30.

44 GUSC: STA GEN 6 Glasgow Workers' Theatre Group Minute Book, 2 August 1938; Tuckett, *The People's Theatre in Bristol*, 12–13; LHASC: CP/ORG/MISC/03/08 *Theatre for the People*, no. 1 (February 1939): 3–7.

45 *Liverpool Weekly Post*, 13 May 1939: 8.

46 Davies, *Other Theatres*, 129.

47 Mackenney, *The Activities of Popular Dramatists in Scotland*, 141–2.

48 Interview in Watson, 'To the Head through The Heart': 12. Producer Sophie Learner reports on this show in *Left News*, no. 40 (August 1938): 1373.

49 On the pageant form see Mick Wallis, 'The Popular front Pageant: Its Emergence and Decline', *New Theatre Quarterly*, vol. 10, no. 4 (1995): 17–32. *Shields Daily News*, 28 July 1931: 5; *Daily Worker*, 22 July 1939: 4.

50 LHASC: CP/ORG/MISC/03/08 *Discussion Paper* (1938): 5. *Left News*, no. 29 (September 1938): 992; no. 40 (August 1939): 1374.

51 *Sheffield Daily Telegraph*, 21 November 1939: 6.

52 GUSC: STA GEN 6 GWTG Minute Book, LBCTG National Committee Meeting Birmingham, 23 October 1938, 3.

53 *Left News*, no. 37 (May 1939): 1282; interview in Chambers, *The Story of Unity Theatre*, 139; Hilliard, *To Exercise Our Talents*, 133–4.

54 Griselda Carr, *Pit Women: Coal Communities in Northern England in the Early Twentieth Century* (London: Merlin Press, 2001), 118–30.

55 Anonymous, 'A Real Workers' Theatre', *Discussion*, vol. 111, no. 2 (1938): 43.

56 *Left News*, no. 29 (September 1938): 981 and no. 36 (April 1939): 1252; *Rugby Advertiser*, 14 March 1939: 3; *Newcastle Evening Chronicle*, 22 February 1939: 10.

57 *Sheffield Daily Telegraph*, 5 May 1939: 5; *Left News*, no. 33 (January 1939): 1135.

58 Samuel, 'Theatre and Socialism in Britain (1880–1935)', in Samuel et al., *Theatres of the Left*, 61; Dawson, *Left Theatre*, 12; Joe Corrie, 'Use the Freedom of the Festival', *The Amateur Theatre and Playwrights' Journal*, vol. 3, no. 66 (1937): 7–8.

59 Dawson, *Left Theatre*, 12–14.

60 MRC: BUP212/A/1/11 Producer's Report September 1938.

61 *Left News*, no. 29 (September 1938): 980.

62 *Left News*, no. 28 (August 1938): 948.

63 V&A: THM/9/6/2/4 Allen, *Notes on Forming Left-Wing Theatre Groups* (1937), 3.

64 On the Club and 1939 see Morgan, *Against Fascism and War*, 85–104.

6 'A remarkable revival in dramatic work and interest': Amateur Theatre during the Second World War

1 Robert Hewison, *Under Siege; Literary Life in London 1939–1945* (London: Weidenfeld & Nicholson, 1977); Angus Calder, *The People's War: Britain 1939–45* (London: Pimlico, 1992), F. M. Leventhal, 'The Best of the Most: CEMA and State Sponsorship of the Arts in War Time', *Twentieth Century British History*, vol. 1, no. 3 (1990): 289–317; Jorn Weingartner, *The Arts as a Weapon of War: Britain and the Shaping of National Morale in the Second World War* (London: Tauris Academic Studies, 2006); Anselm Heinrich, 'Theatre in Britain during the Second World War', *New Theatre Quarterly*, vol. 26, no. 1 (2010): 61–70. Although the focus of this chapter is on theatre CEMA was concerned with all the arts, perhaps especially music.

2 Quoted in Weingartner, *The Arts as a Weapon of War*, 67.

3 PGL: SPE1/C/3/112 unattributed press cutting, 'Win the Winter'.

4 *West Sussex Gazette*, 2 November 1939: 8; *War-time Drama* (November 1940): 1. *War-time Drama* succeeded the BDL journal *Drama*.

5 Whitworth quoted in the *Birmingham Mail*, 24 October 1939: 7; editorials in *War-Time Drama* (November 1939): 1 and (October 1939): 1; Ashwell, 'Keep Up the Standard' in *War-Time Drama* (October 1939): 2.

6 PGL: SPE4/E/2/1 undated article in *Northern Despatch*, 1940.

7 *War-Time Drama* (February 1940): 1. CUSC: Bargoed and Rhymney Valley Educational Settlement *Annual Report 1941/42*, 3.

8 Liverpool report in *War-Time Drama* (July 1940): 7; *Sheffield Daily Telegraph*, 21 November 1939: 6; Ratcliff report in *War-Time Drama* (February 1940): 1.

9 *Motherwell Times*, 8 March 1940: 7; 20 December 1940: 2; 1 January 1942: 6.

10 *War-time Drama* (January 1942): 5; CUSC: Bargoed and Rhymney Valley Educational Settlement *Annual Report 1941/2*, 9–10; *War-time Drama* (January 1942): 8; Mick Wallis, 'Amateur Village Drama and Community in England 1900–50', *New Theatre Quarterly*, vol. 38, no. 3 (2022): 280.

11 PGL: SPE4/E/2/1 undated article in *Northern Despatch*; du Garde Peach in *Theatre World*, vol. 33, no. 189 (1940): 94–5.

12 PGL: SPE4/E/8/1 undated article in *Northern Despatch*, 1941; *Merthyr Express*, 28 March 1942: 5.

13 Weingartner, *The Arts as a Weapon of War*, 112; on the amateur drama and the Theatre Royal issue see MRC: BUP 212/A/1/6-8 Secretary's Report to Bristol Unity Players AGM, June 1944, 2.

14 Sadie Ellerby, 'Fun for the Forgotten Forces', in Barbara Robinson (ed.), *The Swelling Scene: The Development of Amateur Drama in Hull from 1900* (Beverley: Highgate Publications, 1996), 26–33. PGL: SPE 4/E/8/1 undated article in *Northern Despatch*, 1941.

15 *Theatre World*, vol. 33, no. 183 (April 1940): 118; *War-time Drama*, April 1940: 1.

16 *War-time Drama* (November 1941): 1 and (November 1945): 1; Michael Dobson, *Shakespeare and Amateur Performance: A Cultural History* (Cambridge: Cambridge University Press, 2013), 141; PGL: SPE1/A/26/2 Spennymoor Settlement *Annual Report 1941/42*, 2.

17 *War-Time Drama* (May 1942): 2; *The Stage*, 1 April 1941: 5.

18 Rebecca D'Monte, *British Theatre and Performance 1900–1950* (London: Bloomsbury 2015), 166; *War-Time Drama* (October 1939): 3.

19 Oscar L. Lewis in the *Liverpool Weekly Post*, 2 March 1940: 10; DA: D872/1/3 Minutes of the Derbyshire Rural County Council Executive Committee 11 September 1939 and 13 November 1939; also 8 January 1940.

20 Wallis, 'Amateur Village Drama': 280–1. Also details in *Western Morning News*, 27 June 1944: 2.

21 *Yorkshire Observer*, 1 June 1942: 2; *Theatre World*, vol. 34, no. 195 (1941): 14.

22 *Theatre World*, vol. 37, no. 204 (1942): 31; *East London Observer*, 2 January 1942: 3; 16 October 1943: 1 and 30 October 1942: 4.

23 Colin Chambers, *The Story of Unity Theatre* (London: Lawrence & Wishart, 1989), 197–201.

24 Barbara Nixon, *Raiders Overhead* (London: Scolar/Gulliver, 1980), 82, 66. First published 1943.

25 *Port Glasgow Express*, 8 December 1942: 2 and 13 April 1945: 2.

26 NORTHA: NRO 07569/3-5 *Women's Land Army Quarterly Bulletins* April–October 1944; *Berwick Advertiser*, 13 May 1943: 6; *Newcastle Journal*, 5 April 1944: 3.

27 *War-Time Drama* (January 1941): 5.

28 *War-Time Drama* (July 1942): 2; *Barnoldswich and Earby Times*, 16 October 1942: 3 and 21 April 1944: 1.

29 DA: D872/1/3 Minutes of the Derbyshire Rural County Council Executive Committee, 12 July 1943.

30 On CEMA and the scheme see Weingarten, *The Arts as a Weapon of War*, 111; *Sunderland Echo*, 9 July 1943: 5; *Hull Daily Mail* 23 June 1943: 4; *Western Mail*, 17 June 1943: 2; *Liverpool Daily Post*, 21 June 1943: 2.

31 Heinrich, *Theatre in Britain*, 65–6.

32 *Merthyr Express*, 19 October 1940: 6; John Casson, *Lewis and Sybil* (London: Collins, 1972), 218.

33 *Merthyr Express*, 19 October 1940: 1, 6 and 8; *Western Mail*, 13 November 1940: 3.

34 PGL: SPE1/C/3/113 unattributed press cutting, 6 April 1941: 'Shakespeare Tours the Durham Coalfields'; *Sunderland Echo*, 14 April 1941: 3; Ashcroft quoted in the *Daily Herald*, 24 February 1947: 2.

35 *The Stage*, 22 October 1942: 4 and 9 November 1943: 4.

36 B. Ifor Evans and Mary Glasgow, *The Arts in England* (London: The Falcon Press, 1949), 44; *The Stage*, 17 June 1943: 4.

37 Quoted in Jack Lindsay, *The British Achievement in Art and Music* (London: The Pilot Press, 1944), 21.

38 Walter Hudd, 'New Audiences for Old', *Our Time*, vol. 3, no. 2 (1943): 15–18. *Our Time* succeeded *Left Review*.

39 Geoffrey G. Field, *Blood, Sweat and Toil: Remaking the British Working Class, 1939–1945* (Oxford: Oxford University Press, 2013), 244–8. Beth Brewer, 'Drama in a Factory Hostel', *War-Time Drama* (November 1943): 7; and her 'Where Is the Audience?', *Theatre Newsletter*, no. 12 (1946): 14.

40 On the West End see D'Monte, *British Theatre and Performance*, 173.

41 On Shakespeare see *Aberdeen Press and Journal*, 6 May 1944: 4. An example is the anthology Elizabeth Everard (ed.), *Ten One-Act Plays for Women* (London: George Harrap, 1944); *Sunderland Echo*, 14 May 1943: 5. On see Evans *Glamorgan Advertiser*, 27 October 1944: 1.

42 LUSC: Alec Brown Papers A14-16 Leeds Unity Theatre Reports, 1940–1.

43 Steve Nicholson, 'Theatrical Pageants in the Second World War', *Theatre Research International*, vol. 18, no. 3 (1993): 186–96; Jerry Dawson, *Left Theatre: Merseyside Unity Theatre – a Documentary Record* (Liverpool: Merseyside Writers, 1985), 21–2.

44 On the play see Claire Warden, *Migrating Modernist Performances: British Theatrical Tours Through Russia* (London: Palgrave Macmillan, 2016), 149–51; *Yorkshire Post*, 2 May 1942: 6.

45 *Western Times*, 20 July 1945: 7; *Falkirk Herald*, 23 February 1944: 3.

46 *Motherwell Times*, 1 January 1942: 6.

47 *The Stage*, 30 October 1941: 7; Chambers, *The Story of Unity Theatre*, 209–10; Alexei Afinogenev, *Distant Point* (London: Pushkin Press, 1941).

48 *Yorkshire Evening Post*, 10 October 1941: 2; *Surrey Mirror*, 16 April 1943: 5; MRC: BUP 212/A/1/6-8 BUP Reports and Minutes 1941/42 to 1944 Letter from WEA and Unity Players to Editor of *Soviet War News*, 4 August 1942.

49 PGL: SPE1/C/3/1 Spennymoor Settlement Circular, 16 May 1942, and 1/C/14 – cutting from *Auckland Chronicle*, 15 January 1942. *Nottingham Journal*, 14 June 1944: 2.

50 *Manchester Evening News*, 28 August 1941: 2; *The Stage*, 17 December 1942: 2.

51 *War-Time Drama* (March 1943): 1; (May 1944): 1; (November 1944): 3

52 *The Scotsman*, 2 April 1945: 2.

53 *Port Glasgow Express*, 28 March 1945: 3; D'Monte, *British Theatre and Performance*, 176; Linda Mackenney, *The Activities of Popular Dramatists and Drama Groups in Scotland, 1900–1952* (Lampeter: Edwin Mellen Press, 2000), 213–19.

54 *Richmond Herald*, 15 April 1944: 7; *Birmingham Daily Post*, 3 July 1944: 4; *Belfast Telegraph*, 2 July 1945: 6.

55 *Pontypridd Observer*, 23 October 1943: 1–3; *The Scotsman*, 1 May 1944: 3. *The Scotsman*, 11 April 1945: 3.

56 *Pontypridd Observer*, 14 April 1945: 2.

57 Evidence for this is summarized in Paul Laity (ed.), *Left Book Club Anthology* (London: Victor Gollancz, 2001), xxx–xxxi.

58 Paul Addison, *The Road to 1945: British Politics and the Second World War* (London, Quartet Books, 1977), 212–24.

59 *Our Time*, vol. 3, no. 8 (1944): 2.

60 J. B. Priestley, *They Came to a City: A Play in Two Acts* (London: Samuel French, 1972).

61 Ibid.

62 Maggie B. Gale, *J.B. Priestley* (London: Routledge, 2008), 23, 118.

63 *Theatre World*, vol. 39, no. 222 (1943): 19; *Birmingham Mail*, 20 December 1945, 2; PGL: SPE 1/A/30/2 Spennymoor Settlement *Annual Report 1944/45*, 2; *Eastbourne Herald*, 25 November 1945: 7.

64 Chambers, *The Story of Unity Theatre*, 232–6.

65 Ted Willis, *Buster: A Play in Three Acts* (London: Fore Publications, 1943).

66 Ibid.

67 Gill Plain, *Literature of the 1940s: War, Postwar and 'Peace'* (Edinburgh: Edinburgh University Press, 2015), 22.

68 Angela Tuckett, *The People's Theatre in Bristol 1930–45* (London: Our History Pamphlet, no. 45, 1980), 22. *War-Time Drama* (November 1945): 7; *South West Independent*, 4 May 1945: 3.

69 Chambers, *The Story of Unity Theatre*, 246

70 James Barke, *When the Boys Come Home* (unpublished script, BL/LCP 1945/18).

71 Ibid. See also D'Monte, *British Theatre and Performance*, 191.

72 Don Watson, 'Where Do We Go From Here? Theatre, Politics and Education in the British Army 1942–1945', *Labour History Review*, vol. 59, no. 3 (1994): 57–68. See also *A Theatre at War*, BBC Radio 4, 13 March 1975, producer Arnold Goldmann (script, BBC Play Library).

73 *Where Do We Go from Here?* (unpublished script, BL/LCP 1945/17). No author credited but Lindsay and Willis are cited as authors in *A Theatre at War*, BBC Radio 4, 13 March 1975. Ratcliff's involvement in the Unit is mentioned in *Theatre Newsletter*, vol. 2, no. 43 (March 1948): 10.

74 *Coventry Evening Telegraph*, 2 June 1945: 2; *Coventry Standard*, 9 June 1945: 5.

75 *War-time Drama* (November 1942): 1 and (November 1945): 1.
76 PGL: SPE 4/E/18/1 unattributed press cutting, 28 March 1941.

Conclusion: The Contribution of Theatre with a Purpose

1 Whitworth quoted in *Theatre Newsletter*, vol. 2, no. 40 (February 1948): 2; BDL proposals in *War-Time Drama* (January 1943): 3–5; Cambridge conference reported in *Peterborough Standard*, 7 December 1945: 4.

2 *Daily Herald*, 5 February 1948: 2.

3 A booklet reporting the conference accompanies *Theatre Newsletter*, vol. 2, no. 41 (February 1948).

4 See, for example, *The Stage*, 7 March 1940: 7.

5 For example Jack Lindsay's interview with Mary Glasgow of the ACGB in *Our Time*, vol. 7, no. 5 (February 1948): 108.

6 *Theatre Newsletter*, vol. 1, no. 1 (July 1946): 7; vol. 2, no. 26 (July 1947): 5; William Robertson, *Welfare in Trust: A History of the Carnegie United Kingdom Trust 1913–1963* (Dunfermline: The Carnegie United Kingdom Trust, 1964), 179.

7 *Taunton Courier*, 26 December 1958: 8; Barbara Robinson, 'The Crit', in Barbara Robinson (ed.), *The Swelling Scene: The Development of Amateur Drama in Hull from 1900* (Beverley: Highgate Publications, 1996), 64.

8 Helen Nicholson, Nadine Holdsworth and Jane Milling, *The Ecologies of Amateur Theatre* (London: Palgrave Macmillan, 2018), 58.

9 John Bourne, 'The One-Act Play in England', in William Kozlenko (ed.), *The One-Act Play Today: A Discussion of the Technique, Scope and History of the Contemporary Short Drama* (London: Harrap, 1939), 239, and his article 'Garage-hand by Day, Star by Night', *Daily Herald*, 20 October 1937: 10.

10 Quoted in Norman Marshall, *The Other Theatre* (London: John Lehmann, 1947), 85–6; Allardyce Nicoll, *The English Theatre: A Short History* (London: Thomas Nelson, 1936), 208.

11 Claire Cochrane, *Twentieth Century British Theatre: Industry, Art and Empire* (Cambridge: Cambridge University Press, 2011), 116; *Theatrecraft*, vol. 1, no. 6 (May 1939): 5.

12 Marshall, *The Other Theatre*, 87.

13 *Theatre Newsletter*, vol. 2, no. 41 (February 1948): 7–9; Rebecca D'Monte, *British Theatre and Performance 1900–1950* (London: Bloomsbury, 2015), 177.

Select Bibliography

Unpublished scripts

Anonymous. *Union Button*, circa 1938. (MRC: BUPMSS 212)

Anonymous. *Where Do We Go From Here?*, 1945. (BL/LCP 1945/17)

Barke, James. *When the Boys Come Home*, 1945. (BL/LCP 1945/18)

Bewaldeth, John. *The Yard*, 1934. (BL/LCP 1934/43)

Farrell, Bill. *Art for Everyone*, BBC Pacific Service, 9 April 1945. (PGL: SPE 1/C/5)

Farnin, Frank. *The War Memorial*, 1938. (BL/LCP 1938/5)

Fullard, George. *Cloggs*, 1938. (BL/LCP 1938/59)

Goldmann, Arnold. *A Theatre at War*, BBC Radio 4, 13 March 1975. (BBC Play Library)

Windsor, Enid. *Crossing the Frontier*, 1939. (BL/LCP 1939/11)

Published sources

Aberdare Valley Educational Settlement. *Bulletins*, October and November 1938.

Addison, Paul. *The Road to 1945: British Politics and the Second World War*. London: Quartet Books, 1977.

Adult Education Committee of the Board of Education. *The Drama in Adult Education*. London: HMSO, 1926.

Albaya, Winifred. *Through the Green Door: An Account of the Sheffield Educational Settlement 1918–55 Part One*. Sheffield: Sheffield District Education Committee, 1977.

Albaya, Winifred. *Through the Green Door: An Account of the Sheffield Educational Settlement 1918–55 Part Two*. Sheffield: Sheffield District Education Committee, 1980.

Allen, John. 'The Socialist Theatre', *Left Review*, vol. 3, no. 7 (1935): 417–22.

Amateur Stage, 1945–1947.

Amateur Theatre and Playwrights' Journal, 1930–1939.

Andrews, Maggie. *The Acceptable Face of Feminism: The Women's Institute as a Social Movement*. London: Lawrence & Wishart, 1997.

Anonymous. 'A Real Workers' Theatre', *Discussion*, vol. 111, no. 2 (1938): 43.

Armstrong, Keith, ed. *But the World Goes On the Same: Changing Times in a Durham Pit Village*. Whitley Bay: Strong Words Collective, 1978.

Armstrong, Keith, ed. *Homespun: The Story of Spennymoor and its Famous Settlement, told by Local People*. North Shields: Northern Voices, 1992.

Armstrong, Keith. *Common Words and the Wandering Star: A Biographical Study of Culture and Social Change in the Life and Work of Writer Jack Common, 1903–1968*. Sunderland: University of Sunderland Press, 2009.

Bargoed and Rhymney Valley Educational Settlement. *Annual Report*, 1941/42.

Barber, Eric. 'Durham and Northumberland', *Drama*, vol. 11, no. 10 (1933): 173–4.

Barker, Clive and Gale, Maggie B., eds. *British Theatre between the Wars, 1918–1939*. Cambridge: Cambridge University Press, 2000, 4–38.

Beechcroft Settlement. *Annual Reports*, 1919/20 to 1934/35.

Bell, Sam Hanna. *The Theatre in Ulster*. Dublin: Gill and Macmillan, 1972.

Bensham Grove Settlement. *Annual Reports and Scrapbooks*, 1920/21 to 1937/38.

Beste, R. Vernon. 'Mass Declamations', *Our Time*, vol. 2, no. 11 (1943): 5–6, 29–30.

Birt, Raymond. 'Left Turn Among the Amateurs', *The Amateur Theatre and Playwrights' Journal*, vol. 4, no. 79 (1937): 511.

Bolton, Gavin. *Acting in Classroom Drama: A Critical Analysis*. Portland: Calendar Island Publishers, 1999.

Bourne, John. 'Garage-hand by Day, Star by Night', *Daily Herald*, 20 October 1937, 10.

Bourne, John, ed. *Twenty-Five Modern One-Act Plays*. London: Victor Gollancz, 1938.

Bourne, John. *Drama Festivals and Competitions*. London: Pitman & Sons, 1939.

Box, Muriel: *Odd Woman Out*. London: Leslie Frewin, 1974.

Box, Muriel, and Box, Sydney. *Ladies Only*. London: George Harrap, 1934.

Branson, Noreen. *Poplarism 1919–1925: George Lansbury and the Councillors' Revolt*. London: Lawrence & Wishart, 1979.

Branson, Noreen, and Heinemann, Margot. *Britain in the Nineteen Thirties*. London: Weidenfeld & Nicolson, 1971.

Brasnett, Margaret. *Voluntary Social Action: A History of the National Council of Social Service*. London: National Council of Social Service, 1969.

Brewer, Beth. 'Drama in a Factory Hostel', *War-Time Drama* (November 1943): 7–8.

Brewer, Beth. 'Where is the Audience?', *Theatre Newsletter*, no. 12 (1946): 14–15.

Burchardt, Jeremy. 'State and Society in the English Countryside: The Rural Community Movement 1918–39', *Rural History*, vol. 23, no. 1 (2012): 81–106.

Burnett, John. *Idle Hands: The Experience of Unemployment, 1790–1990*. London: Routledge, 1994.

Callcott, Maureen, ed. *A Pilgrimage of Grace: The Diaries of Ruth Dodds*. Whitley Bay: Bewick Press, 1995.

Carleton, Patrick, ed. *The Amateur Stage: A Symposium*. London: Geoffrey Bles, 1939.

Carr, Griselda. *Pit Women: Coal Communities in Northern England in the Early Twentieth Century*. London: Merlin Press, 2001.

Casson, John. *Lewis and Sybil*. London: Collins, 1972.

Chambers, Colin. *The Story of Unity Theatre*. London: Lawrence & Wishart, 1989.

Cochrane, Claire. 'The Persuasiveness of the Commonplace: The Historian and Amateur Theatre', *Theatre Research International*, vol. 26, no. 3 (2001): 233–43.

Cochrane, Claire. *Twentieth Century British Theatre: Industry, Art and Empire*. Cambridge: Cambridge University Press, 2011.

Cochrane, Claire, and Robinson, Jo, eds. *The Methuen Drama Handbook of Theatre History and Historiography*. London: Methuen, 2020.

Corrie, Joe. 'Use the Freedom of the Festival', *The Amateur Theatre and Playwrights' Journal*, vol. 3, no. 66 (1937): 7–8.

Corrie, Joe. *Poems, Plays and Theatre Writings*. Edited and introduced by Linda MacKenney, Edinburgh: 7:84 Publications, 1985.

Corrie, Joe. *In Time O' Strife*. London: Bloomsbury Methuen Drama, 2013. (First published in 1926.)

Croft, Andy. *Red Letter Days*. London: Lawrence & Wishart, 1990.

Croucher, Richard. *We Refuse to Starve in Silence: A History of the National Unemployed Workers' Movement 1920–1946*. London: Lawrence & Wishart, 1987.

Davies, Andrew. *Other Theatres: The Development of Alternative and Experimental Theatre in Britain*. London: Macmillan, 1987.

Davies, John. 'John Davies and the Workers' Educational Association in South Wales', *Llafur*, vol. 8 no. 1 (2000): 45–69.

Dawson, Jerry. *Left Theatre: Merseyside Unity Theatre – a Documentary Record*. Liverpool: Merseyside Writers, 1985.

Derbyshire Rural Community Council Music and Drama Sub-Committee. *Minutes*, 1926–1943.

Dewar, Katherine. 'Report of Harkness House', *Social Services Review*, vol. 13, no. 8 (1932): 50–1.

D'Monte, Rebecca. *British Theatre and Performance 1900–1950*. London: Bloomsbury, 2015.

Dobson, Michael. *Shakespeare and Amateur Performance: A Cultural History*. Cambridge: Cambridge University Press, 2013.

Dodds, M. H. 'Our Aristocratic Theatre', *Drama*, no. 26 (March 1923): 113–15.

Dodds, Ruth. *The Pitman's Pay: A Historical Play in Four Acts*. London: The Labour Publishing Company, 1923.

Drama, 1920–39.

Edwards, Keri. *Writers of Wales: Jack Jones*. Cardiff: University of Wales Press, 1974.

Entwistle, Elsie. *Life's Day*. London: W. Deane, 1935.

Evans, B. Ifor, and Glasgow, Mary. *The Arts in England*. London: The Falcon Press, 1949.

Evans, Eynon E. *Cold Coal*. London: Samuel French, 1939.

Farrell, Bill. 'Drama in the Occupation Centres', *National Council of Social Service News Sheet*, September 1938: 1.

Field, Geoffrey G. *Blood Sweat and Toil: Remaking the British Working Class, 1939–1945*. Oxford: Oxford University Press, 2013.

Fieldhouse, Roger, ed. *A History of Modern British Adult Education*. Leicester: National Institute of Adult and Continuing Education, 1998.

Flanagan, John. *Parish-Fed Bastards: A History of the Politics of the Unemployed in Britain 1884–1939*. New York: Greenwood Press, 1991.

Fleming, Horace. *Beechcroft: The Story of the Birkenhead Settlement 1914–1924*. London: Educational Settlements Association, 1938.

Freeman, Mark. 'No Finer School than a Settlement: The Development of the Educational Settlement Movement', *History of Education*, vol. 31, no.3 (2002): 245–62.

Freshwater, Helen. *Theatre & Audience*. London: Palgrave Macmillan, 2009.

Frost, Anthony, and Yarrow, Ralph. *Improvisation in Drama, Theatre and Performance: History, Practice, Theory*. London: Macmillan, 1990.

Gale, Maggie B. *J.B. Priestley*. London: Routledge, 2008.

Gateshead Progressive Players Diamond Jubilee 1920–1980. Gateshead: Gateshead Little Theatre, 1980.

Gale, Maggie B, and Gardner, Viv, eds. *Women, Theatre and Performance: New Histories, New Historiographies*. Manchester: Manchester University Press, 2000.

Gollancz, Victor, ed. *Famous Plays of 1936*. London: Victor Gollancz, 1936.

Goorney, Howard, and MacColl, Ewan, eds. *Agitprop to Theatre Workshop: Political Playscripts 1930–50*. Manchester: Manchester University Press, 1986.

Gregson, James. *The Autobiography of James Gregson*. Brighouse: ER Smith Publications, 2011.

Hannington, Wal. *The Problem of the Distressed Areas*. London: Victor Gollancz Left Book Club, 1937.

Harkness House Hotch-Potch, 1934.

Harris, Bernard. 'Responding to Adversity: Government–Charity Relations and the Relief of Unemployment in Inter-War Britain', *Contemporary British History*, vol. 9, no. 3 (1995): 529–61.

Heinrich, Anselm. 'Theatre in Britain during the Second World War', *New Theatre Quarterly*, vol. 26, no. 1 (2006): 61–70.

Hewison, Robert. *Culture and Consensus: England, Art and Politics since 1940*. London: Methuen, 1995.

Hilliard, Christopher. *To Exercise Our Talents: The Democratization of Writing in Britain*. Cambridge, MA: Harvard University Press, 2006.

Hobsbawm, Eric. *The Age of Extremes, 1914–1991*. London: Abacus, 1995.

Hudd, Walter. 'New Audiences for Old', *Our Time*, vol. 3, no. 2 (1943): 15–18

Jackson, Angela. *British Women in the Spanish Civil War*. London: The Clapton Press, 2020.

Jarrett-Macauley, Delia. *The Life of Una Marson 1905–65*. Manchester: Manchester University Press, 1998.

Jeffrey, Tom. *Mass Observation: A Short History*. Brighton: Mass Observation Archive Occasional Paper no. 10, University of Sussex Library, 1999.

Jones, Jack. *Land of My Fathers: A Play of the Distressed Areas*. London: Samuel French, 1937.

Jones, Jack. *Unfinished Journey*. New York: Oxford University Press, 1937.

Kelly, Mary. *Village Theatre*. London: Thomas Nelson, 1939.

Kershaw, Baz, ed. *The Cambridge History of British Theatre Vol. 3: Since 1895*. Cambridge: Cambridge University Press, 2004.

Kershaw, Baz. *The Politics of Performance: Radical Theatre as Cultural Intervention*. London: Routledge, 2005.

Kozlenko, William, ed. *The One-Act Play Today: A Discussion of the Technique, Scope and History of the Contemporary Short Drama*. London: George Harrap, 1939.

Laity, Paul, ed. *Left Book Club Anthology*. London: Victor Gollancz, 2001.

Lathan, Peter D. *Fifty Years On: Sunderland Drama Club 1925-75*. Newcastle upon Tyne: Campbell Graphics, 1975.

Laybourn, Keith. *Britain on the Breadline: A Social and Political History of Britain 1918-1939*. Stroud: Sutton Publishing, 1998.

Lea, Gordon. 'Music and Drama amongst the Unemployed: An Experiment', *Social Services Review*, vol. 16, no. 1 (1935): 9.

Leask, Margaret. *Lena Ashwell: Actress, Patriot, Pioneer*. Hatfield: University of Hertfordshire Press/Society for Theatre Research, 2012.

Leeworthy, Daryl. *Labour Country: Political Radicalism and Social Democracy in South Wales 1831-1985*. Cardigan: Parthian Press, 2018.

Left News 1936-1939.

Left Review, 1934-1939.

Leventhal, F. M. 'The Best of the Most: CEMA and State Sponsorship of the Arts in War Time', *Twentieth Century British History*, vol. 1, no. 3 (1990): 289-317.

Lewis, John. *The Left Book Club: An Historical Record*. London: Victor Gollancz, 1970.

Lindsay, Jack. *The British Achievement in Art and Music*. London: The Pilot Press, 1944.

Lindsay, Jack. *Who Are the English? Selected Poems 1935-1981*. Middlesbrough: Smokestack Books, 2016.

Littlewood, Joan. *Joan's Book: Joan Littlewood's Peculiar History, as She Tells It*. London: Methuen, 1994.

Mackenney, Linda. *The Activities of Popular Dramatists and Drama Groups in Scotland, 1900-1952*. Lampeter: Edwin Mellen Press, 2000.

Mally, Lynn. 'The Americanization of the Soviet Living Newspaper', *The Carl Beck Papers in Russian and East European Studies*, no. 1903 (2008): 1-44.

Manders, F. W. D. *A History of Gateshead*. Gateshead: Gateshead Corporation, 1973.

Marshall, Norman. *The Other Theatre*. London: John Lehmann, 1947.

Marshalsey, Karen Anne. 'The Quest for a Truly Representative Scottish National Drama: The Scottish National Players', *Theatre Research International*, vol. 17, no. 2 (1992): 109-16.

McArthur, Euan. *Scotland, CEMA and the Arts Council, 1919-1967: Background, Politics and Visual Art Policy*. Abingdon: Routledge, 2016.

McKibbin, Ross. *Classes and Cultures: England 1918–1951*. Oxford: Oxford University Press, 1998.

McManners, Robert and Wales, Gillian. *Way to the Better: The Spennymoor Settlement*. Durham: Gemini Productions, 2008.

Merthyr Tydfil Educational Settlement. *Annual Reports*, 1935/36 to 1936/37.

Mess, Henry A., ed. *Voluntary Social Services since 1918*. London: Kegan Paul, 1947.

Ministry of Reconstruction: *Final Report of the Adult Education Committee*. London: HMSO, 1919.

Morgan, Kevin. *Against Fascism and War: Ruptures and Continuities in British Communist Politics 1935–41*. Manchester: Manchester University Press, 1989.

Naylor, Barrie. *Quakers in the Rhondda 1926–1986*. Malthouse: Maes-yr-haf Educational Trust, 1986.

New Theatre, 1938–9.

Newton, Robert G. *Acting, Improvised*. London: Thomas Nelson, 1937.

Nicoll, Allardyce. *The English Theatre: A Short History*. London: Thomas Nelson, 1936.

Nicholson, Helen, Holdsworth, Nadine and Milling, Jane. *The Ecologies of Amateur Theatre*. London: Palgrave Macmillan, 2018.

Nicholson, Steve. 'Theatrical Pageants in the Second World War', *Theatre Research International*, vol. 18, no.3 (1993): 186–96.

Nicholson, Steve. *British Theatre and the Red Peril: The Portrayal of Communism 1917–1945*. Exeter: Exeter University Press, 1999.

Nicholson, Steve. *The Censorship of British Drama 1900–1968: Volume Two: 1933–1952*. Exeter: Exeter University Press/Society for Theatre Research, 2020.

Nixon, Barbara. 'Theatre Now', *Left Review*, vol. 2, no. 3 (1935): 105–7.

Nixon, Barbara. *Raiders Overhead*. London: Scolar/Gulliver, 1980. (First published in 1943.)

Nottinghamshire Rural Community Council Adult Education Committee. *Minutes*, 1929–38.

Our Time, 1939–46.

Olechnowicz, Andrej. 'Unemployed Workers, "Enforced Leisure" and Education for the "Right Use of Leisure" in Britain in the 1930s', *Labour History Review*, vol. 70, no. 1 (2005): 27–52.

Perry, Matt, ed. *The Global Challenge of Peace: 1919 as a Contested Threshold to a New World Order*. Liverpool: Liverpool University Press, 2021.

Pilgrim Trust. *Annual Reports*, 1930/31 to 1938/39.

Pilgrim Trust. *Men Without Work: A Report Made to the Pilgrim Trust*. Cambridge: Cambridge University Press, 1938.

Plain, Gill. *Literature of the 1940s: War, Postwar and 'Peace'*. Edinburgh: Edinburgh University Press, 2015.

Priestley, J. B. *They Came to a City: A Play in Two Acts*. London: Samuel French, 1972.

Priestley, J. B. *English Journey*. Ilkley: Great Northern Book, 2009. (First published in 1934.)

Quekett, Hugh S. ed. *Eight Prize-Winning One-Act Plays*. London: George Harrap, 1936.

Ratcliff, Nora. *Rude Mechanicals: A Short Review of Village Drama*. London: Thomas Nelson, 1938.

Rees, Goronwy. 'Politics on the London Stage', *New Writing*, vol. 7, no. 1 (1939): 101–12.

Roberts, John. 'The Sheffield Educational Settlement 1918–1955', MA diss., Faculty of Education, Sheffield University, 1961.

Roberts, Stephen K., ed. *A Ministry of Enthusiasm: Centenary Essays on the Workers' Educational Association*. London: Pluto Press, 2003.

Robertson, William. *Welfare in Trust: A History of the Carnegie United Kingdom Trust 1913–1963*. Dunfermline: The Carnegie United Kingdom Trust, 1964.

Robinson, Barbara, ed. *The Swelling Scene: The Development of Amateur Drama in Hull from 1900*. Beverley: Highgate Publications, 1996.

Rose, Jonathon. *The Intellectual Life of the British Working Classes*. London: Yale University Press, 2021.

Rose, Michael E. and Woods, Anne. *Everything Went on at the Round House: A Hundred Years of the Manchester University Settlement*. Manchester: Manchester University, 1995.

Rothkirch, Alyce. Von. *J.O. Francis, Realist Drama and Ethics: Culture, Place and Nation*. Cardiff: University of Wales Press, 2014.

Samuel, Raphael, MacColl, Ewan and Cosgrove, Stuart, eds. *Theatres of the Left 1880–1935: Workers' Theatre Movements in Britain and America*. London: Routledge & Kegan Paul, 1987.

Saville, John and Bellamy, Joyce M, eds. *Dictionary of Labour Biography Vol. VII*. London: Macmillan Press, 1984.

Shepherd, Simon. *The Unknown Granville Barker: Letters to Helen and Other Texts 1915–18*. London: Society for Theatre Research, 2021.

Sherriff, R. C. *No Leading Lady: An Autobiography*. London: Victor Gollancz, 1969.

Sidnell, Michael J. *Dances of Death: The Group Theatre in the Thirties*. London: Faber, 1984.

Snape, Robert. *Leisure, Voluntary Action and Social Change in Britain, 1880–1939*. London: Bloomsbury Academic, 2018.

Social Service Review, 1932–9.

Spennymoor Settlement. *Annual Reports and Circulars* 1932/33 to 1944/45.

Spicer, Andrew. *British Film Makers: Sydney Box*. Manchester: Manchester University Press, 2006.

Stewart, Frida. *Firing a Shot for Freedom: The Memoirs of Frida Stewart*. London: The Clapton Press, 2020. (First published in 1940.)

Stevenson, John and Cook, Chris. *The Slump: Society and Politics during the Depression*. London: Quartet Books, 1979.

Stocks, Mary. *Fifty Years in Every Street: The Story of the Manchester University Settlement*. Manchester: Manchester University Press, 1945.

Storey, Taryn. 'Village Hall Work Can Never Be "Theatre": Amateur Theatre and the Arts Council of Great Britain, 1945–56', *Contemporary Theatre Review*, vol. 27, no. 1 (2017): 76–91.

Stourac, Richard, and McCreery, Kathleen. *Theatre as a Weapon: Workers' Theatre in the Soviet Union, Germany and Britain 1917–1934*. London: Routledge & Kegan Paul, 1986.

Theatrecraft, 1938–9.

Theatre Newsletter, 1946–8.

Theatre for the People, 1938–9.

Theatre World, 1940–5.

Tuckett, Angela. *The People's Theatre in Bristol 1930–45*. London: Our History Pamphlet no. 45, 1980.

Tylee, Claire M, Cardinal, Agnes and Turner, Elaine, eds. *War Plays by Women: An International Anthology*. London: Routledge, 2000.

Tyneside Council for Social Service. *Annual Reports*, 1930–9.

Unemployed Drama News Introductory Issue, 1936.

Veitch, Norman. *The People's: Being a History of The People's Theatre Newcastle upon Tyne 1911–1939*. Gateshead: Northumberland Press, 1950.

Wallis, Mick. 'The Popular Front Pageant: Its Emergence and Decline', *New Theatre Quarterly*, vol. 10, no. 4 (1995): 17–32.

Wallis, Mick. 'Unlocking the Secret Soul: Mary Kelly, Pioneer of Village Theatre', *New Theatre Quarterly*, vol. 16, no. 4 (2000): 347–58.

Wallis, Mick. 'Amateur Village Drama and Community in England 1900–50', *New Theatre Quarterly*, vol. 38, no. 3 (2022): 270–82.

Warden, Claire. *Migrating Modernist Performances: British Theatrical Tours through Russia*. London: Palgrave Macmillan, 2016.

War-Time Drama, 1939–45.

Waters, Chris. *British Socialists and the Politics of Popular Culture, 1884–1914*. Manchester: Manchester University Press, 1990.

Watson, Don. 'To the Head through the Heart: The Newcastle Left Book Club Theatre Guild 1936–1939', *North East Labour History*, no. 23 (1989): 3–22.

Watson, Don. 'Where Do We Go From Here? Theatre, Politics and Education in the British Army 1942–1945', *Labour History Review*, vol. 59, part 3 (1994): 57–68.

Weingartner, Jorn. *The Arts as a Weapon of War: Britain and the Shaping of National Morale in the Second World War*. London: Tauris Academic Studies, 2006.

Whitworth, Geoffrey. *The Making of a National Theatre*. London: Faber and Faber, 1951.

Wilkinson, Ellen. *The Town That Was Murdered: The Life Story of Jarrow*. London: Merlin Press, 2019. (First published in 1939.)

Williams, Keith, and Mathews, Steven, eds. *Re-Writing the Thirties: Modernism and After*. London: Longman, 1997.

Williams, Raymond. *Drama in Performance*. Milton Keynes: Open University Press, 1991. (First published in 1954.)

Willis, Ted. *Buster: A Play in Three Acts*. London: Fore Publications, 1943.

Women's Land Army Northumberland. *Quarterly Bulletins* 1943 to 1944.

Index

Illustrations are shown in *italic* figures.